FORMULA ONE 2023

Published in 2023 by Welbeck

An Imprint of Welbeck Non-Fiction Limited, part of Welbeck Publishing Group.

Based in London and Sydney.

www.welbeckpublishing.com

Text © Welbeck Non-Fiction Limited, part of Welbeck Publishing Group 2023.

A CIP catalogue record for this book is available from the British Library.

ISBN: 978 1 80279 400 7

Editor: Conor Kilgallon
Design: Luke Griffin, Russell Knowles
Picture Research: Paul Langan
Production: Rachel Burgess

Printed in the United Kingdom

10 9 8 7 6 5 4 3 2 1

Above: Rivals Lewis Hamilton and Max Verstappen scrap for position at Marina Bay in 2022.

FORMULA ONE 2023

TEAMS | DRIVERS | TRACKS | RECORDS

BRUCE JONES

WELBECK

CONTENTS

Right: Max Verstappen shows his delight at Suzuka after clinching his second F1 world title.

Carlos Sainz Jr became a winner for the first time last year with Ferrari and wants more in 2023.

ANALYSIS OF THE 2023 SEASON

With Mercedes failing to build a car capable of excelling with last year's new technical rules, the big question is whether it will have caught up for 2023, or should Red Bull Racing be confident of starting as favourite? Ferrari knows that it must work better as a team, while there might yet be points aplenty for Alpine if its French drivers can work together.

Technical changes have been introduced for 2023 with the aim of reducing the porpoising effect that made so many of the cars so difficult to drive last year. To do this, the governing body has changed the rule book so that the edges of the cars' floors have been raised by 25mm, the minimum height of the throat of their undersides has been raised, lateral deflection tests for the floors have been introduced and sensors that are more accurate in checking if vertical acceleration limits are being breached have been included. In addition, Red Bull Racing will start on the back foot, with its penalty for exceeding last year's cost cap being a fine and a ten per cent reduction in its aerodynamic testing allowance.

What must also excite all fans, though, are the movements in the driver market, something that always stirs the pot. None of these involve the top three teams though, namely Red Bull, Ferrari and Mercedes, who have respectively kept their pairings of last year's champion Max Verstappen and Sergio Perez, Charles Leclerc and Carlos Sainz Jr plus Lewis Hamilton and George Russell.

The driver changes are among the teams who are expected to be giving chase. Chief among these is what happened at Alpine when the announcement of Sebastian Vettel's retirement left a vacancy at Aston Martin that Fernando Alonso shocked everyone by accepting. On the face of this, he is moving to a team that was less competitive

last year, but clearly all was not happy at Alpine. Indeed, it may not be happy this year either, as Esteban Ocon is being joined by former childhood rival Pierre Gasly, who has long since become a fierce rival. This move had never been under consideration, as Alpine reckoned that it would slot in its reserve driver Oscar Piastri as Ocon's teammate, but the multi-titled F1 rookie elected to join McLaren instead. So, Alpine's aim this year will be to steady its ship.

Piastri thus joins Lando Norris at McLaren and will at least have the initial buffer of being an F1 rookie. This is something he might need if the 2023 McLaren proves as unpredictable as last year's, when it was a car that a much-shaken Daniel Ricciardo described as making him 'feel like a passenger' at times. It cost him his F1 career.

Valtteri Bottas looked like a changed man in his first year with Alfa Romeo and revelled in the less pressured atmosphere. However, both he and Chinese second-year F1 racer Guanyu Zhou will be aware that their team continues to tail off in the second half of the year as other teams with larger budgets reap the benefit of their development work.

Haas F1 is another team that endures a similar course through a season and knows that neither Kevin Magnussen nor experienced signing Nico Hulkenberg are likely to be able to start with a result like Magnussen's 2022 opener of fifth place, as that was achieved with an entirely new set of technical rules. Having two experienced drivers will at least ensure that any points-scoring opportunities are taken.

AlphaTauri could have the signing of the year in Nyck de Vries. The Dutchman is a driver long overdue his F1 break and he showed in a one-off for Williams last year that he could offer to AlphaTauri what the driver he was standing in for, Alex Albon, does for Williams. Indeed, team advisor Helmut Marko already sees him as the team leader rather than occasionally error-prone Yuki Tsunoda, who is back for a third year.

Williams finished last in 2022, two places down on 2021, but Albon displayed masterful skills in making his tyres last to score points when the car didn't merit them. In Logan Sargeant, Williams has done better than US-based Haas F1 in signing a young American talent, which is precisely what is needed as F1 enjoys a huge surge in popularity in the USA, especially as it is set to hold three Grands Prix next year, in Miami, at COTA and now Las Vegas.

RED BULL RACING

The team from Milton Keynes was simply too good for Mercedes and out-thought Ferrari last year. Encouragingly, it not only propelled Max Verstappen to wins but Sergio Perez too, suggesting a strength in depth it has not always shown in the past.

Max Verstappen was in dominant form last year as he hunted down and beat the Ferraris, making it a far easier run to the title than in 2021.

Sir Jackie Stewart is a man who can't sit still. He is an achiever and three F1 titles – in 1969, 1971 and 1973 – clearly wasn't enough to satisfy his competitive urge, with his post-racing work diary every bit as crammed as before he hung up his helmet at the end of the 1973 season. Then, when his elder son Paul went racing in the late 1980s, he helped him set up a team that took him through FF1600, FF2000, F3 and into F1's feeder formula, F3000. The team ran other drivers too and was extremely professional in all that it did. With their combined ambition and Paul's realisation that F1 would be beyond him as a driver, the pair decided to make that final push, entering a team in F1 with blue-chip corporate backing.

Starting in 1997, Stewart Grand Prix went straight into the midfield, with Rubens Barrichello claiming its first podium finish – second place at Monaco. Pushing to improve on that proved difficult, but victory came in a wet/dry race at the Nürburgring in 1999 when Johnny Herbert was first to the chequered flag.

Ford bought the team and entered it as Jaguar Racing in 2000, but frustration grew as the team couldn't challenge the top three teams, despite the best efforts

KEY PERSONNEL & 2022 ROUND-UP

ADRIAN NEWEY

Trained in aeronautics, Adrian was soon revolutionising F1 design, taking March to new heights in the late 1980s. Williams snapped him up in 1991 and Adrian was behind the FW14B with which Nigel Mansell dominated in 1992. Four constructors' titles in five years made him the pre-eminent F1 designer and he was coaxed to move to McLaren in 1997 and to Red Bull Racing in 2006, giving the team its first constructors' title in 2010 as Sebastian Vettel won for fun. Since then, either side of a Mercedes golden age, the team has added four more.

COMING OUT WITH BOTH GUNS BLAZING

Having both of its cars retire from the opening race was a concern, both with the same late-race fuel pump problem. Yet, despite further occasional mechanical fallibility, the RB17s were fast everywhere. This gave Verstappen the tool with which to beat the Ferraris, with the team's tally boosted by Sergio Perez, who proved a stronger number two than the team has had in years.

2022 DRIVERS & RESULTS

Driver	Nationality	Races	Wins	Pts	Pos
Max Verstappen	Dutch	22	15	454	1st
Sergio Perez	Mexican	22	2	305	3rd

of Eddie Irvine and Mark Webber. One major problem was Ford's corporate executives trying to interfere with the way that the team was run. So, when Red Bull energy drink company founder Dietrich Mateschitz looked to buy a team, it was the obvious choice. The team would remain based in Milton Keynes, but would race as Red Bull Racing from 2005, run by former F3000 racer Christian Horner.

David Coulthard was the first top driver to race for the team, with Red Bull Racing taking the policy of placing up-and-coming talent alongside him. If these didn't get on the pace quickly, they were ejected, with former F1 racer Helmut Marko responsible for the hiring and firing. This was augmented in 2006 when Mateschitz took over the Minardi team, rebranded it as Scuderia Toro Rosso, and used that as a feeder team.

When ace designer Adrian Newey joined from McLaren, the team found its cutting edge and Sebastian Vettel joined Webber to lead its attack from 2009. A final round sort-out in Abu Dhabi in 2010

gave the team its first drivers' title and Vettel then added the 2011, 2012 and 2013 titles to his pile.

After four years as F1's top team, the Mercedes challenge came on song in 2014, led by Lewis Hamilton, and after Vettel's departure it was left to Daniel Ricciardo to lead the team's attack, which he did, winning races but never the title as the Mercedes steamroller got up to speed.

Engine supply was always a matter that seemed to put Red Bull Racing on the back foot, but the arrival of Max Verstappen after promotion from Toro Rosso during the 2016 season resulted in a win first time out and a new cutting edge. Yet, try as he might, the young Dutchman couldn't take the battle to Mercedes and Hamilton across a full season; until 2021, when it went down to the final race and he won in Abu Dhabi after a controversial call from FIA race director Michael Masi and so pipped Hamilton to the crown.

Red Bull Racing had been notorious for focusing on its lead driver, but the arrival of Sergio Perez brought experience rather than promise and his gathering of

FOR THE RECORD

Country of origin:	England
Team base:	Milton Keynes, England
Telephone:	(44) 01908 279700
Website:	www.redbullracing.com
Active in Formula One:	As Stewart GP 1997-99, Jaguar Racing 2000-04, Red Bull Racing 2005 on
Grands Prix contested:	482
Wins:	92
Pole positions:	79
Fastest laps:	84

THE TEAM

Chairman:	Dietrich Mateschitz
Team principal:	Christian Horner
Motorsport consultant:	Helmut Marko
Chief technical officer:	Adrian Newey
Chief engineering officer:	Rob Marshall
Chief engineer, car engineering:	Paul Monaghan
Chief engineer, technology & analysis:	Guillaume Cattelani
Technical director:	Pierre Waché
Head of performance engineering:	Ben Waterhouse
Head of race engineering:	Guillaume Rocquelin
Sporting director:	Jonathan Wheatley
Test driver:	Daniel Ricciardo
Chassis:	Red Bull RB20
Engine:	Honda V6
Tyres:	Pirelli

points, plus his win in the Azerbaijan GP, meant that Red Bull Racing came close to landing the constructors' title too for the first time since 2013.

Also, encouragingly from a continuity point of view, the team's engine deal with Honda was extended last August by a further two years to last to the end of 2025.

Christian Horner celebrates with Sebastian Vettel, Helmut Marko and Adrian Newey in 2010.

"I'm so thankful to everyone who has been contributing ... everyone constantly working flat out. They're never missing any motivation to try and make the car faster."

Max Verstappen

MAX VERSTAPPEN

Two F1 titles in two years is testament to Max's talent. He didn't start the season with the best car, but the team advanced as Ferrari faltered and Max was merciless in his pursuit of points, even withstanding a quality team-mate.

Max moved up another level in 2022, perhaps inspired by having number one on his car.

Max's father Jos was a prodigy when he hit the racing scene in the 1990s, not only hitting F1 in 1994 in his third year out of karts, but being good enough to join top team Benetton. Max, blessed as well with a mother, Sophie Kumpen, who was also a top kart racer, went one better, getting to F1 in 2015 for his second year out of karts after finishing third in the European F3 series, a category that is far from a starter formula.

It was extraordinary, but Max, still 17, and so the youngest F1 driver ever, was far from overawed. Racing for Red Bull's junior team, Scuderia Toro Rosso, he outscored team-mate Carlos Sainz Jr and peaked with a pair of fourth-place finishes. No one mentioned his age again.

Back for a second campaign with Toro Rosso, Max was given a surprise promotion to Red Bull Racing when Daniil Kvyat was moved down to Toro Rosso after just four races. Then Max floored everyone by seizing the opportunity and winning first time out, in Spain. In 2017, Max finished in a clear sixth place, just behind team-mate Daniel Ricciardo, as the Red Bull pair were only beaten by the Mercedes and Ferrari drivers.

The next few years were all about Mercedes, but Max picked up wins when he could and he ranked fourth in 2018 then third in both 2019 and 2020.

Then came 2021, when Red Bull Racing's form went up a notch and appeared to be on a par with Mercedes' form. Going into the final round of the 22-race season, he and Lewis Hamilton had nine wins and eight wins respectively and, amazingly, were equal on 369.5 points each. Hamilton looked to have done enough at Yas Marina to be on course for his record eighth F1 title, but a late-race safety car deployment led to a strange call from the race director and Max, on fresher tyres, was allowed on to Hamilton's tail and then nipped past on the restart to win the race and the title.

TRACK NOTES

Nationality:	**DUTCH**
Born:	**30 SEPTEMBER 1997, HASSELT, BELGIUM**
Website:	**www.verstappen.nl**
Teams:	**TORO ROSSO 2015-16, RED BULL RACING 2016-23**

CAREER RECORD

First Grand Prix: **2015 AUSTRALIAN GP**

Grand Prix starts: **163**

Grand Prix wins: **35**
2016 Spanish GP, 2017 Malaysian GP, Mexican GP, 2018 Austrian GP, Mexican GP, 2019 Austrian GP, German GP, Brazilian GP, 2020 70th Anniversary GP, Abu Dhabi GP, 2021 Emilia Romagna GP, Monaco GP, French GP, Styrian GP, Austrian GP, Belgian GP, Dutch GP, United States GP, Mexican GP, Abu Dhabi GP, 2022 Saudi Arabian GP, Emilia Romagna GP, Miami GP, Spanish GP, Azerbaijan GP, Canadian GP, French GP, Hungarian GP, Belgian GP, Dutch GP, Italian GP, Japanese GP, United States GP, Mexican GP, Abu Dhabi GP

Poles:	**18**
Fastest laps:	**21**
Points:	**2011.5**

Honours: 2021 & 2022 F1 WORLD CHAMPION, 2013 WORLD & EUROPEAN KZ KART CHAMPION, 2012 WSK MASTER SERIES KF2 CHAMPION, 2011 WSK EURO SERIES CHAMPION; 2009 BELGIAN KF5 CHAMPION, 2008 DUTCH CADET KART CHAMPION, 2007 & 2008 DUTCH MINIMAX CHAMPION, 2006 BELGIAN ROTAX MINIMAX CHAMPION

A SECOND TITLE WITH ROOM TO SPARE

A late-race retirement in the season's opening race at Sakhir was a setback, especially after he won the 2021 title by just eight points. However, of more concern was Ferrari's pace in both qualifying and the race, led by Charles Leclerc. With Lewis Hamilton and Mercedes off the pace, he didn't have to worry about his arch-rival. However, Max needed to apply every bit of pressure that he could as the team got his Red Bull RB19 up to the ultimate pace. Victory at the second race, in Jeddah, was a boost, but it took longer than for Red Bull to match Ferrari. Yet Max kept the pressure on and wins at Imola, Miami and Barcelona put him into the lead in the title race. Further wins in Baku and Montreal, then Paul Ricard, the Hungaroring, Spa-Francorchamps and Zandvoort left him 109 points clear of Leclerc with seven rounds to run. The wins kept coming and he wrapped up the title three races later at Suzuka, but lost popular support by refusing to let Perez by for valuable points in Brazil.

SERGIO PEREZ

Winning the Monaco GP last May was good for two reasons for 'Checo' Perez. Firstly, the obvious prestige that comes with winning that iconic race, but secondly that it also came with a two-year Red Bull Racing contract extension, albeit still to act as its number two.

Sergio proved himself to be more than your usual Red Bull Racing number two driver.

European racers have it easy as there is so much racing on their home scene and then across Europe as they rise up the ranks. For Sergio, it was felt that his best chance to make his name was to head north from Mexico to the USA when he advanced from karts to single-seaters at just 14.

He did a decent job in the Skip Barber Dodge Series, then went racing in Germany the following year. Racing in ADAC Formula BMW, he showed good pace, but needed a second year in the category to gain the consistency that is so vital for the gathering of the points required to mount a title bid.

Sergio then contested the secondary National class of the British F3 Championship in 2007 when he was 17 and won that. In 2008, Sergio aimed for the main title but could rank only fourth as Jaime Alguersuari took the crown.

British F3 was not at its strongest at this time and so it was with interest rather than expectation that people watched Sergio's graduation to GP2 in 2009. He had already dipped his toe in the water over the close season, taking two wins in the Asian series, so he was well acquainted with these more powerful cars when the FIA series kicked off, but he ranked only 12th as Nico Hülkenberg ran out a clear winner. This is why 2010 was such a surprise when Sergio won five races and ended the year second behind Pastor Maldonado.

This, plus a plentiful budget from Mexico, made him attractive to Sauber and so Sergio got his F1 break in 2011. Then two second places in 2012 drew the attention of McLaren, but he stayed there just a year.

Sergio moved on to Force India in 2014 and stayed for seven years, through its name change to Racing Point, earning a reputation for being light on his tyres.

Just when it looked as though his time in F1 was up, he won the Sakhir GP. Then, after joining Red Bull Racing in 2021, he added another win, in Baku.

TRACK NOTES

Nationality:	MEXICAN
Born:	26 JANUARY 1990, GUADALAJARA, MEXICO
Website:	www.sergioperezf1.com
Teams:	SAUBER 2011-12, McLAREN 2013, FORCE INDIA 2014-18, RACING POINT 2019-20, RED BULL RACING 2021-23

CAREER RECORD

First Grand Prix:	2011 BAHRAIN GP
Grand Prix starts:	235
Grand Prix wins:	4
	2020 Sakhir GP, 2021 Azerbaijan GP, 2022 Monaco GP, Singapore GP
Poles:	1
Fastest laps:	9
Points:	1201
Honours:	2010 GP2 RUNNER-UP, 2007 BRITISH FORMULA THREE NATIONAL CLASS CHAMPION

YOU CAN SHINE AS A RED BULL NO. 2

With his F1 career having been saved when he was signed for Red Bull Racing for 2021, Sergio made marked progress in 2022 and showed that not everything in the team has to go Max Verstappen's way. Victory in Monaco was a huge fillip, but already the signs were there that he was going to push his Dutch team-mate harder than ever before. A run of good finishes was somewhat helped though by Ferrari's lack of tactical competence. Then, in the second half of the season, the Mexican veteran raced to second place in the Belgian GP and scored the fourth win of his career in Singapore after absorbing huge amounts of pressure from Charles Leclerc. After backing this up with second place next time out at Suzuka moved him into second place in the points table, Sergio kept pressing on in his quest to end the year as runner-up. However, he showed his displeasure with Verstappen when his team-mate flatly refused to help his quest by letting him by at Interlagos.

FERRARI

Having an uncompetitive car is one thing, but having the fastest car and still blowing its title shot came as a major blow to the team and especially Charles Leclerc, who was let down by both poor reliability and some awful race strategy calls.

Charles Leclerc gathered poles for fun in 2022, but he will only be able to tilt for the title in 2023 if he can achieve equal dominance in the races.

For a team to have been in the World Championship since its inaugural season, 1950, is a remarkable feat. The landscape has been transformed time and again across the years as the rules have changed, and technology has broken new ground and then been superseded, so it's not surprising that Ferrari has had its ups and downs. Thanks to Ferrari's road car division, the money has always been there for the team to be well funded, but the management and the team's brains trust haven't always been at the top level – as shown last year.

Enzo Ferrari was a driven man, an engineer and a driver who had run Alfa Romeo's racing programme before World War II, then running his own team after it. His team had no answer to Alfa Romeo's might in 1950, but Jose Froilan Gonzalez gave the team its first win in the 1951 British GP. Alfa Romeo quit at the end of the year and left the stage to Ferrari. With the championship being run to F2

regulations in 1952, Ferrari had just the car, and Alberto Ascari won pretty much every race for the next two years to land both drivers' titles.

A further rule change for 1954, back to F1 rules, put Ferrari on the back foot, then Mercedes' dominance left them without a further title until 1956, when it had

KEY PERSONNEL & 2022 ROUND-UP

MATTIA BINOTTO

Mattia has been the person shouldering all of the responsibility at Ferrari in recent years. Born in Switzerland to Italian parents, he joined Ferrari in 1995, starting in the F1 team's engine department. As the team found its form with Michael Schumacher at the start of the 21st century, he rose to become head of the department then, in 2016, technical director. However, he was put in the hot seat, as team principal, when Maurizio Arrivabene left in 2019.

A SHOCKING CASE OF WHAT MIGHT HAVE BEEN

Ferrari hit the ground running with the new technical regulations, delighting the *tifosi* by filling the first two positions in the opening round when the Red Bulls retired and the Mercedes were off the pace. Charles Leclerc claimed pole positions by the handful, with Carlos Sainz Jr not far behind. Red Bull Racing got up to speed and started winning at the same time as Ferrari started losing, making the wrong tactical calls again and again, allowing Verstappen to be crowned with four races to spare.

2022 DRIVERS & RESULTS

Driver	Nationality	Races	Wins	Pts	Pos
Charles Leclerc	Monegasque	22	3	308	2nd
Carlos Sainz Jr	Spanish	22	1	246	5th

FOR THE RECORD

Country of origin:	**Italy**
Team base:	**Maranello, Italy**
Telephone:	**(39) 536 949111**
Website:	**www.ferrari.com**
Active in Formula One:	**From 1950**
Grands Prix contested:	**1052**
Wins:	**241**
Pole positions:	**242**
Fastest laps:	**258**

THE TEAM

Chairman:	**John Elkann**
Team principal & technical director:	**tba**
Racing director & head of track area:	**Laurent Mekies**
Head of performance engineering:	**Enrico Cardile**
Head of power unit:	**Enrico Gualtieri**
Head of aerodynamics:	**Loic Bigois**
Driving academy director:	**Jock Clear**
Operations director:	**Gino Rosato**
Chief race engineer:	**Matteo Togninalli**
Reserve driver:	**Antonio Giovinazzi**
Chassis:	**Ferrari SF23**
Engine:	**Ferrari V6**
Tyres:	**Pirelli**

taken over Lancia's D50 chassis and Juan Manuel Fangio used one to good effect. Two years later, Mike Hawthorn pipped Vanwall's Stirling Moss.

A revolution was occurring though, as Cooper and Lotus were now using nimble rear-engined cars. Enzo was disdainful, not considering these to be thoroughbreds, but the writing was on the wall as Jack Brabham used a Cooper to win the drivers' title in 1959 and 1960, so Ferrari had to respond.

A rule change, to smaller 1.5-litre engines, favoured Ferrari in 1961 and Phil Hill won the title after team-mate Wolfgang von Trips was killed at Monza, but the pace of development was so rapid that Ferrari struggled to keep up as BRM and Lotus outpaced it. It took the steely British rider-turned-racer John Surtees to coerce the team into functioning to its full, and he squeaked the 1964 title. But then came a decade of underachievement.

It took another individual of focus and application to bring about its next success, with Niki Lauda combining well with team boss Luca di Montezemolo in the mid-1970s to win the title in 1975 and 1977. He would have won it in 1976 too, but for a fiery accident in Germany.

The decade was brought to a close with Jody Scheckter winning the 1979 crown just ahead of team-mate Gilles Villeneuve, but then came two decades of embarrassment for F1's best-funded team as British constructors Williams, Brabham, McLaren and Benetton provided the drivers' champions right through until 1999.

Like Surtees and Lauda before him, Michael Schumacher's arrival, along with that of team principal Jean Todt and technical director Ross Brawn, led to the team being less Italian in its ways and more open to change. It took until Schumacher's fifth year with Ferrari for a title to come in 2000, but he then added the next four and the image of Ferrari as F1's top team was finally true again.

After Schumacher quit F1 at the end of 2006, Kimi Raikkonen won the title at the final round in 2007, and then Felipe Massa very nearly did the same in 2008, only to be pipped by Lewis Hamilton. Fernando Alonso and Sebastian Vettel came and went, winning races but not titles. However, Charles Leclerc has recently been a bright light since joining in 2019 after a rookie year at Sauber. Yet, like before, it seems that the team's management needs to be sorted out to help him truly achieve.

"We have been competitive at every race in 2022 and have won four of them. Clearly, we are all working as one to get even more in 2023."

Charles Leclerc

Niki Lauda put Ferrari back on track in 1975 when he took the first of two titles in three years.

CHARLES LECLERC

It will have been a long close season for the Monegasque star because it appeared last year that both he and his car were good enough to have taken the crown, but for driver errors, mechanical frailty and tactical blunders. That will have really hurt.

Charles will have worked through the winter to ensure all chances are taken in 2023.

Born into a racing family and treated to the annual thrill of the Grand Prix around his home town of Monaco, it was inevitable that Charles would be drawn to racing. Titles were gathered and he peaked with second places in both the World and European KF kart series in 2012, the year that he turned 15.

His single-seater career began in 2014 in Formula Renault and Charles ranked second in a regional championship before advancing to Formula 3. His pace was as good as his reputation and Charles claimed four wins as he placed fourth overall in the European series ahead of Lance Stroll, George Russell and Alexander Albon.

Moving to GP3, Charles won three times to beat Albon to the title. GP2 was followed by F2 for 2017 and Charles had a fantastic season to land that title too, his seven wins for the Prema Racing team putting him well clear of his rivals.

Ferrari found him a seat with Sauber, to which it supplied engines, for his F1 break in 2018. Charles was hugely impressive in qualifying before the car's pace fell away through the races, peaking with sixth place in Baku, and he easily outscored team-mate Marcus Ericsson.

Ferrari had seen enough and signed him to join Sebastian Vettel in its 2019 line-up. He showed his skill immediately but was denied victory in the second race of the season at Sakhir by an engine hiccough. Charles would go on to win twice – at Spa-Francorchamps and Monza – and this was good enough to rank fourth overall, one place ahead of Vettel, as Lewis Hamilton racked up another title for Mercedes.

This made Charles the de facto team leader, but there were no wins in 2020 as Red Bull Racing became more competitive and claimed any scraps left by Mercedes, and he and Vettel ended the year eighth and 13th. 2021 was better, but again there were no wins and new team-mate Carlos Sainz Jr marginally outscored him.

TRACK NOTES

Nationality:	MONEGASQUE
Born:	16 OCTOBER 1997,
	MONTE CARLO, MONACO
Website:	www.charles-leclerc.com
Teams:	SAUBER 2018,
	FERRARI 2019-23

CAREER RECORD

First Grand Prix:	2018 AUSTRALIAN GP
Grand Prix starts:	102
Grand Prix wins:	5

2019 Belgian GP, Italian GP, 2022 Bahrain GP, Australian GP, Austrian GP

Poles:	18
Fastest laps:	7
Points:	868

Honours: 2017 FIA F2 CHAMPION, 2016 GP3 CHAMPION, 2015 MACAU F3 RUNNER-UP, 2014 FORMULA RENAULT ALPS RUNNER-UP, 2013 WORLD KZ KART RUNNER-UP, 2012 UNDER 18 WORLD KART CHAMPIONSHIP RUNNER-UP & EURO KF KART RUNNER-UP, 2011 ACADEMY TROPHY KART CHAMPION, 2010 JUNIOR MONACO KART CUP CHAMPION, 2009 FRENCH CADET KART CHAMPION

PLENTY OF POLES, BUT ALSO STUMBLES

Six pole positions in last year's first eight rounds ought to have, by the law of averages, resulted in four to five wins. However, they yielded just two wins, in the opening round at Sakhir and the third in Melbourne. That it took a further eight rounds before Charles was first to the chequered flag again after a fabulous drive in Austria was shocking. Certainly, Max Verstappen and his Red Bull Racing RB19 was becoming an ever more competitive ingredient, but a stumble at Imola and then crashing out of the lead in the French GP dented his cause, but not as much as Ferrari's sheer ineptitude with its race tactics. Although Charles would go on to claim another two pole positions, at Monza, which delighted the tifosi, and in the following race at Yas Marina, neither of these yielded another win. Certainly, Mercedes' improving form made life more difficult, but there continued to be poor calls from the pitwall which held him back as Sergio Perez challenged him to be runner-up.

CARLOS SAINZ JR

Despite winning the British GP last year, Carlos has plenty to prove in his third year with Ferrari as his 2022 campaign was patchy. The speed was there, not quite to Charles Leclerc's level, but some days things didn't quite work out.

Carlos started last season with a run of errors, but then began to show his true class.

Being the offspring of a famous actor can't be easy. Neither is being the son of a world champion. The question is whether to follow in their footsteps, and possibly become a poor comparison, or to choose a different path. It might be said that Carlos chose the latter, but only insofar as he chose to race cars rather than to rally them as father Carlos had done, landing two world titles with Toyota in 1990 and 1992.

Carlos Jr had excelled in karts, then headed to single-seaters in 2010. His first notable success was becoming Northern European Countries Formula Renault champion and European series runner-up in 2011. This established him as one to watch and Carlos Jr continued to shine in 2012 as he ranked fifth in the European Formula 3 series.

However, this momentum began to fade in 2013 when Carlos Jr could rank only tenth in GP3 and there was talk that he might lose his backing from Red Bull as one of its scholarship drivers. Fortunately, he went well in a couple of F1 tests and so the backing remained in place and he graduated to Formula Renault 3.5, then duly won that to put his name back up in lights.

Formula 1 followed, Carlos Jr joining Scuderia Toro Rosso in 2015. By 2016, he was going well enough to claim three sixth-place finishes. Then his third year with the Red Bull feeder team was interrupted after he had claimed a fourth place in Singapore by Renault taking him on for the final four races after dropping Jolyon Palmer and keeping him on for 2018.

McLaren liked what it saw, signing Carlos Jr for 2019 and he ranked sixth overall, his best result a third-place finish at Interlagos. He then peaked with second at Monza in 2020, right behind AlphaTauri's surprise winner, Pierre Gasly.

Then Ferrari signed him for 2021 and Carlos Jr finished second in Monaco and third at the Hungaroring, Sochi and Yas Marina, the last of which helped him to outscore team-mate Charles Leclerc.

TRACK NOTES

Nationality:	**SPANISH**
Born:	**1 SEPTEMBER 1994, MADRID, SPAIN**
Website:	**www.carlossainzjr.com**
Teams:	**TORO ROSSO 2015-17, RENAULT 2017-18, McLAREN 2019-20, FERRARI 2021-23**

CAREER RECORD

First Grand Prix:	**2015 AUSTRALIAN GP**
Grand Prix starts:	**163**
Grand Prix wins:	**1**
	2022 British GP
Poles:	**3**
Fastest laps:	**3**
Points:	**782.5**
Honours:	**2014 FORMULA RENAULT 3.5 CHAMPION, 2011 EUROPEAN FORMULA RENAULT RUNNER-UP & NORTHERN EUROPEAN FORMULA RENAULT CHAMPION, 2009 MONACO KART CUP WINNER & EUROPEAN KF3 RUNNER-UP, 2008 ASIA/PACIFIC JUNIOR KART CHAMPION, 2006 MADRID CADET KART CHAMPION**

MAKING STRIDES AFTER A SLOW START

Second and third places in last year's first two races suggested that 2022 was going to be a good year for Carlos. However, he was already in team-mate Charles Leclerc's shadow and clearly struggling to become confident in the handling of what was then the year's fastest car: the F1-75. Then the mistakes began. Full credit to Carlos, though, because he knuckled down, used his analytical approach to find the speed and then built his confidence back up. His reward was a career first, with victory in the British GP to send him into the second half of the year with his tail up. The mistakes weren't all down to Carlos, as shown by his pit crew not having one of his tyres ready at the Dutch GP and then sending him out with an unsafe release. Ferrari had every reason to be delighted with Carlos as his form kept on improving. Pole position for the United States GP gave him great hope, but being squeezed between the McLarens wrecked that. He recovered well to third in Brazil.

Ferrari's pit crew pounces as Charles Leclerc arrives for a pit stop during the Saudi Arabian GP, as VIPs watch from above.

MERCEDES-AMG PETRONAS

The new technical regulations for 2022 were a wake-up call for Mercedes, and the serial title winners were left to play catch-up even to win a race. Expect its gold standard to be regained in 2023, as Mercedes is that sort of team.

It seemed inconceivable that Lewis Hamilton would ever have a winless season, but you can be sure that he won't settle for this in 2023.

It has now been 13 years that this team has raced as Mercedes-AMG, remarkably successful years at that, but its history stretches back to 1999 when it started life as BAR, or British American Racing to give it its full name.

BAR was created by Jacques Villeneuve's skiing coach from his schooldays in Switzerland, Craig Pollock, with money from British American Tobacco. And it started big, indeed boasting in its promotional material that it had 'a tradition of excellence' despite being a brand-new outfit. Although it had Villeneuve – world champion in 1997 – in one of its cars, the team was going nowhere fast and scarcely recorded a race finish in the first half of the 1999 season. In time, though, results started to come, with Jenson Button's four second places in 2004 being its best.

In 2006, rebranded as Honda Racing, Jenson Button achieved its breakthrough by winning the Hungarian GP in a wet/dry race with a performance more down to his ability in changeable conditions than the team's true level of competitiveness.

Then came the global financial slump in 2008 and Honda pulled the plug at the end of the year. A last-minute rescue package put together by technical director Ross Brawn led to its salvation, one that

KEY PERSONNEL & 2022 ROUND-UP

JAMES ALLISON

The high number of F1 teams based in Britain perhaps explains the disproportionate number of British engineers and designers in F1. James is one of the many British F1 designers' and his record since becoming Mercedes' technical director in 2017 has been five straight constructors' titles and then last year's fightback. He began as an aerodynamicist at Benetton and then worked for Larrousse, Benetton again, Ferrari and Benetton for a third time. He then became technical director when it changed to Renault, before a second spell at Ferrari preceded him joining Mercedes.

A BUMPY RIDE GETS SMOOTHED THROUGH THE YEAR

When Mercedes didn't win the first race and was only on the podium in third place after both Red Bulls retired, it was clear that this wasn't going to be another year of Mercedes domination. Other teams had clearly produced cars that worked better, while the W13 was one of those that would porpoise. In time, progress was made but wins remained a step too far until the Brazilian GP.

2022 DRIVERS & RESULTS

Driver	Nationality	Races	Wins	Pts	Pos
George Russell	British	22	1	275	4th
Lewis Hamilton	British	22	0	240	6th

was rewarded by a clever double-decked diffuser giving its cars a performance advantage, which Button and Rubens Barrichello exploited to win eight rounds, with Button crowned champion.

Then Mercedes put its badge on the team for 2010, bringing much-needed finance. This team thus became the second team to carry the Mercedes name in F1, but there was no connection with the works team that took F1 to new levels in 1954 and 1955 with Juan Manuel Fangio the master and Stirling Moss the precociously talented pupil. In reaction to the awful Le Mans disaster of 1955, though, when one of its cars flew into the crowd on the pit straight and killed dozens of people, Mercedes quit motorsport.

For 2010, Michael Schumacher came out of retirement to lead its attack, but it was Nico Rosberg who took its first win. This didn't come immediately though, but in 2012, at the Chinese GP.

The arrival of Lewis Hamilton from McLaren in 2013, taking Schumacher's place, gave the team a sharper edge and Lewis made boss Toto Wolff very happy as he guided the team to second overall, and then, in 2014, landed the drivers' title and moved Mercedes to the top for its first success in the constructors' championship.

There was then no stopping it with a repeat performance in 2015, the team enjoying technical excellence under Paddy Lowe. Extra guile was provided by three-time world champion Niki Lauda, who kept the team tactically sound and motivated by bringing the experience he had gained in the mid-1970s when he helped Ferrari to rediscover its winning ways.

The 2016 season was different as Rosberg attacked like never before, ending the year ahead of Hamilton. Then he surprised everyone by quitting. This left a seat vacant, but the timing of this decision meant that many of the drivers that Mercedes might have chosen were already under contract with other teams. So, Valtteri Bottas was the lucky individual to get a shot with F1's top team. However, the Finn was always made to play a supporting role to Hamilton, albeit landing the odd win. Yet the success kept on coming under

FOR THE RECORD

Country of origin:	**England**
Team base:	**Brackley, England**
Telephone:	**(44) 01280 844000**
Website:	**www.mercedesamgf1.com**

Active in Formula One:
As BAR 1999-2005, Honda Racing 2006-08, Brawn GP 2009, Mercedes 2010 on

Grands Prix contested:	**447**
Wins:	**125**
Pole positions:	**137**
Fastest laps:	**100**

THE TEAM

Head of Mercedes-Benz Motorsport:	**Toto Wolff**
Chief technical officer:	**James Allison**
MD, Mercedes-AMG High Performance powertrains:	**Hywel Thomas**
Director of digital engineering:	**Geoff Willis**
Technology director:	**Mike Elliott**
Chief designer:	**John Owen**
Performance director:	**Loic Serra**
Sporting director:	**Ron Meadows**
Trackside engineering director:	**Andrew Shovlin**
Chief track engineer:	**Simon Cole**
Test driver:	**tba**
Chassis:	**Mercedes F1 W14**
Engine:	**Mercedes V6**
Tyres:	**Pirelli**

new technical director James Allison, the team from Brackley being simply too good and too smart to be toppled. Hamilton resumed his run of titles in 2017 and was set to make it five in succession until being deprived in a controversial 2021 finale in Abu Dhabi that ended with Red Bull Racing's Max Verstappen pipping him.

> **"The team back in Brackley and Brixworth did an amazing job to make our win in Brazil possible, as we had no idea we'd be able to achieve this given where we were at the start of the year."**
>
> Andrew Shovlin

Nico Rosberg gave Mercedes its first win in 2012. Since then, the team has added 123 more.

GEORGE RUSSELL

George moved to Mercedes with a target of beating Lewis Hamilton. That, of course, would make him world champion, but Mercedes failed to produce a car as fast as the Red Bulls and Ferraris, but he was fast and became a winner nonetheless.

George was consistent last year for Mercedes, with victory at Interlagos the highlight.

Anyone who lands a European title in kart racing is worth looking out for, and George did so in 2012 when he was 14. This was when he opted to be home-schooled so that more time could be spent focusing on his racing.

This experience was put to good use in 2014 when he won the British Formula 4 series and was then named the McLaren Autosport BRDC Young Driver of the Year.

Deciding to bypass Formula Renault, George raced in Formula 3 in 2015 and certainly impressed by ranking sixth overall in the European series as Felix Rosenqvist took the title. When he returned for a second attempt in 2016, George rose to third as Lance Stroll dominated.

So, there was no choice but to move on, but with only the budget to graduate to GP3 rather than the more senior GP2. And George did what he had to, by winning four rounds to be a clear champion. Mercedes had seen enough and took him under its wing.

GP2 was renamed as F2 for 2018 and George did what only a few drivers have managed: he won F1's feeder formula at the first attempt, winning seven of the 24 races for ART Grand Prix to be a convincing champion.

With Mercedes having no opening for him for 2019, George was farmed out to Mercedes-powered Williams. Sadly, the team had been on the slide and its car was only good enough for the tail-end of the grid. Still, George showed skill and application, albeit he was never in with a shot at points, his best result being

an 11th place in his first two years. The penultimate race of 2020 saw a change, though, as he moved to Mercedes for the Sakhir GP when Hamilton fell ill, and not only outraced Valtteri Bottas but would have won but for a puncture.

In a third year with Williams in 2021, George scored his first points, for eighth place, in Hungary. He then sensationally qualified second at Spa-Francorchamps and was classified there too when the race was abandoned after one lap because of too much sitting water on the track rendering the conditions unsafe.

TRACK NOTES

Nationality:	**BRITISH**
Born:	**15 FEBRUARY 1998, KING'S LYNN, ENGLAND**
Website:	**www.georgerussellracing.com**
Teams:	**WILLIAMS 2019-21, MERCEDES 2022-23**

CAREER RECORD

First Grand Prix:	**2019 AUSTRALIAN GP**
Grand Prix starts:	**82**
Grand Prix wins:	**1**
	2022 Brazilian GP
Poles:	**1**
Fastest laps:	**5**
Points:	**294**
Honours:	**2018 FORMULA 2 CHAMPION, 2017 GP3 CHAMPION, 2015 F3 MASTERS RUNNER-UP, 2014 BRITISH F4 CHAMPION & McLAREN AUTOSPORT YOUNG DRIVER AWARD, 2012 EUROPEAN KF3 KART CHAMPION**

STRONG FIRST YEAR WITH MERCEDES

George's three years with tail-end Williams were certainly character-building, but all was going to be all right as he was joining the most competitive team on the grid for 2022. However, a tweak of the technical regulations clearly pulled the rug out from under Mercedes' feet. The way that George accepted this and knuckled down to the job of trying to master the porpoising F1 W13 was impressive, and the way that he often out-qualified Lewis Hamilton made people really understand his level of talent. Pole position at the Hungaroring was further proof of his resilience, but it was the way that he achieved good point-scoring drives at every time of asking that really impressed, save for the British GP when he was hit at the first corner and stopped to help the inverted Guanyu Zhou. A mark of his maturity came at Zandvoort when he asked for a new set of tyres for the closing laps and Hamilton didn't, enabling him to finish second, with his team-mate in fourth. Then came that breakthrough win in Brazil.

LEWIS HAMILTON

If neither winning the title nor being in contention for it came as a shock last year as he struggled with a poor Mercedes, not winning a single round was even more so. Another year like this might precipitate his retirement from F1.

Lewis kept his head last year when Mercedes lost form and fell from its F1 pedestal.

Highly skilled at radio-controlled car racing as a kid, Lewis then tried karting and started winning titles for fun, from entry-level cadet karts in 1995 when he was ten through to a European title and the World Kart Cup five years later.

Then came cars, and Lewis had already received a pledge from then McLaren boss Ron Dennis that he would help finance his ascent to F1.

The first step was Formula Renault and he was champion in his second year in the British series. The European F3 series also turned out to be a two-year project and Lewis improved from one win in 2004 to 15 in 2005. Taking that form into GP2, he went straight to the top to edge out Nelson Piquet Jr.

Then came F1 and Lewis impressed from his first race with McLaren in Melbourne and went to the final race of 2007 in with a title shot but, along with team-mate Fernando Alonso, was pipped by Ferrari's Kimi Räikkönen.

Still, Lewis only had to wait a year for his first title, but it was super close in a battle with Ferrari's Felipe Massa. He was lucky that he squeaked that one by a point, for McLaren then fell from the pace and it was a diet of wins but not titles until he elected to join Mercedes.

His second title was claimed in his second year with the Silver Arrows, 2014, and Lewis then took control of F1 to land five of the next six titles, being edged out by team-mate Nico Rosberg in 2016 and then more controversially by Max Verstappen in 2021.

A SEASON OF A DIFFERENT NATURE

After eight years of driving the best car or equal best car on the grid, Lewis knew from before the opening race that his 2022 season was going to be somewhat different. Quite simply, Mercedes had created a car for the new regulations that didn't want to behave. While others offered their drivers a relatively smooth ride, the Mercedes F1 W13 shook its drivers around and made them feel uncomfortable. That new team-mate George Russell did a better job in the first half of the year will have shaken him, but he responded with a run starting at the Canadian GP where he finished third, followed by two more of those and then a pair of seconds. A year without a win would have been unthinkable in the rest of his Mercedes career, but last year really was something else as Mercedes threw everything at getting onto the ultimate pace and Lewis showed dignity when congratulating George for beating him to take a win.

TRACK NOTES

Nationality:	**BRITISH**
Born:	**7 JANUARY 1985, STEVENAGE, ENGLAND**
Website:	**www.lewishamilton.com**
Teams:	**McLAREN 2007-12, MERCEDES 2013-23**

CAREER RECORD

First Grand Prix:	**2007 AUSTRALIAN GP**
Grand Prix starts:	**310**
Grand Prix wins:	**103**

2007 Canadian GP, United States GP, Hungarian GP, Japanese GP, 2008 Australian GP, Monaco GP, British GP, German GP, Chinese GP, 2009 Hungarian GP, Singapore GP, 2010 Turkish GP, Canadian GP, Belgian GP, 2011 Chinese GP, German GP, Abu Dhabi GP, 2012 Canadian GP, Hungarian GP, Italian GP, United States GP, 2013 Hungarian GP, 2014 Malaysian GP, Bahrain GP, Chinese GP, Spanish GP, British GP, Italian GP, Singapore GP, Japanese GP, Russian GP, United States GP, Abu Dhabi GP, 2015 Australian GP, Chinese GP, Bahrain GP, Canadian GP, British GP, Belgian GP, Italian GP, Japanese GP, Russian GP, United States GP, 2016 Monaco GP, Canadian GP, Austrian GP, British GP, Hungarian GP, German GP, United States GP, Mexican GP, Brazilian GP, Abu Dhabi GP, 2017 Chinese GP, Spanish GP, Canadian GP, British GP, Belgian GP, Italian GP, Singapore GP, Japanese GP, United States GP, 2018 Azerbaijan GP, Spanish GP, French GP, German GP, Hungarian GP, Italian GP, Singapore GP, Russian GP, Japanese GP, Brazilian GP, Abu Dhabi GP, 2019 Bahrain GP, Chinese GP, Spanish GP, Monaco GP, Canadian GP, French GP, British GP, Hungarian GP, Russian GP, Mexican GP, Abu Dhabi GP, 2020 Styrian GP, Hungarian GP, British GP, Spanish GP, Belgian GP, Tuscan GP, Eifel GP, Portuguese GP, Emilia Romagna GP, Turkish GP, Bahrain GP, 2021 Bahrain GP, Portuguese GP, Spanish GP, British GP, Russian GP, Sao Paolo GP, Qatar GP, Saudi Arabian GP

Poles:	**103**
Fastest laps:	**61**
Points:	**4405.5**
Honours:	2008, 2014, 2015, 2017, 2018, 2019 & 2020 F1 WORLD CHAMPION, 2007, 2016 & 2021 F1 RUNNER-UP, 2006 GP2 CHAMPION, 2005 EUROPEAN FORMULA RENAULT CHAMPION, 2003 BRITISH FORMULA RENAULT CHAMPION, 2000 WORLD KART CUP & EUROPEAN FORMULA A KART CHAMPION, 1999 ITALIAN INTERCON A CHAMPION, 1995 BRITISH CADET KART CHAMPION

ALPINE

The loss of team leader Fernando Alonso to Aston Martin for 2023 was a blow, but the team's failure to hold down the test driver it had been nurturing, Oscar Piastri, who chose to go to McLaren instead, was an embarrassment.

Esteban had some strong runs last year for Alpine, such as fourth place in the rain at Suzuka and fifth, shown here, at the Red Bull Ring.

This team is like a spade that has had five replacement handles through its 42-year life in F1. It began life simply enough in 1981 when the successful Toleman team wanted to step up from F2, but the path has seldom remained straight since then, with extra confusion caused by being Renault twice through the course of these changes. More confusingly still, it also raced under the Lotus name, but had zero connection with the team that lit up the 1960s and 1970s.

Ted Toleman was a man who made his fortune by transporting cars and he assembled a great band around him as his team rose through racing's ranks. Its first steps in F1 were troubled, but designer Rory Byrne soon had the cars pointing the right way, and then a rookie called Ayrton Senna took the team to the sharp end, finishing second at Monaco in 1984.

It was always clear that Senna would move on and the team next found impetus when it was rebranded as Benetton in 1986, with a considerable financial boost from the knitwear manufacturer and an even bigger boost from flame-spitting BMW turbo engines. Gerhard Berger gave the team its first win, in Mexico in 1986, and Thierry Boutsen, Nelson Piquet and Alessandro Nannini also won during the next four seasons.

KEY PERSONNEL & 2022 ROUND-UP

OTMAR SZAFNAUER

The team principal who joined Alpine last February from Aston Martin started his working life as a Ford management trainee. However, this Romanian-born but American-raised engineer got his break in the motor racing world when he joined BAR for its first year in F1 in 1999, staying on as it became Honda Racing. In 2009, he moved on to Force India, firstly in charge of operations before becoming team principal when it morphed into Racing Point and later Aston Martin.

COMING ON STRONG IN THE FIGHT FOR FOURTH

"To lose one parent may be considered unfortunate, but to lose both looks like carelessness," wrote Oscar Wilde. However, despite having a car that came on strong through 2022, this French-financed, British-based team not only lost former world champion Fernando Alonso's services for 2023 but also those of 2021 F2 champion Oscar Piastri, who had been being groomed to step in. These management woes masked the fact that Alpine had been getting faster.

2022 DRIVERS & RESULTS

Driver	Nationality	Races	Wins	Pts	Pos
Esteban Ocon	French	22	0	92	8th
Fernando Alonso	Spanish	22	0	81	9th

Then the chosen one arrived, with Michael Schumacher joining late in 1991. A winner in 1992, he drove the team forward and won the title in 1994 after an unsavoury clash with Damon Hill's Williams in the final round and again, in less acrimonious circumstances, in 1995. But then he left for Ferrari and the team fell away again.

In order to keep the Renault engine deal it had had since 1995, the team from Oxfordshire was renamed as Renault in 2002, although it had no connection to the works team that the French manufacturer had run from 1977 out of its base at Viry-Châtillon until 1985. Good performances from Jarno Trulli and Fernando Alonso kept it at the front of the midfield, but nowhere close to Ferrari, Williams and McLaren.

Then Alonso took things up a gear in 2005 when he won the drivers' title, with strong support from Giancarlo Fisichella helping the team to take the constructors' title too. In 2006, Alonso did it again, taking his blue and yellow R26 to six wins, with Fisichella adding another as Renault doubled up on the constructors' title, pipping Ferrari by just five points.

The illustrious Lotus F1 team closed its doors in 1994, but entrepreneur Tony Fernandes brought the name back to F1 in 2010. Confusingly, this team, the one that had been Renault, raced as Lotus Renault GP in 2011 against Fernandes' Team Lotus. Then, in 2012, this team changed the name of its cars to Lotus, when Fernandes' team's cars had to race as Caterhams. On track, though, there was no confusion as to which team was which, with Lotus scoring 303 and Caterham none. Then, after returning from a spell in rallying, Kimi Raikkonen gave the team a win in Australia in 2013.

Then it reverted to being Renault in 2016 and also reverted to being the best of the rest behind the top three teams, which were now Mercedes, Red Bull Racing and Ferrari.

Then, with a twist on Renault's involvement, the team was most recently rebranded as Alpine, Renault's sporting division. This was in 2021, with the cars racing in the red, white and blue colours of the French flag. Delighting the company, Esteban Ocon achieved a win, albeit in a topsy-turvy Hungarian GP, but he was still outscored by Alonso, who was back for a third spell with the team.

Hopefully the team will be happy with its identity and keep it for years to come.

FOR THE RECORD

Country of origin:	**England**
Team base:	**Enstone, England**
Telephone:	**(44) 01608 678000**
Website:	**www.alpinecars.com**
Active in Formula One:	**As Toleman 1981-85, Benetton 1986-2001, Renault 2002-11 & 2016-2020, Lotus 2012-15, Alpine 2021 on**
Grands Prix contested:	**716**
Wins:	**49**
Pole positions:	**34**
Fastest laps:	**56**

THE TEAM

Chief executive officer:	**Laurent Rossi**
Team principal:	**Otmar Szafnauer**
Executive director:	**Marcin Budkowski**
Chassis technical director:	**Pat Fry**
Director, power unit:	**Bruno Famin**
Chief aerodynamicist:	**Dirk de Beer**
Sporting director:	**Alan Permane**
Engineering director:	**Matt Harman**
Operations director:	**Rob White**
Chief engineer:	**Ciaron Pilbeam**
Team manager:	**Paul Seaby**
Test drivers:	**tba**
Chassis:	**Renault A523**
Engine:	**Renault V6**
Tyres:	**Pirelli**

25

> "I'm delighted to join Alpine. Driving for a team that has French roots is something very special. I know the strengths of Alpine, having raced against them, and their progress and ambition is very impressive."
>
> Pierre Gasly

Fernando Alonso stopped Michael Schumacher's title run when he won for Renault in 2005 and 2006.

ESTEBAN OCON

There was no repetition of his 2021 win, not even a sniff of it, but this was another solid season from the Frenchman. With Fernando Alonso's departure, though, he will find himself leading the Alpine team for the first time.

Esteban must try to build bridges with his former friend and now team-mate Pierre Gasly.

France – the country that hosted the first ever Grand Prix back in 1906 – went a long time without representation in F1. Then, a decade ago, a flicker of hope was lit, as some of the best young kart racers were French. One of these was Esteban, along with Pierre Gasly and Anthoine Hubert.

Good pace in his second year in Formula Renault, when still 17, saw him rank third in the European series.

This earned Esteban graduation to the FIA F3 Euro Series in 2014, when his nine wins made the racing world pay attention as he landed this prestigious title at his first attempt.

As with many before him, this was followed by a snag – he didn't have the backing to progress to GP2. Instead, he had to make do with the less powerful GP3 series and he did as Valtteri Bottas and Daniil Kvyat had done before him – he won it, to keep his career on track.

Although Esteban showed good pace when testing a Force India F1 car, no doors opened for him in racing's top category so he was placed by Mercedes in DTM, the German touring car series. Then, in an unexpected move, Mercedes gave him his F1 break before the year was out when Manor dropped Rio Haryanto and offered him the seat for the final nine rounds.

Esteban landed a full-time F1 ride for 2017, with Force India. He impressed a great deal by finishing the year eighth overall, boosted by two fifth-place finishes as he challenged team leader Sergio Perez.

After a less fruitful second year, he made way for the well-backed Lance Stroll and spent 2019 on the sidelines, testing for Renault. However, he did get back into a race seat for 2020 and enjoyed his first podium visit after finishing second at Sakhir.

Then the team then morphed into Alpine and Esteban pulled a welcome first win out of nowhere in a chaotic Hungarian GP. He avoided a mass shunt at the first corner then absorbed huge pressure from Lewis Hamilton on his day of days.

ANOTHER YEAR IN ALONSO'S SHADOW

Life wasn't always easy at Alpine last year and Esteban, who had been outscored by Alonso by only 74 points to 81 in 2021, was nowhere near as close to the Spanish former world champion in 2022. It wasn't just the number of cars between them on most grids but the lap time deficit. Certainly, the A522 wasn't always an easy car to drive, but his run of point-scoring drives in the first three races was not repeated until the middle of the season and, even in that five-race run from the Austrian to Dutch GPs, Alonso scored more. Esteban's best result was fourth place in the Japanese GP at Suzuka. Once it became clear that he would be joined by former friend turned fierce rival Pierre Gasly for 2023, you could almost sense an extra desire to shine. Helpfully, the Alpine A522 also became more competitive too and this will give hope for the coming season.

TRACK NOTES

Nationality:	**FRENCH**
Born:	**17 SEPTEMBER 1996, EVREUX, FRANCE**
Website:	**www.esteban-ocon.com**
Teams:	**MANOR 2016, FORCE INDIA 2017-18, RENAULT 2020, ALPINE 2021-23**

CAREER RECORD

First Grand Prix:	**2016 BELGIAN GP**
Grand Prix starts:	**111**
Grand Prix wins:	**1**
	2021 Hungarian GP
Poles:	**0**
Fastest laps:	**0**
Points:	**364**
Honours:	**2015 GP3 CHAMPION, 2014 FIA EUROPEAN FORMULA THREE CHAMPION**

PIERRE GASLY

Having tasted victory with this team in 2020, Pierre must feel as though he is treading water as he continues to wait for a second shot with Red Bull Racing, where wins are attainable. Until then, he must wait and score when possible.

Pierre peaked with fifth in 2022, but will want more as he moved to join a French team.

Racing careers need many ingredients to flourish. Natural speed and racecraft are vital, along with the good fortune to pick the right formula and right team. Sadly, access to a budget is now more important than ever, so for a driver of no notable family wealth to advance through the single-seater formulae is a matter of no little luck.

Pierre is one such driver, one who was a front runner in karting, and it was the ease with which he climbed through the junior formulae, usually as champion or runner-up, that impressed.

Third place in the French F4 series in 2011 was a good start before winning the European Formula Renault title in 2013 at his second attempt. This placed him in Red Bull's talent-spotting scheme and financed his move to Formula Renault 3.5, where Pierre starred, ending the year second to Carlos Sainz Jr.

Pierre then tackled the final step before F1 – GP2. Finishing eighth at his first attempt, he began winning races in 2016 before holding off a challenge from Antonio Giovinazzi to land the title.

Ideally, Red Bull would have promoted him to its junior F1 team, Scuderia Toro Rosso, but there was no drive available, and so Red Bull sent Pierre to Japan to race in Super Formula. Even though he was learning about a new car and new tracks, he impressed with the way that he took two wins to end the year as runner-up, in a year in which he was given his F1 debut after Toro Rosso dropped Daniil Kvyat.

Pierre's first full season in F1, 2018, peaked with a fourth place at Sakhir on only his second outing, and this was enough to clinch his promotion to Red Bull Racing for 2019.

Seventh overall was not considered good enough as team-mate Max Verstappen ranked third – the best of the rest behind the Mercedes drivers. So it was back to Red Bull's junior team, now racing as Scuderia AlphaTauri, for 2020 when he raced to his one win, at Monza, although this wasn't enough to reverse his demotion.

FIFTH PLACE WAS AS GOOD AS IT GOT

This was a year that Pierre couldn't afford, if ever he was going to get another shot with a top team, as his form went backwards. This was down to the AlphaTauri AT03 not being the sharpest tool in the box, but it reflected badly on him and may well have ended his chances of ever getting back into a car capable of competing at the front end of the grid. In the early-season races, Pierre was in a position to tilt at points, with his fifth place on the streets of Baku in the Azerbaijan GP an exception to the team's true form. But then the team's form dropped away by the middle of the season and this left him with a predicament. However, Sebastian Vettel's decision to retire from F1 at year's end suddenly triggered a chain of events that opened the door to a surprise move to more competitive Alpine for 2023. The sticking point was that he and compatriot Esteban Ocon famously don't get on, but the French team decided that this was worth a chance as it tries to fill the gap left by Fernando Alonso's departure.

McLAREN

This became a lopsided team in 2022, with Lando Norris going well whenever the car worked and Daniel Ricciardo being all at sea. Understanding the new technical regulations remained a problem, so the winter will have been a busy one for the design department.

McLaren will be looking to give its drivers a better and more consistent car in 2023, although Lando Norris did take third place at Imola.

Bruce McLaren was a racer first, then an engineer full of ideas and finally a supreme manager of people. He led from the front and asked no one to do what he wouldn't do himself. This is what set his tiny team on the road to success in the 1960s after he followed the example of his former Cooper team-mate Jack Brabham in setting up his own racing car company.

Success was quick to follow and the sale of cars to others financed the push into F1 in 1966, with the money that poured in from its works cars dominating the lucrative Can Am series from 1967 to 1971, with sales to hosts of privateer entries as well, making Bruce's F1 dream possible.

The F1 team was limited to start with but was a winning outfit in its third season when Bruce won the Belgian GP. The victory was fortuitous, but it was welcome all the same as McLaren proved itself to be among the best of the customer teams using the Ford Cosworth

DFV engine in the first year that it was available to teams other than Lotus.

The team might have folded in 1970 when Bruce was killed whilst testing the latest Can Am McLaren, but his lieutenants stepped into the breach, led by Teddy Mayer, and it prevailed. Not only that, but the Gordon Coppuck-designed

KEY PERSONNEL & 2022 ROUND-UP

ZAK BROWN
This Californian wanted to reach the top as a driver, but racing in Formula Opel in Europe in 1992 and then Formula Atlantic back in the USA made it plain that his talents might lie elsewhere. Indeed his strengths were in business and he built up a successful sports marketing firm, which gave him the clout to reach F1, joining McLaren at the end of 2016 as executive director. Zak is also joint owner of the United Autosports sports car team and owns historic racing cars.

A PERPLEXING YEAR OF UPS AND DOWNS
After the strides made in 2021, McLaren struggled to get to grips with the new rules and its MCL36 was sometimes good, but sometimes a handful. Lando Norris got it to work better than Daniel Ricciardo did and the story of the season was how Norris would collect points when they raced on tracks that suited the car while Ricciardo, largely, would not. It was uncomfortable watching a popular racer losing his mojo in the way he did.

2022 DRIVERS & RESULTS

Driver	Nationality	Races	Wins	Pts	Pos
Lando Norris	British	22	0	122	7th
Daniel Ricciardo	Australian	22	0	37	11th

FOR THE RECORD

Country of origin:	**England**
Team base:	**Woking, England**
Telephone:	**(44) 01483 261900**
Website:	**www.mclaren.com**
Active in Formula One:	**From 1966**
Grands Prix contested:	**925**
Wins:	**182**
Pole positions:	**156**
Fastest laps:	**161**

THE TEAM

Chief executive officer:	**Zak Brown**
Team principal:	**Andreas Seidl**
Executive director, technical:	**James Key**
Executive director, racing:	**Andrea Stella**
Executive director, operations:	
	Piers Thynne
Chief engineering officer:	**Matt Morris**
Chief engineer, aerodynamics:	
	Peter Prodromou
Director of design & development:	
	Neil Oatley
Head of design:	**Mark Inham**
Head of race engineering:	**Hiroshi Imai**
Operations director:	**Paul James**
Test driver:	**tba**
Simulator drivers:	**Will Stevens &**
	Oliver Turvey
Chassis:	**McLaren MCL36**
Engine:	**Mercedes V6**
Tyres:	**Pirelli**

M23 helped Emerson Fittipaldi become the first McLaren world champion. Two years later, also in an M23, James Hunt followed suit.

When Lotus introduced ground-effect technology, McLaren was slow to respond and it took the arrival of designer John Barnard's MP4/1 with its carbon-fibre monocoque to put the team back to the front. This was at the start of Ron Dennis's reign and his fastidious approach took the team to new heights, with Niki Lauda and Alain Prost landing a trio of titles in the mid-1980s.

Williams found an advantage with Honda engines, but then McLaren took over the deal and another golden spell arrived. However, Dennis found himself in the middle of an intra-team battle as he had not only the best car but the two best drivers too, and neither Prost nor new signing Ayrton Senna cared to lose to the other. So dominant were they in 1988 that they won 15 of the 16 races as Senna claimed the crown, with Prost on top in 1989 when the battle between the pair came to a climax.

For 1990, Prost opted to lead Ferrari's attack and Senna was so determined not to let Prost get into the first corner at Suzuka in front that he took both of them off en route to becoming champion again. The Brazilian was also champion in 1991.

Williams moved to the front again in remarkable style in 1992 and it took the arrival of Mercedes engines for McLaren to find its form again, with Mika Hakkinen and David Coulthard a potent pairing, the Finn becoming champion in 1998. The Ferrari threat grew stronger in 1999 in a fierce battle with Michael Schumacher until the German broke his leg, although team-mate Eddie Irvine pushed Hakkinen hard. However, McLaren had no answer to Schumacher over the next five years and it took until the arrival of Fernando Alonso and Lewis Hamilton for the team to shine again. This was in 2007 when they were pipped by Ferrari's Kimi Raikkonen, but then Hamilton took control in 2008.

McLaren then struggled to land a deal for a competitive engine, leaving it floundering so much that Hamilton moved to Mercedes and it has been a rebuilding process ever since. Carlos Sainz Jr was pipped at Monza in 2020 then Daniel Ricciardo won at the same venue in 2021 for the team's first victory since the 2012 Brazilian GP.

"We are delighted to welcome Oscar to McLaren. He has an impressive racing career to date, and we are sure that, together with Lando, will be able to help us to move another step forward towards our ambitions."

Andreas Seidl

Lewis Hamilton produced one of the great drives when he dominated a wet/dry 2008 British GP.

LANDO NORRIS

Life wasn't easy for the McLaren drivers last year, their car being rather erratic, but the way that Lando adapted and put team-mate Daniel Ricciardo in the shade was yet more proof that he is made of title-winning material, car allowing.

Lando continued in his role as lead McLaren driver, but will have a rookie to tame in 2023.

Lando was one of those drivers who carved a swathe through the karting scene, gathering titles by the handful while largely missing the tail end of their schooling as they criss-crossed Europe.

Always with a healthy budget supplied by his financier father Adam, Lando was a European kart champion before he advanced to cars. His first step wasn't into single-seaters, but into Ginettas, a special sports car series for 14-year-olds.

The following year, 2015, brought his graduation to single-seaters and the MSA Formula title along with some experience in F4. In 2016, Lando was a very busy 16-year-old, competing in the Toyota Racing Series in New Zealand to get his season going and winning that, then racing in the European Formula Renault series and winning that too. To cap his season, Lando won the prestigious McLaren Autosport BRDC Young Driver award, and so began his connection with McLaren.

F3 came next and Lando won the European title in that too. He also tried F2 and was ready for a title assault in 2018. He was also in with a shout for Carlin in an all-British scrap, although lost out to George Russell but beat Alexander Albon.

Fast, consistent and eager to learn, he thus stepped up to F1 with McLaren in 2019 and instantly looked at home, his ready sense of humour earning him new fans.

Two sixth-place finishes in his rookie season were achieved before kicking off the COVID-affected 2020 season with third place in the opening race in Austria. His more experienced team-mate, Carlos Sainz Jr, would eventually overhaul his points tally and they ended the year sixth and ninth as Mercedes continued to dominate.

For 2021, Sainz Jr moved to Ferrari and was replaced by eight-time race winner Daniel Ricciardo. Yet it was the young British driver who came out ahead in their intra-team battle, 160 points to 115, this time with Lando sixth and Daniel eighth. If there was one frustration, it would be that it was Daniel who gave McLaren its first win in nine years, pipping Lando in a McLaren one-two at Monza.

TRACK NOTES

Nationality:	**BRITISH**
Born:	**13 NOVEMBER 1999,**
	GLASTONBURY, ENGLAND
Website:	**www.landonorris.com**
Teams:	**McLAREN 2019-23**

CAREER RECORD

First Grand Prix:	**2019 Australian GP**
Grand Prix starts:	**82**
Grand Prix wins:	**0 (best result: 2nd, 2021 Italian GP)**
Poles:	**1**
Fastest laps:	**5**
Points:	**428**
Honours:	**2018 F2 RUNNER-UP, 2017 EUROPEAN F3 CHAMPION, 2016 EUROPEAN FORMULA RENAULT CHAMPION & FORMULA RENAULT NEC CHAMPION & TOYOTA RACING SERIES CHAMPION, 2015 MSA FORMULA CHAMPION, 2014 WORLD KF KART CHAMPION, 2013 WORLD KF JUNIOR KART CHAMPION & EUROPEAN KF KART CHAMPION & KF JUNIOR SUPER CUP WINNER**

LANDO WORKS HARD WITH TRICKY CAR

All at sea or not all at sea. That appeared to be the story of McLaren's early season form last year. Lando earned plaudits for wrestling a still clearly far from sorted MCL36 to some decent positions on the grid, and also in the finishing order, such as his third place in the Emilia Romagna GP at Imola, while setting the fastest lap at Monaco was proof that the car was at its best, or at least its least troublesome, on the twistier tracks. It was the way that Lando learnt to handle the car that will have augmented his experience, although he will certainly be hoping that this McLaren car doesn't prove to be such a beast to tame. Some encouragement was taken from racing to fourth place in the Singapore GP, and there were flashes of speed at Interlagos as well, but there was never any likelihood of repeating the second place finish that he achieved at the Italian GP in 2021 on the day that McLaren returned to winning ways after nine years in the wilderness and so he dropped a rank to seventh overall.

OSCAR PIASTRI

This extremely promising Australian racer was caught in a storm last year and, instead of joining Alpine as planned after a year as its reserve driver, he signed for McLaren where he replaces Daniel Ricciardo for his first year in F1.

Oscar will be hoping his decision to avoid Alpine will be rewarded with a superior car.

Jack Brabham and Alan Jones were world champions for Australia, and Mark Webber came close, with Daniel Ricciardo also a Grand Prix winner but not a champion. And now comes along a young Australian with the best pedigree yet, for Oscar has had an almost uniquely titled approach to Formula 1.

Oscar began in karting and raced strongly enough in 2016, when he was 15, to rank sixth in the World OK Junior series.

Wasting no time, he then advanced to single-seaters, starting with the 2016/17 United Arab Emirates Formula 4 series, Even though he missed some of the rounds, he was fast enough to rank fourth.

The 2017 season was spent in British F4 and Oscar ended the year as runner-up, with six wins to his name. His season in Formula Renault European was less successful, as he was only eighth at the end of the year. So, Oscar returned in 2019, this time with R-ace GP, won seven times and did just enough to become champion.

With an eye to adding to its prodigious list of single-seater champions, Prema Racing signed Oscar for 2020 to lead its attack on the FIA Formula 3 series. He again won the title, making it titles in successive years, as he pipped Theo Pourchaire and Logan Sargeant in a final-round shoot-out.

Incredibly, Oscar made it three in a row in 2021, a feat unheard of in the top international single-seater categories, when he won the FIA Formula 2 series for Prema Racing at the first time of asking. He did it in impressively dominant style, quick enough to win six races, but consistent enough to end the year 60.5 points clear of his closest challenger Robert Shwartzman – they ended the season on 252.5 points and 192 respectively.

Having been signed up by the Alpine F1 Team, Oscar was given his first F1 test run and did well. However, there were no vacancies at Alpine for 2022 as the race seats were filled by Fernando Alonso and Esteban Ocon, so all they could offer was for him to be its reserve driver for 2022.

TRACK NOTES

Nationality:	**AUSTRALIAN**
Born:	**6 APRIL 2001,**
	MELBOURNE, AUSTRALIA
Website:	**www.oscarpiastri.com**
Teams:	**McLAREN 2023**

CAREER RECORD

First Grand Prix:	**2023 BAHRAIN GP**
Grand Prix starts:	0
Grand Prix wins:	0
Poles:	0
Fastest laps:	0
Points:	0

Honours: **2021 FIA FORMULA 2 CHAMPION, 2020 FIA FORMULA 3 CHAMPION, 2019 FORMULA RENAULT EUROPEAN CHAMPION, 2017 BRITISH FORMULA 4 RUNNER-UP**

A YEAR SPENT ON THE SIDELINES

F1 teams taking a long-term view like to promote obvious young racing talent. More than that, F1 teams like to make sure that no other teams get to sign them first, so they often take the Red Bull approach of having more drivers on their books than they need. Alpine have been less rapacious, spreading its net less liberally, but taking an option on a driver who had won three single-seaters in three years didn't seem to be much of a risk. So, Oscar spent last year without a race seat, attending Grands Prix as Alpine's third driver. Then, when Alpine was surprised by Fernando Alonso leaving it to join Aston Martin after Sebastian Vettel announced that he was retiring, it moved quickly to announce Oscar as its second driver for 2023, alongside Esteban Ocon. Yet it seems that the Australian had signed only a heads of agreement document and so Alpine didn't have him under contract, leaving him free to join McLaren for this year once the Contract Recognition Board considered him free to change teams.

A change in technical regulations allowed Alfa Romeo a good start to last season but then, as ever, the Swiss team's form fell away in the second half of the year. If this year's car is good, though, Valtteri Bottas will deliver.

Valtteri Bottas scored a run of points last year, such as at Miami, but the team lost its bite as the season wore on. Will this year be any different?

The opening round of the inaugural World Championship at Silverstone in 1950 was all about Alfa Romeo, its cars filling the front row and then, 200 miles later, the top three positions. The title was gathered by team leader Giuseppe Farina and then by Juan Manuel Fangio in 1951. Then the Italian manufacturer quit.

Alfa Romeo resurfaced in 1977 and showed flashes of speed with Bruno Giacomelli, but none of this lasted long enough even to win a race, until 1985.

Then came the third time the Alfa Romeo name graced F1, starting in 2019, yet this was simply badge-engineering the team that had raced previously as Sauber. Indeed, the only Italian element in the cars was the Ferrari V6 in their tail.

To understand how the team got to where it is, one needs to go back to when Peter Sauber gained Mercedes approval for his sports-prototype programme and ran Jochen Mass, Mauro Baldi and Jean-Louis Schlesser, with the latter pair winning the World Championship title in 1990 before racing as mentors to its young guns, including Michael Schumacher and Heinz-Harald Frentzen in 1991.

Understanding that Mercedes would provide engines when the Swiss team graduated to F1 was a mistake as the deal didn't come together, but Sauber

KEY PERSONNEL & 2022 ROUND-UP

XEVI PUJOLAR
There is no substitute for experience as shown by this Spanish engineer. He started in karting, then vaulted up the categories by working in Formula Nissan and then F1's immediate feeder category, Formula 3000, for Helmut Marko's team. He got his F1 break in 2002 when he joined Jaguar Racing. His next move took him to Williams and, apart from a year with Hispania F1 in 2010, he stayed until moving to Scuderia Toro Rosso in 2014 and then Sauber (now Alfa Romeo) in 2016.

STARTING FAST, BUT SLOWING DOWN
Getting both cars into the points in the opening round represented a dream start for Alfa Romeo. And even though Bottas improved on his sixth at Sakhir with a fifth at Imola, it was expected that other teams would begin to adjust to the new regulations and move past them. And so they did. Team mate Guanyu was delighted to be the first Chinese driver to score points and he peaked with eighth in Montreal, but gained most attention for flipping at Silverstone.

2022 DRIVERS & RESULTS

Driver	Nationality	Races	Wins	Pts	Pos
Valtteri Bottas	Finnish	22	0	49	10th
Guanyu Zhou	Chinese	22	0	6	18th

FOR THE RECORD

Country of origin:	Switzerland
Team base:	Hinwil, Switzerland
Telephone:	(41) 44 937 9000
Website:	www.sauber-group.com
Active in Formula One:	As Sauber
1993-2018 (as BMW Sauber 2006-2010),	
	Alfa Romeo 2019 on
Grands Prix contested:	546
Wins:	1
Pole positions:	1
Fastest laps:	6

THE TEAM

Owner:	Finn Rausing
Chairman:	Pascal Picci
Team principal:	Frederic Vasseur
Technical director:	Jan Monchaux
Operations director:	Axel Kruse
Head of aerodynamics:	
	Alessandro Cinelli
Head of track engineering:	Xevi Pujolar
Head of aerodynamic development:	
	Mariano Alperin-Bruvera
Head of aerodynamic research:	
	Seamus Mullarkey
Head of vehicle performance:	
	Elliot Dason-Barber
Team manager:	Beat Zehnder
Head of race strategy:	Ruth Buscombe
Third driver:	tba
Chassis:	Alfa Romeo C43
Engine:	Ferrari V6
Tyres:	Pirelli

made its bow in 1993 anyway, with Ilmor engines. Fifth place on its debut, for JJ Lehto in South Africa, was a dream start, beaten by his fourth at Imola. Mercedes came good with an engine for 1994, then offered the deal to McLaren in 1995. Using Ford engines instead, Frentzen gave the team its first podium at Monza.

A significant change occurred in 1997 when Sauber did a deal to run the previous year's Ferrari engines badged as Petronas units. These didn't fire it up the order, so Sauber remained resolutely in the midfield. This all changed in 2001 when it rose four places in the rankings to end the season fourth overall, albeit far behind Ferrari, McLaren and Williams, with Nick Heidfeld outscoring rookie Kimi Raikkonen who finished sixth on his debut.

The team's breakthrough came in 2006 when it was rebranded as BMW Sauber and enjoyed proper manufacturer involvement for the first time. No instant results were expected, but fifth overall was a good start, with Heidfeld peaking with third in Hungary. Their second year together was outstanding, ending up second behind

Ferrari as Heidfeld and Robert Kubica starred, with the best coming at Montreal where Heidfeld was second behind first-time winner Lewis Hamilton.

This Canadian circuit would yield even more in 2008 when Kubica became the team's first winner in 2008, followed home in second by Heidfeld in a race at which Hamilton threw away victory by crashing when leaving the pits. More strong results cemented third place in the constructors' points table.

BMW didn't stay long, however, and left after 2010, leaving Sauber to revert to Ferrari power when Mexican investment kept it afloat and brought Sergio Perez in alongside Kamui Kobayashi. The Mexican came close to winning in Malaysia in the second race of 2012, but the team suffered its annual slide away from being competitive. Part of this stemmed from a lack of budget, but mostly because the best F1 brains won't be coaxed away from F1's base in a sweep around London.

By 2016, the inevitable happened and Peter Sauber was made to stand aside as investment from Finn Rausing gave him a

majority shareholding and he brought in Frederic Vasseur to run the team.

Charles Leclerc gave Sauber reason to be optimistic in 2018 when he shone in his rookie year before joining Ferrari. Then, as a way of bringing in more money, the team was renamed as Alfa Romeo in 2019.

The team's day of days came when it took a Canadian one-two in 2008 when it raced as BMW Sauber.

"From day one with the team, Zhou has had the humility to ask questions and learn, from the engineers as well as from Valtteri ... to improve race after race."

Frederic Vasseur

VALTTERI BOTTAS

Despite not being in a position to go for wins, Valtteri looked to be enjoying life more in his first year with Alfa Romeo than having to play a supporting role at Mercedes, before his car became increasingly less competitive.

Valtteri appeared rejuvenated by life after Mercedes, but will be praying for a better car.

Formula Renault was the best pan-European series when Valtteri stepped up from karts at the age of 17. That was in 2007, and he pipped Daniel Ricciardo to the European title in 2008. This set Valtteri up for graduation to Formula 3, and he ranked third in both 2009 and 2010, with his highlight being two wins in the separate Marlboro Masters race.

The next step should have been to GP2, but he didn't have the budget, so he made the smaller leap to GP3 and saved his career by winning the title. The part of the champion's prize that had attracted Valtteri to GP3 was an F1 test run with Williams, and his performance impressed hard-to-please team founders Frank Williams and Patrick Head.

This led to a year as the Williams test driver and then a race seat for 2013. He scored points before having a more competitive car in 2014, twice finishing second to rank fourth at the end of the year.

Two solid seasons followed and Valtteri was set to continue with Williams in 2017 when Nico Rosberg surprised everyone by quitting after winning the title, and so Valtteri found himself with the top team. Presented with the best car in the field, Valtteri won three times but was in team leader Lewis Hamilton's shadow. And this was how it continued through the next four seasons, with occasional days when he could beat Lewis, others when he wasn't allowed to try and many others when he couldn't get close. Life as a number two was lucrative but not that enjoyable. There was also the spectre of

Mercedes junior driver George Russell in the wings, and Valtteri's currency dipped when Russell had a one-off outing in the 2020 Sakhir GP when Lewis was unwell and overtook him several times in a race that the understudy would have won if his car hadn't suffered a puncture. This, unfortunately, showed that Valtteri was good but not good enough to become a world champion, and so it was a matter of when, not if, he would be replaced.

TRACK NOTES

Nationality:	**FINNISH**
Born:	**28 AUGUST 1989,**
	NASTOLA, FINLAND
Website:	**www.valtteribottas.com**
Teams:	**WILLIAMS 2013-16, MERCEDES**
	2017-21, ALFA ROMEO 2022-23

CAREER RECORD

First Grand Prix:	**2013 AUSTRALIAN GP**
Grand Prix starts:	**200**
Grand Prix wins:	**10**
2017 Russian GP, Austrian GP, Abu Dhabi	
GP, 2019 Australian GP, Azerbaijan GP,	
Japanese GP, US GP, 2020 Austrian GP,	
Russian GP, 2021 Turkish GP	
Poles:	**20**
Fastest laps:	**19**
Points:	**1787**
Honours:	**2019 & 2020 F1 RUNNER-UP,**
	2011 GP3 CHAMPION, 2009 & 2010
	FORMULA 3 MASTERS WINNER, 2008
	EUROPEAN & NORTHERN EUROPEAN
	FORMULA RENAULT CHAMPION

STARTING WELL, BUT THEN TAILING OFF

Sixth place in last year's opening race was way better than Valtteri would have expected as he adjusted to life after Mercedes, but the Finn really showed his worth by scoring points in six of the season's first seven races. The team's Ferrari engines were strong and the Alfa Romeo C42 didn't porpoise as much as, say, the Mercedes, so Valtteri looked happy at the start of his life after Mercedes. However, as other teams sorted their early-season problems, Alfa Romeo did as the team before it did when it raced as Sauber – it lost ground and became less competitive. Suddenly, not only did improving on his fifth place finish in the Emilia Romagna GP at Imola look unlikely, but so too did even scoring a point for tenth. Valtteri would have enjoyed racing the Mercedes duo at Miami, but not clipping the wall while doing so, falling to seventh place. Valtteri's manner was obviously more relaxed that it had been when he was racing alongside Lewis Hamilton, and he enjoyed being the team leader rather than being made to take a supporting role.

GUANYU ZHOU

The most memorable moment of this Chinese driver's first year in F1 was his car's inversion at the start of the British GP, but there was enough progress made for him to stay on for a second year with Alfa Romeo.

Zhou bounced back from his inversion at Silverstone to add experience to his speed.

Heading overseas very early in his karting career made Zhou different to his Chinese contemporaries and proved to be the foundation stone to him being more international in his approach and, eventually, more successful.

Having hosted a Grand Prix every year since 2004, China was desperate for an F1 star of its own and Zhou performed well enough on the World and European karting scene to merit advancing to car racing when he was a precocious 15-year-old. His first year of single-seaters was in the Italian Formula 4 series and Zhou ended the season as runner-up. Not only did this earn him selection for Ferrari's driver academy, but it set him up for spending the northern hemisphere winter racing in New Zealand's Toyota Racing Series, a championship won by Lando Norris.

Formula 3 came next for Zhou's career and this turned into a three-year project in the FIA European series as, despite reaching the podium in 2016 and 2017, it took until 2018 for Zhou to start winning races, but he was still far away from eventual title winner Mick Schumacher.

For most drivers, that would signal time for a career change, but backing from Chinese sponsors enabled Zhou to step up to F2, the last level before F1, and he impressed by gathering a few podium finishes in 2019. In 2020, he took a win, at Sochi, but F1 was still little more than a dream as drivers need to win and score consistently to merit making that final step to the sport's top category. Clearly, Zhou's third year in F2 was pivotal and he won two of the first four races, first at Sakhir and then at Monaco. Although Zhou only won once more in the remaining 20 races, at Silverstone, he did enough to rank third overall as UNI-Virtuosi team-mate Oscar Piastri took the crown.

And so he had earned the right to step up to F1 and, with his nationality working for him as sponsors reckoned the publicity would be huge in China, Zhou was in the fortunate position of having the backing behind him to make the move.

TRACK NOTES

Nationality:	**CHINESE**
Born:	**30 MAY 1991, SHANGHAI, CHINA**
Website:	**www.zhou-guanyu.com**
Teams:	**ALFA ROMEO 2022-23**

CAREER RECORD

First Grand Prix:	**2022 BAHRAIN GP**
Grand Prix starts:	**22**
Grand Prix wins:	**0**
	(best result: 8th 2022 Canadian GP)
Poles:	**0**
Fastest laps:	**1**
Points:	**6**
Honours:	**ASIAN FORMULA 3 CHAMPION, 2015 ITALIAN FORMULA 4 RUNNER-UP**

SURVIVING HIS SILVERSTONE FLIP

Starting his F1 career by guiding his Alfa Romeo into the points with tenth place at Sakhir was something of a surprise, but the team was relatively competitive at the outset, with rejuvenated team-mate Valtteri Bottas finishing in sixth that day. However, in a year peppered with retirements, it took Zhou until the ninth round to score again, this time with eighth place in Montreal. There was gradual progress, though, as his deficit to Bottas came down. Yet for all that, the image that sticks is his freakish accident at the first corner of the British GP when his car flipped across the gravel trap and ended up wedged between the rear of the barriers and an earth bank. Since then, Zhou pressed on and became more consistent and did everything required to learn the particular craft required to shine in F1. He did well to score again, by finishing 10th in the Italian GP, suggesting that the Chinese driver's rookie F1 season was a fair one.

Sebastian Vettel marked his retirement after 16 years in F1 by performing a flamboyant series of donuts in Abu Dhabi.

⟩⟩ ASTON MARTIN F1 TEAM

When one world champion, Sebastian Vettel, announced that he was retiring, Aston Martin pulled off a master stroke by replacing him with another, Fernando Alonso. This surprise move emphasises the team's ambition and it now must provide a car worthy of advancement.

Lance Stroll pushed hard through 2022, such as taking a point at home in Canada, but he will want to be scoring more consistently this year.

As this team enters its third campaign as the Aston Martin F1 Team, it still doesn't feel quite right to the older F1 fans, many of whom feel that Aston Martin is a sports car brand. Indeed, its most notable motorsport success is still its victory in the Le Mans 24 Hours back in 1959. However, the marque from Newport Pagnell did try F1 around that time, entering the World Championship in 1959, albeit with a front-engined car just as Cooper and Lotus had already proved that putting the engine behind the driver's shoulders was the way to go. Indeed, the best result achieved by the time that Aston Martin quit F1 midway through 1960 was Roy Salvadori's sixth place in the British and Portuguese GPs in 1959. Any link to the current cars is simply the name, the finance behind the team and the metallic green livery rather than any continuous or rediscovered bloodline.

The team that exists today stems from the ambition of Eddie Jordan when he elected to make the jump from successful Formula 3000 entrant into F1 in 1991. With a simple and effective Gary Anderson-designed chassis, the team was an instant hit as it ranked fifth at the end of the season.

The traditionally trickier second season was just that, a result of being so

KEY PERSONNEL & 2022 ROUND-UP

MIKE KRACK

This engineer from Luxembourg joined BMW in 1998 before entering F1 with Sauber in 2001. Starting off in data analysis, he became a race engineer for Felipe Massa from 2004. He rose to become chief engineer during the team's BMW Sauber days before working in F3. He then joined BMW's DTM team and later Porsche's team in the World Endurance Championship. He returned to BMW to work on assorted projects before joining Aston Martin at the start of 2022.

ASTON MARTIN AWAITS ITS GREAT REVIVAL

The team's second season racing as Aston Martin didn't bring great strides forward, but they did improve as they got to grips with the new technical regulations. Unlike 2021, there were no podium finishes, but Sebastian Vettel appeared to find an extra spring in his step as he counted down to the end of his career, showing form in his late-race battle with fellow former champion Fernando Alonso at Suzuka. Lance Stroll raced but didn't excite, although the Canadian's drive to sixth place in Singapore showed that he can occasionally shine.

2022 DRIVERS & RESULTS

Driver	Nationality	Races	Wins	Pts	Pos
Sebastian Vettel	German	20	0	37	12th
Lance Stroll	Canadian	22	0	18	15th
Nico Hulkenberg	German	2	0	0	22nd

FOR THE RECORD

Country of origin:	**England**
Team base:	**Silverstone, England**
Telephone:	**(44) 01327 850800**
Website:	**www.astonmartinf1.com**
Active in Formula One:	**As Jordan 1991-2004, Midland 2005-06, Spyker 2007, Force India 2008-18, Racing Point 2019-20, Aston Martin 2021 on**
Grands Prix contested:	**579**
Wins:	**5**
Pole positions:	**4**
Fastest laps:	**7**

busy in its maiden season that planning the next car wasn't afforded as much attention as the first, plus the decision to take paid-for Yamaha engines in place of the Ford units it used in 1991, thus claiming just one point.

As the decade progressed, so did Jordan, with both drivers – Rubens Barrichello and Eddie Irvine – on the podium in Canada in 1995 with Ferrari's race winner Jean Alesi. Ever ambitious, though, Peugeot engines were replaced with Mugen Honda units for 1998 and that long-desired first win was taken by Damon Hill in a wet Belgian GP, with team-mate Ralf Schumacher right behind him. The 1999 season was even better as Heinz-Harald Frentzen led the attack and won twice to help Jordan rank third. This remains its best season.

Although Giancarlo Fisichella won in Brazil in 2003, retrospectively, after an appeal was upheld that he had been in the lead when the race was stopped early, Eddie Jordan decided to sell up and so the team raced as Midland in 2005, then was renamed after Dutch sports car manufacturer Spyker in 2007. Its main rebrand, though, came in 2008 when the cars went racing in a white, green and orange livery as Force India. This was because Indian drinks company owner Vijay Mallya had bought the team. It remained based opposite the gates of Silverstone and continued under the technical guidance of James Key. Continuity of staff remained a strong point, but a constant input of money remained a weak point. However, achieving more points per pound than most rivals, the team produced good results for Fisichella, Sergio Perez, Paul di Resta and Nico Hulkenberg. But the threat of closure was constant as Mallya was sought by the Indian tax authorities.

Lawrence Stroll rescued the team from financial peril and had it renamed as Racing Point for 2019, with its 2020 season a great one as Perez and Lawrence's son Lance Stroll helped the team rank fourth, a highlight being Perez's second place in Turkey, and his consistent scoring left him fourth in the drivers' championship table.

THE TEAM

Chief executive officer:	**Martin Whitmarsh**
Team principal:	**Mike Krack**
Chief technical officer:	**Andrew Green**
Technical director:	**Dan Fallows**
Sporting director:	**Andy Stevenson**
Engineering director:	**Luca Furbatto**
Head of trackside engineering:	**Bradley Joyce**
Production director:	**Bob Halliwell**
Chief designers:	**Akio Haga & Ian Hall**
Aerodynamics director:	**Simon Phillips**
Operations manager:	**Mark Gray**
Chief mechanic:	**Curtis Stones**
Test driver:	**Stoffel Vandoorne**
Chassis:	**Aston Martin AMR23**
Engine:	**Mercedes V6**
Tyres:	**Pirelli**

However, Stroll Sr had become a shareholder of Aston Martin and money from the luxury car manufacturer triggered the latest name change and the arrival of Sebastian Vettel. Their first year together resulted in a slide to seventh overall, with Vettel's surprise second place in Baku in a race affected by blowouts being a highlight.

This is the moment, celebrated by Damon Hill, when the team took its first win, as Jordan.

"I have watched as the team has attracted people with winning pedigrees ... no one in F1 is demonstrating a greater vision and commitment to winning."

Fernando Alonso

FERNANDO ALONSO

One of the biggest shocks in F1 in recent years came when Fernando surprised the F1 paddock as it took in the news of Sebastian Vettel's retirement by announcing that he would quit Alpine to replace him. The speed remains.

Fernando shocked Alpine when he elected to move to Aston Martin.

Fernando's record in karting was brilliant, culminating in the world title in 1996 when he was 15 and the Italian and Spanish titles the following year.

Then came the move to cars in 1999 and Fernando won the Formula Nissan title at his first attempt. Next stop was the Formula 3000 category, where he made drivers with much greater experience look pedestrian when he blitzed the field at Spa-Francorchamps to help him to rank fourth.

Benetton had him under contract and he was found a ride with Minardi for a learning year. There was no vacancy with the team as it morphed into being Renault for 2002, but he got in plenty of testing and so was more than ready when the team gave him a race seat for 2003. Indeed, he was a winner before the year was out, taking the first of his 32 career wins in Hungary.

In 2005, Fernando won seven rounds and the title, then repeated the feat the following year, again with seven wins.

Moving to McLaren for 2007 was expected to produce more titles, but he scrapped all year with rookie team-mate Lewis Hamilton and both were pipped by Ferrari's Kimi Räikkönen.

So, it was back to Renault and, unfortunately, a less competitive car, taking two wins in 2008 but none in 2009. He then left for Ferrari where he achieved five wins but ended up being pipped by Red Bull's Sebastian Vettel at the final round. The next three years were less fruitful, but then a second spell at McLaren was a disaster.

Fernando tried to win the Indy 500 and the World Endurance Championship, taking two titles and two wins in the Le Mans 24 Hours, before returning to F1 in 2021.

TRACK NOTES

Nationality:	**SPANISH**
Born:	**29 JULY 1981, OVIEDO, SPAIN**
Website:	**www.fernandoalonso.com**
Teams:	**MINARDI 2001, RENAULT 2003-06, McLAREN 2007, RENAULT 2008-09, FERRARI 2010-14, McLAREN 2015-18, ALPINE 2021-22, ASTON MARTIN 2023**

CAREER RECORD

First Grand Prix:	**2001 AUSTRALIAN GP**
Grand Prix starts:	**358**
Grand Prix wins:	**32**

2003 Hungarian GP, 2005 Malaysian GP, Bahrain GP, San Marino GP, European GP, French GP, German GP, Chinese GP, 2006 Bahrain GP, Australian GP, Spanish GP, Monaco GP, British GP, Canadian GP, Japanese GP, 2007 Malaysian GP, Monaco GP, European GP, Italian GP, 2008 Singapore GP, Japanese GP, 2010 Australian GP, German GP, Italian GP, Singapore GP, Korean GP, 2011 British GP, 2012 Malaysian GP, European GP, 2013 Chinese GP, Spanish GP

Poles:	**22**
Fastest laps:	**23**
Points:	**2061**
Honours:	**2019 DAYTONA 24 HOURS WINNER, 2018/19 WORLD ENDURANCE CHAMPION, 2018 & 2019 LE MANS 24 HOURS WINNER, 2005 & 2006 F1 WORLD CHAMPION, 2012 & 2013 F1 RUNNER-UP, 1999 FORMULA NISSAN CHAMPION, 1997 ITALIAN & SPANISH KART CHAMPION, 1996 WORLD & SPANISH KART CHAMPION, 1994 & 1995 SPANISH JUNIOR KART CHAMPION**

GOING WELL, THEN THE BOMBSHELL

The early season races were nothing special last year, but then Fernando got into synch with the Alpine A522 and the points began to flow from his home Grand Prix onwards. He began to look more like the Fernando of old, a double world champion don't forget. Fifth place in the British GP was a highlight, but so too was the way that he put his respected team-mate Esteban Ocon firmly in his place. Mechanical fallibility certainly cost him points, but Fernando applied himself with ever increasing vigour and appeared to relish taking the role of underdog. A further fifth place finish at Spa-Francorchamps was backed up by sixth places at Paul Ricard and Zandvoort, then another fifth in the penultimate round at Interlagos. However, it was when he qualified second in Canada that Fernando really smiled. Life wasn't happy enough to keep him for 2023 though.

LANCE STROLL

It's a strange thing to have a driver in an inviolable position on a grid restricted to 20 drivers, but this is Lance's position. He's quick but not the best and not consistent enough, but his father bankrolls the team.

Lance learnt from Sebastian Vettel and will do the same with new mentor Alonso.

Lance's father Lawrence is a hugely successful businessman who loves motor racing. Although he has recently bought a major stake in Aston Martin, Lawrence did his racing in Ferraris in the North American Championship.

With this filling the weekends of his early childhood, it's not surprising that Lance was soon racing karts. He was, in fact, exceptionally good, finishing sixth in the World KF series in 2013. This was his springboard to graduate to single-seaters when he was just 14 in the Ferrari-funded Florida Winter Series. This was his homework before racing in the Italian Formula F4 championship, something that he won by a distance.

With the benefit of his substantial backing, Lance then spent the close season contesting New Zealand's Formula Toyota Series and won that title to carry valuable momentum into setting up his entry to the FIA European F3 series. This proved to be a harder nut to crack and Lance displayed his raw pace but a lack of finesse in 2015, ranking fifth. What Lance needed to do in 2016 was to cut out the accidents, which he did and this landed him the title at his second attempt with a tally of 14 wins.

So, armed with a plentiful budget, he skipped F2 and went straight to F1 in 2017, starting with Williams which his father was helping to keep afloat financially. He learnt well from experienced team-mate Felipe Massa, even finishing third in Baku.

With Williams in retreat, Lance joined the Force India team as it became Racing Point for 2019, this time being mentored by Sergio Perez. Lance appeared to have cut out the mistakes by 2020 and matched his 2017 Baku finish with a pair of thirds at Monza and Sakhir.

The team was renamed again, as Aston Martin, for 2021 but the results were not good, with his best a seventh-place finish at Monza. He matched strides with his team-mate Sebastian Vettel in the early part of the season, but this did wane as the season wore on, albeit he ended the year 13th overall just behind Vettel's 12th.

TRACK NOTES

Nationality:	**CANADIAN**
Born:	**29 OCTOBER 1998,**
	MONTREAL, CANADA
Website:	**www.lancestroll.com**
Teams:	**WILLIAMS**
	2017-18, RACING POINT 2019-20,
	ASTON MARTIN 2021-23

CAREER RECORD

First Grand Prix:	**2017 AUSTRALIAN GP**
Grand Prix starts:	**122**
Grand Prix wins:	**0 (best result: 3rd, 2017**
	Azerbaijan GP, 2020 Italian GP, Sakhir GP)
Poles:	**1**
Fastest laps:	**0**
Points:	**194**
Honours:	**2016 FIA EUROPEAN**
	FORMULA THREE CHAMPION, 2015 TOYOTA
	RACING SERIES CHAMPION, 2014 ITALIAN
	FORMULA FOUR CHAMPION

SOLID, BUT STILL ACCIDENT-PRONE

The question last year was whether Sebastian Vettel, with retirement already in his mind, was something of a spent force. If not, fine, but if he was, then this was a less than sparkling campaign from the 24-year-old Canadian who seldom bettered him. There were high points, such as Lance's cluster of tenth-place finishes at Imola, Miami, Montreal, Paul Ricard, Zandvoort and Interlagos, and peaked with an excellent sixth place at the Singapore GP. However, Vettel peaked with a sixth place and outscored him across the season, which really ought not to be happening in Lance's sixth year in F1, if ever he finds himself in a season in which he gets to be driving a truly competitive package. Having a father who owns the team is fine, but perhaps Lance has ambitions to one day join a team that is habitually at the sharp end of the grid so that he can take a shot at winning.

43

HAAS F1

A fifth place at last year's opening round was a false dawn, but Kevin Magnussen starred and then Mick Schumacher came on strong, suggesting that better things may lie in store for this American team in 2023, but don't bank on it.

Kevin Magnussen hit the ground running on his return to F1 with Haas last year, finishing fifth at Sakhir, but this was to be as good as it got.

McLaren has a team in IndyCar and another in Formula E in addition to its F1 programme, and Ferrari is about to join Alpine in the World Endurance Championship, but Gene Haas's team is the one with the most different sideline: its NASCAR team. It could not be more diametrically opposed from the high-tech world of F1 to the resolutely low-tech world of stock car racing. Yet this was the arena in which Gene Haas first set up a racing arm of his business empire.

Haas made his fortune with a machining business and NASCAR proved to be the best place to promote this, with its blue-collar fan base, starting in 2002. Success soon came the Haas team's way, but this was accelerated by going into partnership with driver Tony Stewart in 2009, with Stewart landing the title in 2011. Three years later, Kevin Harvick took their second crown.

Having established the Haas name across the USA, Gene then looked for a global push and decided that F1 was

the best way to do this. And so the seeds were sown for a team of his own, starting in 2016. This was set up to run from a base right alongside his NASCAR team's

headquarters in Kannapolis in North Carolina. Of course, some technology could be shared, but not that much. When F1 insiders pointed out that no

KEY PERSONNEL & 2022 ROUND-UP

BEN AGATHANGELOU

There has been much change through the past three decades, and this Anglo-Greek aeronauticist has been there to witness it. After joining McLaren in 1994, Ben worked for Tyrrell then Honda's stillborn F1 programme. Benetton came next, then Jaguar Racing, becoming chief aerodynamicist when it morphed into Red Bull Racing. After Adrian Newey arrived, he moved on to HRT F1 team, then Ferrari, before joining Haas F1 in 2015 as it prepared to enter F1 the following year.

TECH CHANGES LEAD TO IMPROVED FORM

Russia's invasion of Ukraine gave the team an unexpected start, as it meant that Russian driver Mazepin had to be dropped, and Magnussen returned. With the change in technical regulations for 2022 putting some teams on the back foot as their cars porpoised, Haas found itself competitive and the Dane raced to fifth place in the opening round. More points followed and then, in the second half of the year, Schumacher got into the points too.

2022 DRIVERS & RESULTS

Driver	Nationality	Races	Wins	Pts	Pos
Kevin Magnussen	Danish	22	0	25	13th
Mick Schumacher	German	22	0	12	16th

FOR THE RECORD

Country of origin:	USA
Team bases:	Kannapolis, USA, & Banbury, England
Telephone:	(001) 704 652 4227
Website:	www.haasf1team.com
Active in Formula One:	From 2016
Grands Prix contested:	144
Wins:	0
Pole positions:	1
Fastest laps:	3

team operating from the USA had shone in F1, an operating base in England was added.

The car for that first F1 campaign made use of experienced hands, being designed by racing car constructor Dallara and fitted with a Ferrari engine and mechanical parts. The benefit of this was shown when Romain Grosjean immediately put a smile on Gene's face by advancing from 19th on the grid at the team's debut in Melbourne to finish sixth. When this was followed by fifth place in the second round, hopes were high. These were not duly met, but nevertheless outscoring Renault, Sauber and Manor at their first attempt was a strong start.

The arrival of Kevin Magnussen in place of Esteban Gutierrez for 2017 gave the team a boost, and he and Grosjean formed a rapid pairing. In 2018, they gathered more points than before as Haas ranked a remarkable fifth overall, peaking with Grosjean's fourth place in Austria.

However, the foot has to be planted firmly on the throttle at all times to keep up in F1, and 2019 was a setback when the team dropped back to rank ninth of the ten teams, with team principal Guenther Steiner infuriated by his drivers running into each other more than once in their internal battle for supremacy. Matters got worse in 2020 when Haas remained ninth overall, but this time scored just three points after 2019's tally of 28.

The obvious way to try and counter this decline was to redouble efforts and recruit a superior design team. Yet Haas did something rather different: it disposed of its drivers, both of whom were able to deliver with a competitive car, and brought in two drivers from F2. These were Nikita Mazepin, courtesy of his billionaire father's wealth, and Mick, son of seven-time world champion Michael, Schumacher, placed with the team by Ferrari as part of its engine package. The result was zero points and last position, with neither driver being able to learn from an experienced hand.

THE TEAM

Team owner:	Gene Haas
Team principal:	Guenther Steiner
Chief operating officer:	Joe Custer
Technical director:	Simone Resta
Team manager:	Mark Lowe
Head of engineering operations:	
	Ben Agathangelou
Director of engineering:	Ayao Komatsu
Group leader aerodynaicist:	
	Christian Cattaneo
Operations manager:	Peter Crolla
Test driver:	tba
Chassis:	Haas VF-23
Engine:	Honda V6
Tyres:	Pirelli

With ever more Grands Prix now being held in the USA, it is really time that the team at least opted for the publicity that would be gained by introducing a young American driver as it strives to work its way towards the midfield. In NASCAR, however, race wins are guaranteed, as Harvick continues to be one of the leading drivers.

45

> "Kevin's pole position at Interlagos was a great moment for Haas F1 Team. We'd waited seven years for that and it shows again that hard work and determination pays off."

Guenther Steiner

Romain Grosjean's escape from this accident at Sakhir in 2020 remains one of F1's greatest escapes.

KEVIN MAGNUSSEN

Having received an 11th-hour call-up to return to F1, Kevin did a great job at the start of the year, but the team will want a more sustained attack in 2023 as his form certainly dropped away as Mick Schumacher began to catch him.

Kevin proved his worth last year as he steadied Haas, but points became hard to find.

Jan Magnussen was a driver tipped for the top. While he reached F1 with Stewart in 1997, after a one-off for McLaren in 1995, he didn't continue his progress and so left F1 at the end of 1998, largely to race in the USA.

His son, Kevin, was seven that year and soon took to karts. Yet, with Jan still a current driver, it was hard for the family to mount a championship bid.

This had to wait until 2008 when Kevin was 15 and he raced in the Danish Formula Ford series.

Second place in the 2009 Northern European Countries Formula Renault series was followed by graduation to F3 for 2010. This was the category in which his father had swept all before him, but it took Kevin to secure third place in the German series to land a ride in the British series for 2011. Seven wins left him in second place behind Felipe Nasr, but that was enough for him to move up with Carlin to Formula Renault 3.5. This proved to be a two-year project before Kevin was crowned champion for DAMS in 2013.

After impressive test runs, McLaren gave Kevin his F1 break in 2014 and he shocked by finishing second on his debut in Melbourne, a result he has never matched. It looked as though his F1 career would be as short as his father's as Kevin was dropped for 2015, but he made his return with Renault in 2016 before moving on to join Haas F1 for its second season, starting a fiery partnership with team-mate Romain

Grosjean that ended when they were replaced by Mick Schumacher and Nikita Mazepin for 2021.

Kevin then tried a different sort of racing by spending the year in the IMSA Sports Car series in the USA, pedalling a Cadillac for Chip Ganassi Racing. Partnered by Renger van der Zande, he won on Detroit's Belle Isle circuit and ranked seventh overall in a year in which the smile was back on his face.

Kevin also contested the Le Mans 24 Hours alongside his father, clearly enjoying life beyond F1.

TRACK NOTES

Nationality:	DANISH
Born:	5 OCTOBER 1992, ROSKILDE, DENMARK
Website:	www.kevinmagnussen.com
Teams:	McLAREN 2014, RENAULT 2016, HAAS F1 2017–20, HAAS 2022–23

CAREER RECORD

First Grand Prix:	2014 AUSTRALIAN GP
Grand Prix starts:	141
Grand Prix wins:	0 (best result: 2nd, 2014 Australian GP)
Poles:	0
Fastest laps:	2
Points:	183
Honours:	2013 FORMULA RENAULT 3.5 CHAMPION, 2011 BRITISH FORMULA THREE RUNNER-UP, 2009 FORMULA RENAULT NORTHERN EUROPE RUNNER-UP, 2008 DANISH FORMULA FORD CHAMPION

LATE CALL-UP GIVES ANOTHER CHANCE

One person who clearly benefited from Russia's invasion of Ukraine was Kevin. In a flash, with Nikita Mazepin's father's company, Uralkali, hit by sanctions, he was offered the chance to return to F1 after a year racing sports cars. Typically, he grabbed the opportunity with both hands and made the team smile when he was fifth in the opening round at Sakhir. The team knew that this result was a false dawn as established rivals got to grips with the new technical regulations rather better, but ninth-place finishes in the second and fourth rounds at Jeddah and Imola respectively showed his worth. These were bettered by Kevin's eighth place at the Red Bull Ring, but it was noticeable how team-mate Mick Schumacher began to match him and then gradually move ahead, especially when the German finished sixth at Silverstone. However, Kevin's form came back and he triggered the biggest smile the F1 paddock enjoyed all year when he read the changing conditions right at Interlagos and took pole.

NICO HULKENBERG

There was much clamour for a young American to fill the second seat at Haas. However, the team has opted for a known performer whose experience and speed count for so much – points in F1 mean prize money.

Nico returns to a full season of racing for 2023 – his vast experience will be invaluable.

Rising to the top in racing is like scaling a pyramid. There are many championships and a huge number of competitors in karting, but these narrow down when young drivers step up to single-seaters. Not only does the price to compete increase with each step, but so does the kudos of winning.

For most, talent is simply not enough. Of course, the offspring of millionaires will keep rising, but often the very best have to rely on people backing them for their future potential. Nico was one such driver.

He won national karting titles in his native Germany before storming to the Formula BMW ADAC title in his first year out of karts. He then seemed to stumble in German F3 when he had a slim budget and was entered in an uncompetitive car. However, the A1GP series, which had much more powerful cars in which drivers raced their national teams, was another option. One impressive test got him a drive and he starred to win Germany the 2006/2007 title.

Third in European F3 in 2007, he then won the title in 2008 and found the backing to step up to GP2. Most drivers take several years win this title (the last step before F1) but Nico won it first time out and F1 beckoned.

Starting with Williams in 2010, he ended an uncompetitive year with pole in Brazil but lost his ride to wealthy Pastor Maldonado in 2011. Back in F1 in 2012 with Force India, Nico then found himself with only midfield drives. There

was talk of him being signed by Ferrari, but they felt that this tall German would be too heavy. He ranked ninth in 2014 and 2016 for Force India. In between those results, he won the Le Mans 24 Hours for Porsche in 2015.

Nico raced for Renault from 2017 to 2019, ranking seventh in 2018, but drivers with more money edged him aside until this new opportunity with Haas.

TRACK NOTES

Nationality:	**GERMAN**
Born:	**22 19 AUGUST 1987, EMMERICH, GERMANY**
Website:	**www.nicohulkenberg.net**
Teams:	**2020 RACING POINT, 2022 ASTON MARTIN, 2023 HAAS**

CAREER RECORD

First Grand Prix:	**2021 BAHRAIN GP**
Grand Prix starts:	**181**
Grand Prix wins:	**0 (best result: 4th, 2012 Belgian GP, 2013 Korean GP, 2016 Belgian GP)**
Poles:	**1**
Fastest laps:	**2**
Points:	**521**
Honours:	**2015 LE MANS 24 HOURS WINNER, 2009 GP2 CHAMPION, 2008 EUROPEAN F3 CHAMPION, 2007 F3 MASTERS WINNER, 2006/07 A1GP CHAMPION, 2005 GERMAN FORMULA BMW ADAC CHAMPION, 2003 GERMAN KART CHAMPION, 2002 GERMAN JUNIOR KART CHAMPION**

LIFE ON THE FORMULA 1 SIDELINES

To say that a driver with 181 F1 starts to his name hasn't had the breaks seems perverse, but Nico has never really had the drives worthy of the talent that shone so brightly on his ascent to F1. However, his appeal to F1 teams since his last full-time ride in 2019 with Renault is clear, hence his stand-in role with Racing Point in 2020 and then the same team under its most recent name, Aston Martin, last year. Nico was brought in to cover for Sebastian Vettel for the first two races while his compatriot recovered from COVID. He was given next to no warning and had had no testing or simulator work, but arrived in Bahrain and did a steady job. He then went better in Saudi Arabia next time out, heading home team-mate Lance Stroll, albeit with neither driver netting any points as the team struggled in the early races to get its cars to work to the new-generation technical rules.

Kevin Magnussen guides his Haas VF-22 to another point-scoring finish at one of the team's two home races in the USA.

SCUDERIA ALPHATAURI

The descent from sixth position in the constructors' championship in 2021 to ninth overall last year tells a story. There were certainly no repeats of Pierre Gasly's 2020 win at Monza and it's hard to see any change for 2023.

Yuki Tsunoda endured an up and down campaign in 2022, but will surely be smiling this year if he can repeat results like his seventh at Imola.

It is incredible how soon after a team changes its identity that people forget what went before. For example, F1's youngest fans will probably have no idea that Scuderia AlphaTauri isn't how this Italian team started life. Before this incarnation, of course, the team spent 14 seasons racing as Scuderia Toro Rosso. Yet, of course, it had a long if not illustrious life before even that, when it was plain and simple Minardi.

Although a Fiat dealer by profession, Giancarlo Minardi wanted more to be a race entrant and ran cars in the Italian junior formulae before stepping up to F2. His team designed and built its own car and started winning with rising star Michele Alboreto in 1981. Alessandro Nannini was the team's next star, but Minardi elected not to change to F3000 when that replaced F2 in 1985 and so entered F1 instead.

Although deeply uncompetitive when it started in F1 in 1985, the team plodded on, held back notably by its heavy Motori Moderni engines. By the late 1980s, though, it had Ford engines and a chassis designed by Aldo Costa and finally began to progress, getting both cars home in the top six at the 1989 British GP.

It looked as though Minardi had made a quantum leap when Pierluigi Martini

KEY PERSONNEL & 2022 ROUND-UP

JODY EGGINTON

Technical director since 2019, Jody is one of those working in F1 who has benefited from working in other spheres of motor racing. After starting with Tyrrell as a junior designer in the 1990s, he worked for the Xtrac automotive engineering firm and then for the Opel and Aston Martin motorsport divisions before returning to F1 with Force India in 2005. He moved on to the short-lived Caterham team before joining Scuderia Toro Rosso, forerunner of AlphaTauri.

TAKING SEVERAL STRIDES IN THE WRONG DIRECTION

Some teams coped with the technical regulation changes better than others and it's safe to say that this Italian team is one that came out on the wrong side of the equation. Although Pierre Gasly scored in the opening round and peaked with fifth place in the Azerbaijan GP, the Red Bull junior team lost ground as rival teams caught up and, unfortunately, usually finished just outside the points, with Yuki Tsunoda simply too erratic in the second car to be much help to the team's cause.

2022 DRIVERS & RESULTS

Driver	Nationality	Races	Wins	Pts	Pos
Pierre Gasly	French	22	0	23	14th
Yuki Tsunoda	Japanese	22	0	12	17th

qualified on the front row for the first race of 1990, but that was down to the excellence of Pirelli's qualifying tyres on the Phoenix street circuit, putting more competitive rivals on Goodyear rubber behind it. Martini ultimately finished in seventh place.

Doing a deal to run with a competitive engine was always a problem, but the team earned the respect of the paddock by championing young Italian drivers in a way Ferrari has seldom done, with Minardi giving F1 breaks to Giancarlo Fisichella and Jarno Trulli. Its best find, though, was a young Spaniard called Fernando Alonso.

By 2001, Minardi had handed the team over to Paul Stoddart, but the big change came in 2006 when Red Bull owner Dietrich Mateschitz wanted a junior team, and so bought the team and named it Scuderia Toro Rosso, with the express aim of bringing on drivers to see how they coped in the F1 environment and whether they might be good enough to join the senior team. To make its role clear, the cars were painted in a livery not dissimilar to Red Bull Racing's, and former F3 team chief Franz Tost was brought in to oversee proceedings.

This waiting room for drivers who might prove good enough to step up to Red Bull Racing produced its first fruit when not only did Sebastian Vettel win the 2008 Italian GP, but it meant that Toro Rosso took a win before the senior team did. Naturally, this earned Vettel promotion.

This mantra of doing well and being given a shot with the senior team continued when Max Verstappen stepped straight from just one year in F3 after he stopped karting to start his F1 career at 17. He had a solid first year with Toro Rosso, settling in so quickly that he took a couple of fourth places in 2015 before getting a sudden promotion after just four races in 2016 and immediately winning.

Going up to Red Bull Racing doesn't mean a driver will stay there, though, as Daniil Kvyat and Pierre Gasly discovered, with the Russian being the one dropped to make way for Verstappen. Still, Gasly got to have the last laugh after the team was rebranded

FOR THE RECORD

Country of origin:	Italy
Team base:	Faenza, Italy
Telephone:	(39) 546 696111
Website:	www.scuderia.alphatauri.com
Active in Formula One:	As Minardi 1985-2005, Toro Rosso 2006-19, AlphaTauri 2020 on
Grands Prix contested:	670
Wins:	2
Pole positions:	1
Fastest laps:	2

THE TEAM

Team owner:	Dietrich Mateschitz
Team principal:	Franz Tost
Technical director:	Jody Egginton
Chief designer:	Paolo Marabini
Head of aerodynamics:	tba
Head of vehicle performance:	Guillaume Dezoteux
Team manager:	Graham Watson
Operations manager:	Michela Fabbri
Team co-ordinator:	Michele Andreazza
Chief engineer:	tba
Chief race engineer:	Jonathan Eddols
Test driver:	tba
Chassis:	AlphaTauri AT04
Engine:	Honda V6
Tyres:	Pirelli

51

for 2020 as Scuderia AlphaTauri, when he scored a remarkable win at Monza in one of the now dark blue and white cars. Gasly's form was then good enough through 2021 to finish the year ranked ninth overall, something of which no Minardi driver could ever have dreamt.

Pierre Gasly gave the team its first victory as AlphaTauri, in the 2020 Italian GP at Monza.

"We had a very successful time with Pierre [Gasly], but we are pleased to start a new chapter with Nyck, who's a very highly skilled driver as he has won in all of the categories he has competed in, and so deserves a seat in F1."

Franz Tost

YUKI TSUNODA

The explosive start that Yuki made to his F1 career in 2021 seemed long forgotten through much of last season, as this natural racer seemed to rein it back in as results didn't go his way. However, he's back to put that right.

Yuki found life harder in his second year and will have the challenge of a new team-mate.

If you think that Yuki is small now, a genuine pocket rocket, then imagine how minute he was when he started racing karts at the age of six. He was quick, though, and numerous titles followed, with a highlight being finishing second overall in the World FP Junior series in 2012 when he was 12.

With his schooling still ongoing, it took until 2016 for Yuki to step up to single-seaters, starting with Japan's Formula 4 series and finishing on the podium in one of only two races he competed in. Back for a full campaign in 2017, Yuki became a winner and ranked third. Ordinarily, a driver would then have tried to move up a level, but he took the decision to have a second full F4 campaign and it paid off as he won seven times and was crowned champion.

Signed up to Red Bull's driver scholarship programme, Yuki moved to Europe in 2019 and ran concurrent campaigns in the FIA Formula 3 series and the Euroformula Open for similar cars, ranking ninth in the former and fourth in the latter.

This amount of track time served Yuki well as he kept fresh through the winter by contesting the Toyota Racing Series in New Zealand. He then stepped up to F2 in 2020 and soon looked at home, taking three wins for the Carlin team and ending the year third overall behind Mick Schumacher and Callum Ilott.

Ordinarily, this might have led to a second year in F2, but F1 was keen to have a Japanese driver for the first time since 2014, and so the door opened for Red Bull Racing to place Yuki with its junior team, Scuderia AlphaTauri for the 2021 season.

Yuki didn't disappoint with his speed, scoring points on his debut by finishing ninth at Sakhir, but he was mistake-prone and needed to knuckle down and learn from team-mate Pierre Gasly. Fortunately, Yuki gave himself a more relaxed off-season by finishing fourth in the last race of the year in Abu Dhabi to prove that he was prepared to temper his exuberance.

TRACK NOTES

Nationality:	**JAPANESE**
Born:	**11 MAY 2000, KANAGAWA, JAPAN**
Website:	**www.yukitsunoda.com**
Teams:	**ALPHATAURI 2021-23**

CAREER RECORD

First Grand Prix:	**2021 AUSTRALIAN GP**
Grand Prix starts:	**43**
Grand Prix wins:	**0 (best result: 4th, 2021 Abu Dhabi GP)**
Poles:	**0**
Fastest laps:	**0**
Points:	**44**
Honours:	**2018 JAPANESE F4 CHAMPION, 2017 EAST JAPAN F4 CHAMPION, 2012 WORLD FP JUNIOR KART RUNNER-UP, 2011 & 2010 NEW TOKYO NTC KART CHAMPION, 2006 JAPANESE KID KARTS CHAMPION**

SUFFERING SECOND YEAR BLUES

Yuki certainly had some highs, such as eighth place at the opening race in Bahrain, seventh at Imola and tenth in the Spanish GP. However, he had lows too, in a way that he shouldn't have had in his second year in F1. One low point was hitting the wall as he left the pits at the Canadian GP to bring out the safety car. However, the weekend that he will want to forget from 2022 was the very next one, the one spent at the British GP, as he did little right at Silverstone. Firstly, Yuki crashed with team-mate Pierre Gasly, something that drivers with Red Bull's feeder team are very much recommended not to do... Especially if debris left from this collision is then driven over by Max Verstappen just after he had put his Red Bull into the lead, wrecking his race. Certainly, the AlphaTauri AT03 was not the most competitive car out there, but the team was anxious that Yuki dropped the driver errors and was rewarded with 20th place in Singapore.

NYCK DE VRIES

Mentored by McLaren, it looked as though this fast-rising star was going to hit F1 at a canter, yet it failed to happen and so he took his talents to Formula E. But one surprise opening was all it took for him to land a drive for 2023.

Nyck's maiden F1 outing last year, at Monza, showed his worth as he scored in a Williams.

Even regular fans who pay little heed to karting had heard the name Nyck de Vries long before he started racing single-seaters, as he had a habit of winning world titles. Stepping up to cars when he was 17, huge things were expected, but things didn't go quite as effortlessly as expected.

Starting in Formula Renault in 2012, Nyck reached the podium but needed to come back in 2013 to record his first wins in the European series, although he ranked fifth again. Few F1 stars need a third year at this level, but Nyck came back and racked up six wins en route to the 2014 European title.

Formula Renault 3.5 offered more power in 2015 but less of a challenge for this diminutive Dutchman as he scooped a win at the final round to end up third overall. Unfortunately, Nyck didn't have the money to move up to GP2, so tried GP3 in 2016 instead. Two wins were only good enough for sixth in the standings, where he was topped by his team-mates, Charles Leclerc and Alex Albon.

This was enough for Nyck to get to F2 for 2017, but although he won at Monaco in his first year and ranked seventh, he then had a poor start to 2018, and his three wins were not enough to finish higher than fourth. So, back Nyck came for 2019 and four wins earned him the crown.

There were no F1 openings, so Mercedes placed Nyck in Formula E and he won that title at his second attempt, in 2021, by which time he had also contested the Le Mans 24 Hours as he still looked to F1.

Signed as a reserve driver for Mercedes in 2021, Nyck gained useful experience, although few of these runs yield an F1 seat. However, due to the Mercedes engine connection, Nyck had runs for Williams in practice at last year's Spanish GP and at the Italian GP for Aston Martin. Then, a day later, Albon was hit by appendicitis. One minute Nyck was sipping coffee at Williams, just over a day later he was an F1 point scorer...

TRACK NOTES

Nationality: **DUTCH**
Born: **2 FEBRUARY 1995, UITWELLINGERGA, HOLLAND**
Website: **www.nyckdevries.com**
Teams: **WILLIAMS 2022, ALPHATAURI 2023**

CAREER RECORD

First Grand Prix: **2022 ITALIAN GP**
Grand Prix starts: **1**
Grand Prix wins: **0 (best result: 9th, 2022 Italian GP)**
Poles: **0**
Fastest laps: **0**
Points: **2**
Honours: **2021 FORMULA E CHAMPION, 2019 FIA FORMULA 2 CHAMPION, 2014 EUROPEAN FORMULA RENAULT CHAMPION, 2010 & 2011 WORLD KART CHAMPION, 2009 EUROPEAN KF2 KART CHAMPION, 2008 WORLD KF3 KART CHAMPION**

SHINING ON HIS ONE OPPORTUNITY

The 2022 season was going to be all about defending his Formula E title. Of course, there was Nyck's F1 reserve role for Mercedes, but he kicked off in winning style at Formula E's opener at Diriyah in Saudi Arabia, suggesting that it would be another great year with Mercedes EQ. And yet it wasn't as only one more win followed, in Berlin, and that meant a disappointing ninth place overall as team-mate Stoffel Vandoorne won the title. With no apparent F1 openings available at the end of August, Nyck might have felt glum. Then, four weeks later, Alex Albon was hit by appendicitis and so Nyck got an unexpected F1 break and he didn't waste his chance by finishing ninth at Monza. It proved to be incredibly timely as there were a couple of F1 rides still up for grabs. His performance there proved that he was still a very valid option, having once shone brightly before being on the verge of being edged out of the picture at the age of 27.

Still continuing to rebuild after its change of management, the team was not competitive last year, having struggled with the new regulations, but Alex Albon produced some outstanding drives to score points that the car didn't merit.

Alex Albon produced remarkable results when he made his tyres last like no other. For 2023, he'd like a car that can do more of the work.

Formula 1 fans owe Keith Duckworth a huge debt, as the double four-valve V8 that he designed in the mid-1960s is the reason that some of the sport's greatest teams came into being. Financed by Ford, the Ford DFV was a competitive engine that could be bought off the shelf for a reasonable price. Therefore, it gave ambitious team owners their best ever chance to have a crack at F1.

Frank Williams was one such individual. Having been a racer but lacking the funds to proceed beyond F3, he worked out that his best way of staying involved was to run cars for others. His greatest success was running a Brabham for Piers Courage, peaking with second place at Monaco in 1969. Yet he wanted more and started running cars bearing his own name from 1972, all powered by DFVs. Money was always tight and success was hard to achieve, but he plugged on.

What changed the Williams momentum in F1 came in 1977 when he teamed up with designer Patrick Head, and Clay Regazzoni became the first driver to win in a Williams. This was at the 1979 British GP and then team-mate Alan Jones ended the year with a string of wins. In 1980, the Australian became the team's first champion as he and Carlos

KEY PERSONNEL & 2022 ROUND-UP

FRANÇOIS-XAVIER DEMAISON
Not to be confused with a French actor by the same name, Williams' technical director is an engineer of wide experience. He honed his skills in F1, touring cars and rallying for Renault and Peugeot before becoming the chief engineer on Subaru's rally programme. From there, he was part of Volkswagen's world rally programme as it dominated from 2013 to 2016. After that, François worked on its ID. R Pikes Peak car, then joined Williams at the start of 2021.

THERE WERE NO BONUS PODIUM VISITS IN 2022
Looking back over the team's 2021 season still elicits a gasp that it contained a second place in the Belgian GP. This was gifted in a rain-struck race that never got going. Last year, however, there were no such handouts and each of the five point-scoring drives was achieved by tyre management by Alex Albon and his Monza stand-in de Nyck Vries, as well as great tactics by Nicholas Latifi in Japan. In fact, Latifi's points came just after the Canadian had been told that he hadn't performed well enough to keep his drive for a fourth year.

2022 DRIVERS & RESULTS

Driver	Nationality	Races	Wins	Pts	Pos
Alex Albon	British/Thai	21	0	4	19th
Nyck de Vries	Dutch	1	0	2	21st
Nicholas Latifi	Canadian	22	0	2	20th

Reutemann also combined to give it its first constructors' title.

With backing from Saudia, the team was on a firm financial footing for the first time. Although Reutemann blew his chance to land the 1981 title in a final-round flop at Las Vegas, 1982 produced the team's second champion, Keke Rosberg, in an extraordinary year in which 11 drivers won races.

The team was dealt a body blow in 1986 when Frank crashed on his way back from a pre-season test at Paul Ricard and would spend the rest of his life in a wheelchair. If anything, this hardened his resolve and only a blowout in the last round at Adelaide denied Nigel Mansell the world title. Nelson Piquet got the job done in 1987.

Then Williams lost the Honda engine deal to McLaren and it took until 1992, now with Renault engines and a high-tech chassis from Adrian Newey and his design team, to get the team back to the front. And how. The FW14B in Mansell's hands was massively dominant, the pair winning as they pleased.

However, Williams reckoned that it was the car more than the driver, and so Mansell was replaced by Alain Prost for 1993. He too won the title, and he too was replaced. His replacement, Ayrton Senna, was a driver that Frank had wanted since he had tested him at the end of 1983 when the Brazilian was still in F3. Cruelly, after car problems in the first two races of 1994, Senna was then killed at Imola, leaving Damon Hill to lead the team.

Hill stepped up to the challenge and would have been champion had Michael Schumacher not clipped a wall in the Adelaide finale and then swerved intentionally into his car. In 1996 though, he landed the title. And in Williams fashion, got fired. Jacques Villeneuve landed the 1997 title. But then Williams went off the boil and Newey left for McLaren, and it wasn't until it landed a BMW engine deal that its drivers even won races again. Indeed, landing a competitive engine deal has been a perennial problem ever since, and the team's relative slide down the order has

resulted in less prize money and thus of course less budget with which to play.

Frank Williams could have sold up, but he loved F1 and stayed on until late 2020, with daughter Claire running the team, before a third year spent at the back of the grid forced him to agree to sell.

The team's most recent win, a big shock, was when Pastor Maldonado triumphed in Spain in 2012.

"Alex brings a great blend of skill and insightful learnings that will help bring the team greater success. He's a fierce competitor, has proved a popular and loyal team member, and will provide us a stable base."

Jost Capito

» ALEX ALBON

The start of Alexander's return to F1 last year was very impressive, with this British/Thai driver producing some incredible drives in which his ability to make his tyres last took his Williams to unexpected points. All he needs now is a better car.

Alex was able to collect unlikely points in 2022 and deserves a better car in 2023.

Put into karts by his father Nigel, who had raced in the British Touring Car Championship, Alexander was soon gunning for titles. His first came in 2009 when he was 13, landing the Super 1 Honda series. He then landed the European KF3 championship before being runner-up in the 2011 World KF1 series.

Not surprisingly, car racing was Alexander's next stop and he moved into Formula Renault in 2012 with Red Bull backing. However, the results didn't flow and Alexander was dropped from the scholarship scheme after he ranked 16th in the European series in 2013. But Alexander wasn't beaten yet and stayed on to rank third in 2014. He also had a fair year in F3 in 2015, then tried GP3 in 2016 and finished runner-up to Charles Leclerc.

Good enough for a couple of podium visits but no wins in his first year in F2, Alexander really came good in a three-way, all-British shootout in 2018 when he won four times but ended up third behind George Russell and Lando Norris.

Alexander was brought back into the Red Bull fold when he was able to extricate himself from a contract to race for Nissan in Formula E to graduate to F1 with Scuderia Toro Rosso. His form was so good, including a sixth place at Hockenheim, that he was promoted midway through the year to Red Bull Racing, with Pierre Gasly going in the opposite direction. He then rounded off the year with a run of fifths and sixths plus fourth at Suzuka to do enough to stay on for the 2020 season.

However, two third places aside, 2020 was a disappointment and Alexander was dropped from F1 as the team brought in Sergio Perez to be a more consistent points scorer.

Alexander did keep Red Bull backing, though, albeit racing for Ferrari in the DTM series and for mentoring Yuki Tsunoda in his maiden year of F1 with Scuderia AlphaTauri.

Yet Alexander's F1 days weren't over forever, because when Williams went into new ownership he was selected for an F1 return in 2022.

TRACK NOTES

Nationality:	**BRITISH/THAI**
Born:	**23 MARCH 1996,**
	LONDON, ENGLAND
Website:	**www.alexalbon.com**
Teams:	**TORO ROSSO 2019, RED BULL**
	2019-2020, WILLIAMS 2022-23

CAREER RECORD

First Grand Prix:	**2019 AUSTRALIAN GP**
Grand Prix starts:	**59**
Grand Prix wins:	**0 (best result: 3rd,**
	2020 Tuscan GP & Bahrain GP)
Poles:	**0**
Fastest laps:	**0**
Points:	**201**
Honours:	**2016 GP3 RUNNER-UP,**
	2011 WORLD KF1 KART RUNNER-UP, 2010
	EUROPEAN KF3 KART CHAMPION, 2009 SUPER
	1 HONDA KART CHAMPION

A MAESTRO AT MAKING HIS TYRES LAST

The Williams FW44 was the slowest of the 20-car field last year, sensitive to many influences that restricted its performance. With points being scored only down to tenth place, they were unlikely to be going Williams' way. And yet, somehow, almost unnoticed at the back of the field, Alex chipped away, light on his tyres and prepared to take on crazily long runs. And then, as others pitted for a third set, he kept going to the chequered flag, taking tenth place in Melbourne and then ninth two races later, in Miami. A further tenth-place finish was earned at the Belgian GP and he was bolstered by the signing of a contract extension. This seemed to give Alex even more confidence as he took on and beat rivals in more competitive machinery. He was disappointed to have to miss the Italian GP through illness and will have been both intrigued and perhaps a little concerned to see stand-in Nyck de Vries finish ninth. However, he returned and shone again but scored no more points.

LOGAN SARGEANT

Last October's United States GP was huge for Logan as he became the first American driver since 2015 to have a run in F1 practice. Williams then announced that he would race for them in 2023 if he scored enough super-licence points.

Logan is hitting F1 as the appetite for and interest in F1 in the USA hits new heights.

The 22-year-old Floridian followed in the wheel tracks of older brother Dalton, first into racing karts and then cars. Logan was clearly a major star in kart racing, finishing sixth in the European KF Junior series in 2014 when he was 13, and then winning the world series the following year.

At the end of 2016, as he approached his 16th birthday, Logan gained his first experience of single-seaters by contesting the United Arab Emirates Formula 4 series through the winter. Taking 15 podium finishes from 18 starts to finish as runner-up showed that he was ready for 2017, when he ranked third in the British F4 championship, just a few points behind Oscar Piastri.

The European Formula Renault title was his target for 2018, but Logan had to settle for three wins and fourth overall. He had shown enough promise to merit stepping up to the FIA Formula 3 championship in 2019, but it wasn't rewarded as his best result was only a ninth-place finish as he ranked just 19th. However, third place in the end of season F3 race around the streets of Macau was a fillip and Logan bounced back in 2020. He joined the crack Prema Racing team and vaulted forward to win twice and end the year third overall, with that man Piastri again taking the title in a final round shootout.

Whether it was wise to remain for a third year in F3 in 2021 is open to debate, but the hoped-for title didn't materialise and, after a terrible start to the year with Charouz Racing System, he claimed a solitary win at Sochi and was only seventh at year's end. Logan also contested the F2 races supporting the Saudi Arabian GP and even a couple of sports-prototype races in the European Le Mans Series, finishing fourth at Paul Ricard as he gained useful experience gaining track time and knowledge.

Finally, Logan had his first taste of F1, testing for Williams and making his ultimate ambitions clear as he lined up his deal to graduate to F2, the last step before F1, in 2022.

Being given the opportunity to run in the first practice sessions at Circuit of the Americas, Mexico City and Interlagos let Logan display that he was ready to make the step to the sport's top level in 2023.

STEPPING UP IN A COMPETITIVE F2 YEAR

Formula 2 seemed to suit Logan better than F3 had, taking to the extra power with aplomb and showing his potential by taking pole position for the third round at Imola. He had to wait until the following round before he claimed his first podium for Carlin, though, and then until the second Silverstone race for his first victory. Two races later, at the Red Bull Ring, Logan won again. It was an unusual year in F2 as the wins were spread between 12 drivers, and so consistency was a must for any driver with title ambitions. When Logan's 'other job', as reserve driver for Williams, bore fruit at the United States GP, he rose to the occasion and impressed in the first of the three practice sessions at the Circuit of the Americas, albeit as the slowest of four F1 rookies being given a shot. Knowing that a Williams race seat would be his if he could clinch enough points in the final round to finish in the top-five in the F2 series, Logan pressed on.

TRACK NOTES

Nationality:	**AMERICAN**
Born:	**31 DECEMBER 2000,**
	BOCA RATON, USA
Website:	**tba**
Teams:	**WILLIAMS 2023**

CAREER RECORD

First Grand Prix:	**2023 BAHRAIN GP**
Grand Prix starts:	0
Grand Prix wins:	0
Poles:	0
Fastest laps:	0
Points:	0

Honours: **2016/17 F4 UAE RUNNER-UP, 2015 CIK WORLD KF JUNIOR KART CHAMPION**

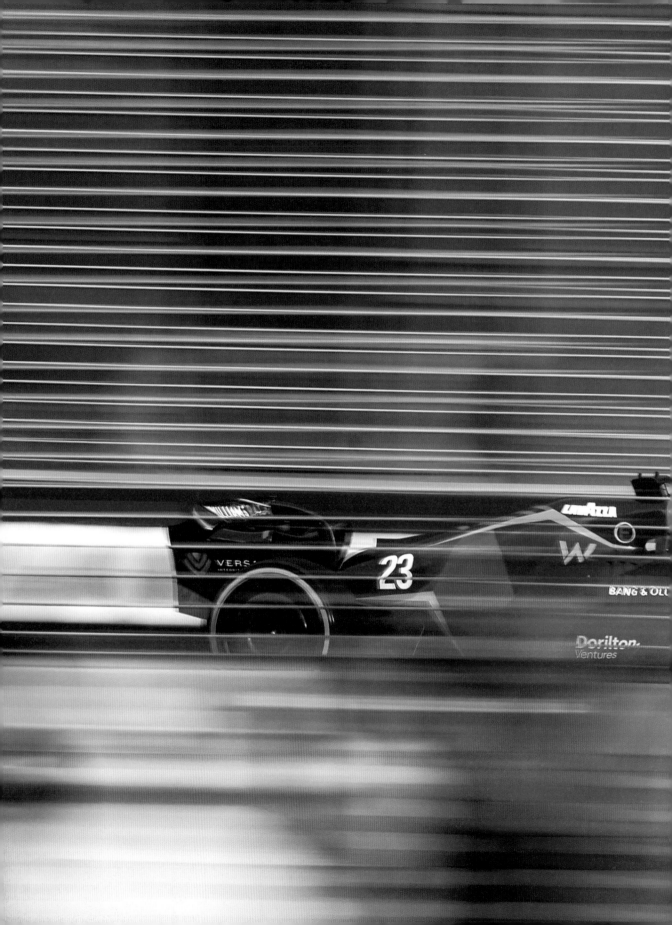

Alex Albon led the way at Williams in 2022 but has rookie Logan Sargeant for company in 2023.

TALKING POINT: **NEW MANUFACTURERS AIM FOR F1 GLORY**

The arrival of new engine regulations to be introduced in 2026 looks to have attracted two new manufacturers to Formula 1. Audi has gone into partnership with the team that started life as Sauber but raced more recently as Alfa Romeo. Excitingly, Porsche was expected to join forces with Red Bull Racing, but its deal fell through.

For a while last summer, it appeared that two of the biggest names in motorsport, Audi and Porsche, were going to join the World Championship in 2026. This was seen as affirmation that F1 was the place to be, with not one but two of the Volkswagen Group's brands looking to join the F1 show to take on the best from Mercedes, Ferrari, Renault and Honda. However, nothing is as simple as it seems in F1 and one of this pair of manufacturers who have had so much success in sports car racing, each winning the Le Mans 24 Hours multiple times, chose to reverse out of its deal.

Audi announced its plans to join the F1 grid in 2026 towards the end of last summer, albeit confusingly having a car with its own name on it at the announcement, suggesting that it might build its own cars rather than just the engine and associated components. The cars will not be built by Audi but will continue to be built by the team based at Hinwil in Switzerland, the team that started life as Sauber but was renamed as Alfa Romeo for 2019 in a deal that will come to an end at the end of this season. Audi will have a 50 per cent share in the team, which is fantastic news as it will give the team security in tricky financial times. More than this, Audi is a manufacturer that truly understands motorsport, having shone in rallying, sports prototypes, GTs and touring cars, and so it is more likely to have informed and constructive input into the team once it bears its name.

Then Porsche's plans to follow suit, also starting in 2026 when it sought to take a 50 per cent stake in Red Bull Racing, began to unravel at the end of August as it became apparent that the team's management were having second thoughts about handing over this level of control to an outside factor. Equally, Porsche wanted to be more than simply an engine supplier and so withdrew when Red Bull's owners pointed out that the deal wasn't for 50 per cent of the team but for 50 per cent of its engine division, Red Bull Powertrains. So, without the right deal in place that would give them some control over the direction that the team would take, Porsche was left high and dry. Building its own engine for 2026 wouldn't be an option, as it has no facility in place to do so. This means that Porsche won't, as planned, use its F1 involvement to showcase its focus on synthetic fuels.

This scrapped deal was less than ideal, but the Honda element of Red Bull Racing appeared to be beefed up last year, with the team's deal to run Honda-based engines having been extended to the end of 2025. Beyond that, Honda's renewed interest may or may not lead to it staying on with the team.

At this point, Stefano Domenicali, chief executive officer of the Formula One Group, said that there were other manufacturers watching on, looking to see if an opening might occur that would suit their entry to F1. Indeed, there is talk that the Lotus name might return to

the sport in which it shone so brightly in the 1960s and 1970s then less so in its second incarnation in the 2010s. Equally, Renault may be open to having another company's name on its F1 engines in the near future, with Geely – the Chinese owners of Lotus and other brands – looking to get involved with the Renault engine project, as might the team known as Aston Martin.

One matter of note as F1 lost one of its main potential contenders is that the World Endurance Championship has done considerably better than F1 in attracting manufacturers to its ranks, with Toyota, Ferrari, Peugeot, Porsche, Cadillac and Glickenhaus entering cars in 2023, with more to come from 2024, including BMW and Lamborghini. So, the WEC is set to enter a new golden age. However, F1 continues to struggle with the balancing act of trying to satisfy the wants and desires of both nimble teams and less fast-moving manufacturers who both need each other, but the devil is in the detail or, in this case, the proportion of any deal done.

Opposite top left: Porsche entered F1 in 1962 when Dan Gurney gave it its only F1 win in the French GP at Rouen.

Opposite top right: Ayrton Senna, shown leading at Monaco, gave Honda great success when it powered McLaren in 1988.

Opposite middle: Audi Sport is looking to make its F1 bow in 2026.

Opposite bottom: Audi's F1 concept car was unveiled at Spa last August and it is likely to be run by Sauber.

#Future Is An Attitude

Audi Sport

TALKING POINT: **THE SHORTAGE OF AMERICAN F1 DRIVERS**

The Netflix *Drive to Survive* series in the past few years has given F1 an image boost in the USA like nothing before. This is reflected in the fact that there will be three Grands Prix in the USA this year, and yet there is still a lack of American drivers on the grid. The burning question on the lips of new American fans is why.

The United States has had a long but less than steady relationship with Formula 1. Its Grand Prix has been held at 11 circuits dotted around the country, which can either be seen as a way of spreading the message or perhaps the fact that F1 has never truly taken hold of the interest of American motor racing fans. After all, they have their own IndyCar series and the mighty stock car racing beast, NASCAR, to follow. They are popular with polar opposite sectors of society but are both undeniably American.

From the first year of the World Championship in 1950 through until 1960, the Indianapolis 500 counted as a round of the World Championship, but there was no crossover. Ironically, this was not the case after the race was dropped from the championship, as Lotus in particular then added it to their schedule, attracted by the prestige of a possible win there but even more so by the winner's purse.

Just before this partnership came to a close, there was a stand-alone United States GP in 1959, held at the Sebring circuit built on a Florida airbase. This was won by Bruce McLaren and was notable for attracting the regular racers. It was so successful that the next US GP was held on the other side of the country, at Riverside in California, before moving to Watkins Glen in upstate New York in 1961. And there it found a home, until 1980 at least.

The Long Beach street circuit was an additional event from 1976, and it started a trend of temporary street circuits. And these, in a way, were part of the problem,

as F1 cars weren't in their natural habitat in these point-and-squirt environments. Leading IndyCar driver Rick Mears tested impressively for the Brabham F1 team and, had he been convinced to come to F1, this might have broken the dam and attracted more of America's best, but the deal fell through.

American drivers had been as well represented as most in the early 1960s and Phil Hill became the USA's first world champion when he landed the title for Ferrari in 1961. Then Dan Gurney was a race-winning front runner through to the middle of the decade, even starting his own team.

IndyCar star Mario Andretti dabbled in F1 from 1968, becoming a winner for Ferrari in 1971. However, his Atlantic-hopping time was rewarded in 1978 when he became America's second world champion after a dominant season with Lotus.

And yet, F1 was still seen as exotic, as a 'cheese and wine' circus rather than a 'beer and a burger' environment, and so America's best remained on the banked ovals. Indeed, since Andretti's 1978 title win, 44 years have passed, not only without a third American world champion but there hasn't even been any chance of one, and the big question is why.

One clear hurdle for American drivers was evident last year, namely that they are not currently eligible to qualify for the FIA super-licence required to compete in F1. This was thrown into focus midway through last year when Colton Herta was tipped to take the second seat at AlphaTauri. As a

22-year-old second-generation American racer with seven IndyCar wins to his name, this seemed a good fit and would certainly give Red Bull's junior team plenty of publicity on F1's visits to Miami, COTA and Las Vegas. However, the FIA wouldn't grant him a super-licence, sticking with its rule that they are for drivers who have achieved notable success in the FIA F2 and F3 championships.

American drivers have traditionally not headed overseas to further their careers, but this is changing and the one who shone last year in F2 was Logan Sargeant who won races at Silverstone and Red Bull Ring, while also getting first-hand F1 experience by spending race weekends with Williams which helped him land a race seat for 2023.

He was backed up last year by five Americans competing in the FIA F3 Championship, led by Jak Crawford who won once to rank seventh overall. Alone among them, Reece Ushijima was a rookie and he showed promise by not only qualifying on pole at Silverstone but finishing third.

F1 needs to think hard about opening its doors to America's best.

Opposite top: The first American World Champion, Phil Hill, in 1961.

Opposite middle left: America's second world champion was Mario Andretti, shown after winning the 1978 French GP.

Opposite middle right: Logan Sargeant is one of only a few Americans who leave the USA to pursue F1 ambitions.

Opposite bottom: Colton Herta aimed for F1, but will remain in Indycars.

TALKING POINT: **SEBASTIAN VETTEL STEPS INTO RETIREMENT**

Sebastian Vettel was a boy wonder who came, saw and conquered in F1, becoming a winner with Scuderia Toro Rosso then claiming four world titles with Red Bull Racing. He then matured from a fast and entertaining character as he raced with Ferrari into one of F1's elder statesmen, a man with mature views of the wider world.

The World Championship is going to miss Sebastian. Not only was he a four-time world champion, but he was much more than that in that he chose to see the larger picture.

Racing drivers are, necessarily, focused on what they do, from childhood through until the very best of them, finances allowing, reach the foothills of F1 before they have matured into adulthood. For some, like Lando Norris and George Russell, it means that families take the latter stages of their schooling on so that they are free to travel, to test and to race. Yet Sebastian is different, as shown by developing views on more worldly matters and being prepared to state them in public on BBC's *Question Time*, being erudite, even in his second language, about a range of matters including his discomfort about travelling the world burning hydrocarbons to race in F1.

What makes this more surprising is that Sebastian came from an ordinary background and was, like his rivals, soon out of school, racing everywhere. He was exceptionally good too, gathering titles for fun as he advanced through karting and then the junior single-seater categories. What stood out as much as his string of wins was Sebastian's apparent ability to have mental capacity to spare to help him process those vital outer elements of performance that helped him sort a car, drive it fast and win the tactical battle too, all the elements of a champion.

Any driver who can win 18 out of 20 races, as Sebastian did in Formula BMW in 2004, has something special about them and, unsurprisingly, he found it easy to advance to the European F3 Championship. There, he learnt from Lewis Hamilton and then was edged out of the title in 2006. However, he had already stepped up to the more powerful Formula Renault 3.5 and impressed by collecting a win and a second on his first outing. More than that, BMW Sauber snapped him up as a reserve driver for the remainder of the year, with people in the paddock amazed by the pace of this baby-faced individual.

When holding a clear lead in the Formula Renault 3.5 series in 2007, Sebastian got his F1 break when Robert Kubica was injured in Montreal, making his F1 debut in the United States GP at Indianapolis. He became not only what was then the youngest ever F1 starter, at 19 years and 349 days, but a point-scorer too.

Scuderia Toro Rosso signed him for the season's final seven races and Sebastian rewarded them with fourth place in China. Then he rewarded them a whole lot more in 2008 by giving the team its first win, at Monza. Red Bull Racing, slightly miffed that its junior team had won before it did so itself, signed Sebastian for 2009. Three races into the season, he made Red Bull Racing winners as well, going on to be runner-up to Jenson Button in Brawn GP's *annus mirabilis*.

Then, truly engrained at RBR, thanks in no part to his popular humour as well as his speed, Sebastian set about his 2010 campaign, but it was peppered with mishaps until three wins in the last four races were enough for him to sneak the title. Then he followed this with three more, with his 2011 and 2013 campaigns truly dominant. However, he then found himself outperformed by team-mate Daniel Ricciardo in 2014 and this ruffled his feathers.

Most drivers who have reached the top appear to want to prove themselves further by winning a title for Ferrari, and so Sebastian moved across for 2015, but it wasn't to be as his six-year spell there corresponded with the Hamilton/Mercedes years.

Having discovered the downside of Ferrari team politics as he was edged from favour by Charles Leclerc, Sebastian elected to go back to racing for a British team, Aston Martin. Here, his main role was to mentor Lance Stroll, but his flashes of speed showed that he could still, 16 seasons in, get the best from his machinery.

So, with 299 Grand Prix starts and four F1 titles to his name, a wild hairstyle and a wide range of interests, Sebastian starts a fulfilling onward journey that you just know won't be boring.

Opposite top left: Sebastian was given his F1 break by BMW Sauber in the 2007 US GP.

Opposite top right: Design chief Adrian Newey and team boss Christian Horner congratulate Sebastian after another race win.

Opposite middle: Sebastian won races but not titles with Ferrari. This is at Suzuka in 2018.

Opposite bottom: Sebastian's final F1 spell was with Aston Martin, with Lance Stroll.

KNOW THE TRACKS 2023

Liberty Media has made a concerted effort to increase the number of Grands Prix since taking over Formula 1. The COVID pandemic held them back in 2020 and 2021, but this year's 24-race calendar is a sign of their intent and is notable for the fact that the United States has gained a third Grand Prix, with Las Vegas following last year's addition of Miami.

Make no mistake, the ever-increasing number of races is going to stretch the team personnel to breaking point as they will be away both from home and their team headquarters for fully half of the year. Most teams, to prevent burn-out, will have to cycle their staff through a rota system.

Putting the 24-event calendar together is much more difficult than it was several decades ago when there were typically only 16 Grands Prix to apportion. This was usually a more user-friendly pattern of a few flyaway races, then spring and summer spent dotting around Europe before a few more flyaways at year's end.

Now, with so many races, it is a real puzzle, and the sequence of events achieved for 2023 is not entirely logical as Liberty Media has bent a little to accommodate the hosts' various date demands.

This long but exciting season starts with the Bahrain GP at Sakhir, followed a fortnight later by another race in the Middle East in Jeddah before it heats up too much.

Then, a fortnight later, the teams head to Australia for the ever-popular round held in Melbourne's Albert Park, where there is a tremendous package of supporting races and an enthusiastic crowd which really adds to the atmosphere.

The fourth round pencilled into the calendar is for Shanghai, but this may not happen if China continues to keep its borders closed. Working its way back west, the next stop is in Azerbaijan on the last weekend in April to charge around the streets of capital city Baku.

The idea of America having more than one Grand Prix per season started in the mid-1970s, when the USA's regular race at Watkins Glen in autumnal upstate New York was augmented by a spring race on the streets of Long Beach in California. This year, the first of its trio of races will be in Miami, a city which came out in force to support its maiden race last year.

Then comes the European leg, starting at Imola, and this is where the logistics start to become intense as it is followed on consecutive weekends by races in Monaco and just outside Barcelona.

It would have made sense for the next race, in Montreal, to have been paired with the one in Miami. However, it wasn't, and so the teams then have to cross the Atlantic again for the 11th round at the Red Bull Ring in Austria, and then on to the British GP.

Races at the Hungaroring and Spa-Francorchamps are paired together and then the teams have a much-needed three weekends off before resuming at the Dutch GP at Zandvoort, followed immediately by the annual pilgrimage to Monza.

Then the team transporters are used only to ferry their teams' gear to the airport for the run of eight flyaway races that conclude the season. Kicking off with the popular street race in the downtown location of Singapore's Marina Bay, this journey is followed by a visit to one of F1's greatest challenges, old-school Suzuka in Japan.

Then it's time to double back and head to Losail in Qatar for the season's third race in the Middle East, a region that remains relatively disinterested in F1 but has the funds to bring the show to town. The location between Asia and Europe certainly works well in terms of viewing times in F1's core markets.

The third race in the USA comes on the penultimate weekend of October, at the Circuit of the Americas in Texas. Then it's on south for races in Mexico City and São Paulo's Interlagos on consecutive weekends, before turning back north and travelling to the season's only new venue laid out on the streets of Las Vegas.

Finally, the season is due to come to an end in Abu Dhabi with the recently improved Yas Marina Circuit. Then, a month later, it will be Christmas.

SAKHIR

This is a circuit that left the teams confounded by its dual nature when they first visited, but F1 fans have grown to like the place, especially for its superb downhill esses.

The first thing that marks out this circuit from venues in more temperate climes is that it was designed to be a lap of two halves, one true to the nature of its desert environs and the other representing that of an oasis, with grass verges and buildings. In Arab style, the pit complex is topped out with towers designed with a nod to the local vernacular architecture.

F1 fans will find it easy to identify the hand of circuit architect Hermann Tilke when they look at the shape of the first corner complex, as a tight first turn feeds, just like Sepang, into a more open second. On the opening lap, no move is completed until the second corner is behind, although some don't even get that far...

From here, it is 'out into the desert',

with the gentle climb to the right-hand hairpin at turn 4 followed by a brilliant descent through the esse from turn 5 to turn 7.

The lap's flow is slowed at tight turn 8 and then another tight one at turn 10. This brings the cars on to a short straight behind the paddock and a poor entry to this can offer potential to pass into the tight corner at its end, turn 11.

From here, the track rises again, drivers accelerating hard all the way to the end of the second of its three timing sectors.

A good exit from turn 13 at the circuit's highest point can help a driver catch a tow down the return slope that would be really useful if it wasn't for the last two tightish corners. As it is, a good exit from turn 15 can still help a driver line up a pass into turn 1.

INSIDE TRACK

BAHRAIN GRAND PRIX

Date:	**5 March**
Circuit name:	**Bahrain International Circuit**
Circuit length:	**3.363 miles/5.412km**
Number of laps:	**57**
Email:	**info@bic.com.bh**
Website:	**www.bahraingp.com.bh**

PREVIOUS WINNERS

2014	**Lewis Hamilton** MERCEDES
2015	**Lewis Hamilton** MERCEDES
2016	**Nico Rosberg** MERCEDES
2017	**Sebastian Vettel** FERRARI
2018	**Sebastian Vettel** FERRARI
2019	**Lewis Hamilton** MERCEDES
2020	**Lewis Hamilton** MERCEDES
2020*	**Sergio Perez** RACING POINT
2021	**Lewis Hamilton** MERCEDES
2022	**Charles Leclerc** FERRARI

* As the Sakhir GP

Location: Heading south out of Manama, a main road leads to a turn-off towards low hills, and it is among the folds of these that the circuit nestles.

How it started: There was a push to get the World Championship to spread itself beyond its European base. Not only did the Middle East have the oil wealth to build new circuits, but being located midway between Europe and Asia made it attractive in terms of its time zone working for the largest number of fans. Sakhir's first Grand Prix was in 2004.

Its greatest Grand Prix: The 2019 race should have produced a first win for Charles Leclerc, on only his second outing for Ferrari, but an engine glitch slowed him and he had to settle for third behind the two Mercedes.

Its most memorable Grand Prix: No one who ever witnessed Romain Grosjean's accident in 2020 will forget it, as his first lap accident was one of the most violent in F1 history. Incredibly, after touching Daniil Kvyat's AlphaTauri, his Haas slammed into the barriers, with the rear half snapping off as the front half went through the barriers. If the halo saved his life, then so did the speedy extrication moments after that.

BAHRAIN INTERNATIONAL CIRCUIT

Speed
0   100   200   300
321km/h maximum

⏱1 Timing sector   ▬ DRS   🔲 DRS detection   ⚙4 Gear   ▲ Overtaking opportunity

2022 POLE TIME: **LECLERC (FERRARI), 1M30.558S, 133.685MPH/215.146KPH**
2022 WINNER'S AVERAGE SPEED: **117.792MPH/189.568KPH**
2022 FASTEST LAP: **LECLERC (FERRARI), 1M34.570S, 128.013MPH/206.018KPH**
LAP RECORD: **M SCHUMACHER (FERRARI), 1M30.252S 134.262KPH/216.074KPH, 2004**

JEDDAH

Drivers don't often suggest that a circuit might be just a little too fast, but this is something that has been considered since this seafront track made its debut in 2021.

It always felt as though it was just a matter of time before Saudi Arabia was brought into the World Championship fold and, after earlier plans came to nothing, a circuit was finished just in time for its debut at the end of 2021.

Anxious to be seen as more open to the outside world, the Saudi Arabian government financed a stopgap circuit just outside Jeddah, until a permanent facility could be built.

The brief given to circuit architect Hermann Tilke was to design a track that would give opportunities for overtaking. He went beyond that and produced a circuit that was quite the opposite of Monaco, with endless fast sweepers and esses and precious few points of heavy braking. With corner after corner being taken at over 150mph (240kph), drivers

voiced opinions after the inaugural event that they were concerned that cars would arrive at full pelt through the esses, and any driver who might have crashed around the next turn might be a sitting duck.

The lap is thin in shape, inserted in a narrow strip of land between the buildings and a drop down to the lagoon, forcing the lap to be shaped like a much-crimped hairpin. What makes it so tricky is how the corners come in long sequences, like the high-speed run of twists from turn 4 to turn 12, all of which are taken at more than 150mph (240kph), and then again in a more open run from turn 14 to turn 20 on the return leg.

The only point of the lap that is slow, apart from the hairpins at either end, is the opening corner, which is an accident magnet on lap 1.

SAUDI ARABIAN GRAND PRIX

Date:	19 March
Circuit name:	**Jeddah Street Circuit**
Circuit length:	**3.830 miles/6.175km**
Number of laps:	**50**
Email:	tickets@saudimotorsport.com
Website:	**www.saudiarabiangp.com**

PREVIOUS WINNERS

2021	**Lewis Hamilton**	MERCEDES
2022	**Max Verstappen**	RED BULL

Location: The track is on the corniche, sitting above a man-made lagoon located eight miles to the north of Jeddah.

How it started: Saudi Arabia has watched infinitely smaller neighbours Bahrain and Abu Dhabi host rounds of the World Championship and decided that it was time to join them, building a purpose-built facility solely to do this.

Its greatest Grand Prix: For sheer drama, the inaugural Saudi Arabian GP in 2021 will take some beating. Hosting the penultimate round of the World Championship decider on your debut, with a fierce title scrap raging between Lewis Hamilton and Max Verstappen, meant that drama was sure to be part of the show. The pair didn't disappoint in a race interrupted by two red flags and controversy provided by Verstappen gaining an advantage by running off the track at turn 1 and regaining the lead by coming back on at turn 2. This happened again, and when he slowed to let Hamilton by, the Mercedes driver wasn't ready and hit him up the back. Then he let him by and immediately dived past by using his DRS. Eventually, the tyres on Verstappen's Red Bull were shot and Hamilton won to set up a furious finale in Abu Dhabi.

Its toughest corner: With a choice of 27 corners, this isn't an easy one, especially as many of these feed almost immediately into the next twister. However, the run from turn 7 to turn 10 as the cars pile on ever more speed, often around blind bends, certainly focuses the drivers' minds.

69

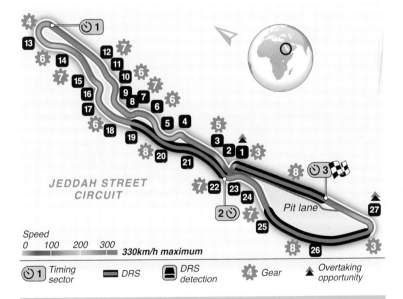

JEDDAH STREET CIRCUIT

Pit lane

Speed
0   100   200   300   **330km/h maximum**

🕐1 Timing sector   ▬ DRS   ▢ DRS detection   ◆ Gear   ▲ Overtaking opportunity

2022 POLE TIME: **PEREZ (RED BULL), 1M28.200S, 156.585MPH/252.000KPH**
2022 WINNER'S AVERAGE SPEED: **136.379MPH/219.481KPH**
2022 FASTEST LAP: **LECLERC (FERRARI), 1M31.634S, 150.717MPH/242.556KPH**
LAP RECORD: **HAMILTON (MERCEDES), 1M30.734S, 152.212MPH/244.962KPH, 2021**

» MELBOURNE

It was good to be back at Melbourne last year, and the popularity of this venue with teams and drivers alike comes not just from the newly improved circuit but from the atmosphere too.

INSIDE TRACK

AUSTRALIAN GRAND PRIX

Date:	**2 April**
Circuit name:	**Albert Park**
Circuit length:	**3.280 miles/5.278km**
Number of laps:	**58**
Email:	enquiries@grandprix.com.au
Website:	**www.grandprix.com.au**

The atmosphere at the Australian GP has always been exceptional and last year, after a two-year hiatus, was the first time that the fans were treated to a circuit with real flow. This came from the previously stop-start Albert Park layout being tweaked by a handful of corners being made more open, starting with the first turn, opening out what had always been something of a tight right/left combination.

The third corner has been widened too, by fully four metres, on its inside edge and given a more positive camber to help drivers get through this 110-degree right. It is still one of the best places to watch the racing as the drivers brake hard.

The circuit is still very much broken into sectors and the slowish run to turn 6 is now brought to an end by a far easier right-hander. Cars are now able to travel around 45mph (72kph) faster to enter a sector around the far side of the lake, shorn of the old Clark chicane and thus made flat-out all the way from turn 6 to what used to be turn 12. In addition, the left/right esses at the far side of the lake have been opened to help drivers carry more speed through there and approach that 90-degree right at over 200mph (320kph).

The final sector of the lap is a slower stretch between the trees and two of the corners have been offered more width at their apex, again adding to a little more speed being used, making the show more spectacular for the fans, although not really providing any more overtaking spots for the drivers.

However, if you look at the new, more open layout, the most likely passing spots remain turns 1 and 3.

PREVIOUS WINNERS

2011	**Sebastian Vettel**	RED BULL
2012	**Jenson Button**	McLAREN
2013	**Kimi Raikkonen**	LOTUS
2014	**Nico Rosberg**	MERCEDES
2015	**Lewis Hamilton**	MERCEDES
2016	**Nico Rosberg**	MERCEDES
2017	**Sebastian Vettel**	FERRARI
2018	**Sebastian Vettel**	FERRARI
2019	**Valtteri Bottas**	MERCEDES
2022	**Charles Leclerc**	FERRARI

Location: With the push to increase F1's spread, many future circuits will be street venues with their associated shortcomings. Albert Park does it better, its parkland setting being a mile from the city centre.

How it started: Adelaide had hosted Australia's Grand Prix since it joined the World Championship in 1985, but state pride meant that Victoria snatched it from South Australia, starting at Albert Park in 1996.

Its greatest Grand Prix: It was hard to pick out the cars in the spray in 2013, but it was harder still to understand the new range of Pirelli tyres as almost no one – aside from Kimi Raikkonen, who rose from seventh to win for Lotus – could make the softer compound last.

A local hero: Three F1 world titles – in 1959, 1960 and 1966 – make Jack Brabham the stand-out, and the fact that he spearheaded the rear-engined revolution with Cooper and later won his final crown in a car bearing his own name puts him right in F1's pantheon.

Rising national star: Oscar Piastri spent 2022 on the sidelines, not racing but attending Grands Prix as Alpine's reserve driver. His three different titles in the previous three years mark him out as a star.

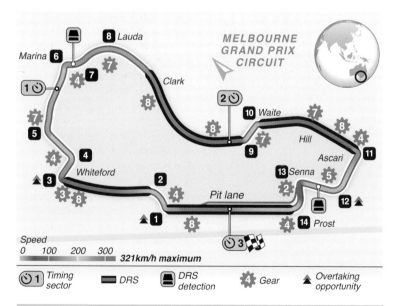

MELBOURNE GRAND PRIX CIRCUIT

Speed
0   100   200   300
321km/h maximum

Timing sector — DRS — DRS detection — Gear — Overtaking opportunity

2022 POLE TIME: **LECLERC (FERRARI), 1M17.868S, 151.622MPH/244.012KPH**
2022 WINNER'S AVERAGE SPEED: **130.024MPH/209.254KPH**
2022 FASTEST LAP: **LECLERC (FERRARI), 1M20.260S, 147.103MPH/236.740KPH**
LAP RECORD: **LECLERC (FERRARI), 1M20.260S, 147.103MPH/236.740KPH, 2022**

BAKU

The Baku City Circuit is an extremely unusual venue, as it's a street circuit that combines the traditional weaving between buildings with straights along which the cars can top 200mph (320kph).

Few knew what to expect when F1 turned up in Azerbaijan for the first time in 2016. What they found was impressive, as the organisers had produced a street circuit with a difference. In fact, with many differences.

The main difference to, say, Monaco is that this track starts off in a modern section of the city, where the block layout of its streets means 90-degree corners but straights between. In Monaco, nothing is straight. The roads used are wider too.

The second difference is the two-part nature of the lap, with the transition coming at turn 8 where the circuit reaches the ramparts and enters the citadel. At this point, the lap loses those 90-degree corners and becomes more free-form as it starts to climb a slope and snake its way through a small park lined

with grandstands alongside the city walls, before opening out for a blast through two fast kinks and then a slower corner at turn 15.

Running past some of the capital's grandest buildings, the track then turns hard left by the opera house at turn 16 and plunges back down the slope towards the level of the starting straight.

The rest of the lap is a flat-out blast, through four kinks – one to the left and three to the right – the cars topping 200mph (320kph) as they flash past the pits and the park that lines the seashore in eighth gear before the drivers have to brake hard for the first corner, the first of a run of four 90-degree corners. Not surprisingly, the braking zone for turn 1 is the best spot of the 3.75-mile lap for drivers to line up an overtaking move.

AZERBAIJAN GRAND PRIX

Date:	**30 April**
Circuit name:	**Baku City Circuit**
Circuit length:	**3.753 miles/6.006km**
Number of laps:	**51**
Email:	**info@bakugp.az**
Website:	**www.bakugp.az**

PREVIOUS WINNERS

2016	**Nico Rosberg** MERCEDES
2017	**Daniel Ricciardo** RED BULL
2018	**Lewis Hamilton** MERCEDES
2019	**Valtteri Bottas** MERCEDES
2021	**Sergio Perez** RED BULL
2022	**Max Verstappen** RED BULL

Location: The capital of Azerbaijan, it sits in the middle of the country on a peninsula jutting into the Caspian Sea, and the circuit is spread between the modern buildings and park on the seashore and the walled area of the old city.

How it started: The Grand Prix is in Azerbaijan because of one thing: oil money. The country has no history of motor racing but decided to finance a round of the World Championship to gain international recognition. That it's midway between Europe and the Far East made its time zone attractive too from a TV audience perspective. A version of the circuit had already been tried when the FIA GT held a race there in 2013, which was won by a Team WRT Audi driven by Laurens Vanthoor and 1998 Le Mans victor Stephane Ortelli.

Its greatest Grand Prix: Surprise happenings can make a Grand Prix memorable and the 2021 running of the Azerbaijan GP had just that. The problem was tyres that blew in dramatic fashion. Lance Stroll was the first to suffer this fate, on the main straight no less, at 190mph (304kph)... Then, the same fate befell leader Max Verstappen. This brought out the red flag and at least Red Bull Racing came away with the win as team-mate Sergio Perez controlled the restart, at which Lewis Hamilton knocked his brake bias fully forward and skidded off at the first corner.

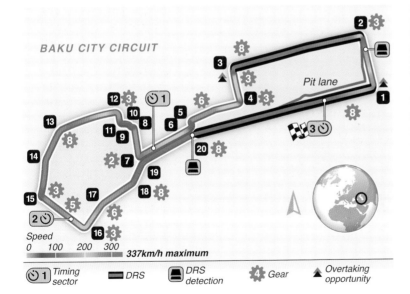

BAKU CITY CIRCUIT

Pit lane

Speed
0   100   200   300
337km/h maximum

🕐 1 Timing sector	DRS
DRS detection	4 Gear
▲ Overtaking opportunity	

2022 POLE TIME: LECLERC (FERRARI), 1M41.359S, 132.482MPH/213.210KPH
2022 WINNER'S AVERAGE SPEED: 121.257MPH/195.144KPH
2022 FASTEST LAP: PEREZ (RED BULL), 1M46.046S, 126.627MPH/203.787KPH
LAP RECORD: LECLERC (FERRARI), 1M43.009S 130.360MPH/209.795KPH, 2019

MIANI

People laughed at the seascapes painted on the run-off areas around the circuit before its maiden event last year, but they weren't laughing after it proved to be a real hit.

The American owners of Formula 1 want more American races, and so do the sponsors, especially now that F1 has a new, much younger audience thanks to the success of the Netflix show *Drive to Survive*. This is why the people behind the Miami GP were keen for their circuit to prove itself before the addition of a third Grand Prix in the USA settles at Las Vegas.

The flow of the 3.36-mile circuit is slow to start with, as the first corner is very tight. This at least provides scope for overtaking on the opening lap. However, it is then followed by a run of medium-speed esses before the long left-hander at turn 7. A good exit from there is vital as the track then opens out through kinks at turns 9 and 10, and then a straight to turn 11.

There are two principal passing points in the lap. The first comes at turn 11, a tight left-hander, and the second, after a very twisty section from there into a 90-degree left, opens out on to the lap's longest straight. This takes the cars down to turn 17 and passing is most likely into this hairpin as the drivers brake heavily after exceeding 200mph (320kph) on the approach.

For this year, the drivers will be hoping that the track surface can be made less bumpy, as finding a set-up was tricky.

The second thing that F1 would do well to reduce for 2023 would be the flocks of minor celebrities who bulldozed their way up and down the grid last year, happy to take any adulation that came their way, but too rude to contribute to the show by not deigning to be interviewed.

INSIDE TRACK

MIAMI GRAND PRIX

Date:	**7 May**
Circuit name:	**Miami International Autodrome**
Circuit length:	**3.362 miles/5.411km**
Number of laps:	**57**
Email:	**info@f1miamigp.com**
Website:	**www.f1miamigp.com**

PREVIOUS WINNERS

2022   **Max Verstappen** RED BULL

Location: Miami is a sprawling city and the circuit is to be found, but only for race weekend, laid out in open space around the Hard Rock Stadium in the Miami Gardens suburb on the northern side of the city.

How it started: There have been races held on temporary circuits in city settings around Florida for decades, as well as on the banked oval at Daytona, but Miami was long tipped as a city where F1 would do well. Earlier bids all failed until last year's breakthrough when it settled instead on being hosted in an area with space to fit a temporary circuit, in the car park of the Hard Rock Stadium.

Its greatest Grand Prix: Well, with only one held so far, that will be last year's, when Max Verstappen won for Red Bull Racing after catching and passing Charles Leclerc's Ferrari, although he then had that lead annulled when a safety car period was required after Lando Norris and Pierre Gasly clashed. However, he controlled the restart.

A local hero: Logan Sargeant from Boca Raton further up Florida's east coast is the USA's new single-seater hero, winning several rounds of last year's FIA F2 series in a manner not seen before from a young American driver. As a result of this, he is sure to be a much-needed American contender in F1 in years to come. It hasn't been an overnight vault up the order like Max Verstappen, but is the result of six years racing in Europe, because America's single-seater ladder is relatively poorly supported.

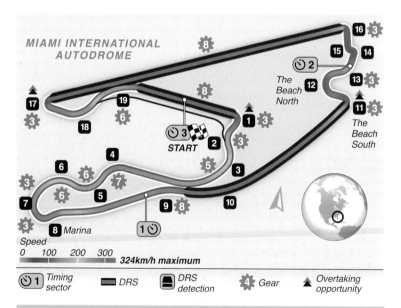

MIAMI INTERNATIONAL AUTODROME

The Beach North

The Beach South

START

Marina

Speed
0 100 200 300
324km/h maximum

⏱1 Timing sector   🔲 DRS   🔲 DRS detection   ⚙4 Gear   ▲ Overtaking opportunity

2022 POLE TIME: **LECLERC (FERRARI), 1M28.796S, 136.338MPH/219.415KPH**
2022 WINNER'S AVERAGE SPEED: **121.764MPH/195.960KPH**
2022 FASTEST LAP: **VERSTAPPEN (RED BULL), 1M31.361S, 132.510MPH/213.255KPH**
LAP RECORD: **VERSTAPPEN (RED BULL), 1M31.361S, 132.510MPH/213.255KPH, 2022**

IMOLA

This circuit is very much in an earlier style, intimate in the way that it is spread across a hillside and uses the gradient change to make each of its corners different. It is old school and all the better for that.

EMILIA ROMAGNA GRAND PRIX

Date:	**21 May**
Circuit name:	**Autodromo Enzo e Dino Ferrari**
Circuit length:	**3.048 miles/4.906km**
Number of laps:	**63**
Email:	**info@autodromoimola.it**
Website:	**www.autodromoimola.it**

PREVIOUS WINNERS

2000*	**Michael Schumacher**	FERRARI
2001*	**Ralf Schumacher**	WILLIAMS
2002*	**Michael Schumacher**	FERRARI
2003*	**Michael Schumacher**	FERRARI
2004*	**Michael Schumacher**	FERRARI
2005*	**Fernando Alonso**	RENAULT
2006*	**Michael Schumacher**	FERRARI
2020**	**Lewis Hamilton**	MERCEDES
2021**	**Max Verstappen**	RED BULL
2022**	**Max Verstappen**	RED BULL

* Run as the San Marino GP
** Run as the Emilia Romagna GP

Some circuits are marked by the sheer speed that the cars can reach, but the Autodromo Enzo e Dino Ferrari isn't one of these. It's certainly no Silverstone and its identity comes from the way that it runs close to the banks of a river then gets interesting as it turns back on itself and scales the hillside, bisecting the orchard-clad slope.

The fastest part of the lap comes early in its three-mile length, with drivers having to brake heavily for the first corner of consequence, the left flick into the Tamburello chicane. This is one of the chief passing points.

It might be said that Imola is too tight for the speed of F1 cars, but the racing action is always close as heavy braking for the 150-degree uphill left at Tosa bunches the field.

The flow of the lap is magnificent from there up to a crest at Piratella before a steep drop to Acque Minerali, with the track then flicking up again just as rapidly to make it the most challenging corner.

With the track entering a narrow funnel between concrete walls, it flattens out over a lower crest and the drivers have to drop down to second gear as they throw their cars in to the right/left flick at Variante Alta, the slowest point of the lap.

It's the proximity of trees along the track's flanks that give it its nature, but this feeling of being simply in a park is shattered when the cars descend to the first of the Rivazza left-handers and the drivers are confronted by giant grandstands.

The rest of the lap is on the level, with drivers able to accelerate from here all the way to the first chicane.

Location: Although it long hosted the San Marino GP, the circuit is not in the principality at all, but in Castellaccio Park on the southern edge of Imola.

How it started: The circuit was opened in 1952 and remained a national level circuit until hosting a non-championship F1 race in 1963, won for Lotus by Jim Clark. Sixteen years later, it hosted another, won by Niki Lauda for Brabham, before it hosted the Italian GP instead of Monza in 1980 and got its own race in 1981.

Its first Grand Prix: Given a one-off shot of hosting the Italian GP in 1980, the *tifosi* poured in, hoping for a Ferrari win, but it went to Brabham instead, with Nelson Piquet dominant.

A race to remember: 1994 was tragic. First Rubens Barrichello crashed his Jordan in practice and was lucky to survive. In qualifying, Simtek's Roland Ratzenberger was unfortunate not to. Then JJ Lehto stalled on the third row and was hit hard from behind. However, the one that every F1 fan remembers is when Ayrton Senna crashed and was fatally injured at the restart. The F1 world was left in shock.

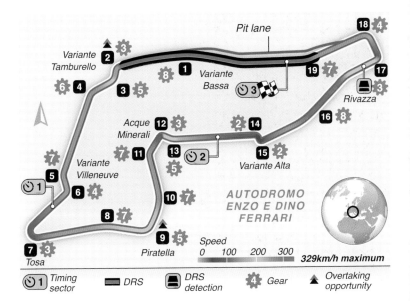

2022 POLE TIME: **NOT APPLICABLE AS SPRINT RACE ORDER DEFINED THE GRID**
2022 WINNER'S AVERAGE SPEED: **125.058MPH/201.262KPH**
2022 FASTEST LAP: **VERSTAPPEN (RED BULL), 1M18.446S, 139.983MPH/225.281KPH**
LAP RECORD: **HAMILTON (MERCEDES), 1M15.484S 145.476MPH/234.121KPH, 2020**

MONACO

There was much talk last year that Monaco had run its course as an F1 venue. Certainly, the track has clear limitations, and always has had, but its importance to F1's identity remains.

Think Monaco GP, and most people think of the staggeringly large yachts in the harbour and the 'beautiful people' partying in the principality. The teams and drivers, though, think of a crazily tight and narrow track and awkward working conditions. However, the sponsors love it for entertaining VIPs and F1 needs it for its eternal glamour.

The lap scarcely has a straight worthy of the name as it weaves its way around the buildings, with just arcing stretches between the corners. The start/finish straight, for example, is nothing of the sort, and famously, those on the back row struggle even to see the starting lights on the gantry.

The first corner, Sainte Devote, is a constriction, turning slightly to the left before going right. Contact and a bent front wing or two seems almost inevitable on the opening lap.

The track then goes uphill all the way to Massenet, the tricky and high-speed left-hander that feeds the cars into a rare open space as they cross Casino Square. This is the high point and it's then downhill to Mirabeau, a sharp right, and on down to the left-hand Grand Hotel hairpin. Carrying on downhill from there, the track drops through a right and then another to get back on to the level. This is at Portier, right by the sea wall, but drivers are more focused on the curving tunnel that follows, fortunately well lit these days.

A gentle drop to harbour-front level follows and then the blast past the yachts, the swimming pool and on to the lap's tight finish at La Rascasse and Virage Antony Noghes.

INSIDE TRACK

MONACO GRAND PRIX

Date:	**28 May**
Circuit name:	**Circuit de Monaco**
Circuit length:	**2.075 miles/3.339km**
Number of laps:	**78**
Email:	**info@acm.mc**
Website:	**www.acm.mc**

PREVIOUS WINNERS

2012	**Mark Webber**	RED BULL
2013	**Nico Rosberg**	MERCEDES
2014	**Nico Rosberg**	MERCEDES
2015	**Nico Rosberg**	MERCEDES
2016	**Lewis Hamilton**	MERCEDES
2017	**Sebastian Vettel**	FERRARI
2018	**Daniel Ricciardo**	RED BULL
2019	**Lewis Hamilton**	MERCEDES
2021	**Max Verstappen**	RED BULL
2022	**Sergio Perez**	RED BULL

Location: The heart of Monte Carlo is its harbour, beneath the castle, and this is where the circuit is to be found, its pit lane right next to the swimming pool.

How it started: Cigarette manufacturer Antony Noghes proposed to the royal family a race be held around the streets to bring people and much-needed money to the principality. This was in 1929 and it brought Monaco international appeal that it has never lost.

Its greatest Grand Prix: Nigel Mansell never won at Monaco, but it wasn't for the want of trying. The closest he came was in his title-winning year, 1992, when he had to pit with seven laps left with a suspected puncture. The team wasn't prepared for his arrival and this let Ayrton Senna take the lead, which Nigel then tried to wrestle back in every way possible, ending up 0.2 seconds short.

A local hero: For decades, Louis Chiron was the greatest Monegasque F1 driver, having finished third in the 1950 Monaco GP. Olivier Beretta peaked with a seventh place in the 1994 German GP. Then came Charles Leclerc, easily outstripping both.

Rising national star: One Leclerc clearly isn't enough, as there's another on the way, with 21-year-old Arthur becoming a front runner in his second year in F3.

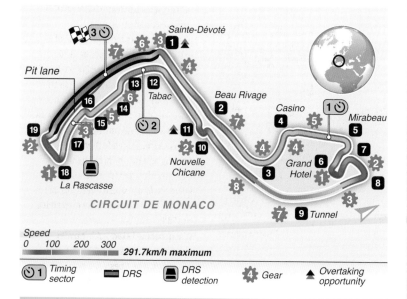

CIRCUIT DE MONACO

Sainte-Dévoté · Pit lane · Tabac · Beau Rivage · Casino · Mirabeau · Nouvelle Chicane · Grand Hotel · La Rascasse · Tunnel

Speed
0 100 200 300   **291.7km/h maximum**

Timing sector · DRS · DRS detection · Gear · Overtaking opportunity

2022 POLE TIME: LECLERC (FERRARI), 1M11.376S, 104.582MPH/168.308KPH
2022 WINNER'S AVERAGE SPEED: 68.343MPH/109.987KPH
2022 FASTEST LAP: NORRIS (MCLAREN), 1M14.693S, 99.937MPH/160.834KPH
LAP RECORD: HAMILTON (MERCEDES), 1M12.909S, 102.383MPH/164.769KPH, 2021

BARCELONA

If a European venue needs to be culled from the F1 calendar, perhaps this one would be the least missed, except by the home fans of Fernando Alonso and Carlos Sainz Jr.

SPANISH GRAND PRIX

Date:	**4 June**
Circuit name:	**Circuit de Barcelona-Catalunya**
Circuit length:	**2.892 miles/4.654km**
Number of laps:	**66**
Email:	**info@circuitcat.com**
Website:	**www.circuitcat.com**

PREVIOUS WINNERS

2012	**Pastor Maldonado** WILLIAMS
2013	**Fernando Alonso** FERRARI
2014	**Lewis Hamilton** MERCEDES
2015	**Nico Rosberg** MERCEDES
2016	**Max Verstappen** RED BULL
2017	**Lewis Hamilton** MERCEDES
2018	**Lewis Hamilton** MERCEDES
2019	**Lewis Hamilton** MERCEDES
2021	**Lewis Hamilton** MERCEDES
2022	**Max Verstappen** RED BULL

Location: Built 15 miles north of Barcelona, the Circuit de Barcelona-Catalunya is located in gentle hills near Montmelo, albeit with the fields fast disappearing under factories.

How it started: Spain couldn't settle on a home for its Grand Prix, trying four other venues between 1951 and 1991 when it settled on here.

Its greatest Grand Prix: In terms of achievement, the wet race in 1996 stands out. It was Michael Schumacher's first year with Ferrari and he made an awful start to fall from third to ninth. However, he then charged to the front as others slid off and won by 45 seconds.

A local hero: Fernando Alonso is from Spain's far north, but he was immediately adopted as the local hero, being the first Spanish driver capable of winning in F1. Of course, he then added the 2005 and 2006 F1 titles.

Rising national star: 2021 IndyCar champion Alex Palou, a McLaren test driver, but, if he doesn't cross over, then David Vidales is the pick of Spain's rising stars, winning a round of the FIA F3 series. However, 2015 Manor F1 driver Roberto Merhi popped back one weekend last year and finished third in an F2 race in Austria.

Back in the early 1990s, this was a modern circuit, the best that Spain had ever offered, although sadly there were no Spanish drivers to help fill the stands. Indeed, Spain was more into motorbikes, so there wasn't much of a buzz. However, the teams tested here in the weeks between Grands Prix, when F1 testing was the norm rather than a rarity. Seeking to develop their cars for the full range of circuits, they liked the wide variety of corners that it offered, from fast to slow.

As a race venue, though, the flow was wrecked when it was decided that the sweep down the hill from turn 13 on to the start/finish straight was too open, meaning that the cars would carry so much speed that the approach to the next braking point, turn 1, would be reached at astonishing speed and was thus thought to be too dangerous, so a chicane was inserted, wrecking the lap's best passing place.

As it remains, the rest of the lap is little changed, with the downhill approach to the first corner still offering the best chance for passing, especially on the opening lap. It is really a two-part corner, as turn 2 follows immediately. If a driver is slow out of there, a rival might be able to tail them up the hill through turn 3 and try to pass into turn 4.

Turn 5, from where the track dips again, also offers a possibility to pass. But the best part of the lap is where the climb starts again at turn 7, through to the best corner, Campsa at the top of the hill, where a good exit can help down the dipping infield straight before the climb to turn 12.

CIRCUIT DE BARCELONA-CATALUNYA

Renault · Repsol · Campsa · Banc Sabadell · Seat · Würth · Pit lane · La Caixa · Elf · New Holland

Speed 0 100 200 300
322.7km/h maximum

Timing sector · DRS · DRS detection · Gear · Overtaking opportunity

2022 POLE TIME: LECLERC (FERRARI), 1M18.750S, 132.795MPH/213.714KPH
2022 WINNER'S AVERAGE SPEED: 118.127MPH/190.108KPH
2022 FASTEST LAP: PEREZ (RED BULL), 1M24.108S, 124.336MPH/200.099KPH
LAP RECORD: VERSTAPPEN (RED BULL), 1M18.149S 133.816MPH/215.357KPH, 2021

The backdrop at Singapore's Marina Bay Circuit is one of F1's most spectacular. But for the drivers, it's eyes down.

MONTREAL

One of the trickiest things to do in F1 is to find anyone who doesn't love going to Montreal. The track layout is tight, but the weather is usually good and the city fabulous fun.

The Circuit Gilles Villeneuve packs quite a punch for a track built on such a small plot of land. Even though it's hemmed in on one side by the river and on the other by the rowing lake used when Montreal hosted the Olympic Games in 1976, the track manages to offer not only some points at which the drivers really have to work, but also a straight long enough for them to consider making a passing manoeuvre.

The start of the lap has a swerve to the right before a hard left that is often the scene of trouble on the opening lap, particularly since it feeds almost immediately into a right-hand hairpin as the drivers jockey for position.

A sequence of esses follows, with the track then disappearing between trees and everything feeling very hemmed in before tight turn 6.

Then comes a decent run down to the turn 8/9 esse before heavy braking into L'Epingle. This is a hairpin in front of huge grandstands packed with people expecting to see passing moves, both working and not, as the drivers change down to second gear, dive in and hope for the best…The run from there down to the final corner is very fast, with the cars clearing 200mph (320kph) before the drivers have to throw out the anchors to drag their speed down enough for the right/left chicane, as they attempt to make the most of the lap's best passing point. There is a concrete wall right across from its exit and this has become known as the"champions' wall", as even the greatest, such as Michael Schumacher, have run wide over the kerbs and clattered it.

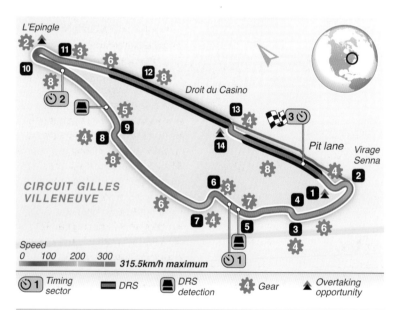

CIRCUIT GILLES VILLENEUVE

L'Epingle · Droit du Casino · Pit lane · Virage Senna

Speed
0   100   200   300
315.5km/h maximum

⏱1 Timing sector   ▬ DRS   ▢ DRS detection   ⚙4 Gear   ▲ Overtaking opportunity

2022 POLE TIME: VERSTAPPEN (RED BULL), 1M21.299S, 119.992MPH/193.109KPH
2022 WINNER'S AVERAGE SPEED: 118.107MPH/190.075KPH
2022 FASTEST LAP: SAINZ JR (FERRARI), 1M15.749S, 128.784MPH/207.258KPH
LAP RECORD: BOTTAS (MERCEDES), 1M13.078S, 133.491MPH/214.833KPH, 2019

INSIDE TRACK

CANADIAN GRAND PRIX

Date:	**18 June**
Circuit name:	**Circuit Gilles Villeneuve**
Circuit length:	**2.710 miles/4.361km**
Number of laps:	**70**
Email:	**info@circuitgillesvilleneuve.ca**
Website:	**www.circuitgillesvilleneuve.ca**

PREVIOUS WINNERS

2011	**Jenson Button** McLAREN
2012	**Lewis Hamilton** McLAREN
2013	**Sebastian Vettel** RED BULL
2014	**Daniel Ricciardo** RED BULL
2015	**Lewis Hamilton** MERCEDES
2016	**Lewis Hamilton** MERCEDES
2017	**Lewis Hamilton** MERCEDES
2018	**Sebastian Vettel** FERRARI
2019	**Lewis Hamilton** MERCEDES
2022	**Max Verstappen** RED BULL

Location: Montreal sits on the northern bank of the St Lawrence River and Île Notre-Dame, on which the circuit is located, just off the southern bank, linked by road bridges and by the metro.

How it started: Built in 1978 when Mosport Park was becoming unsafe as F1 cars grew ever faster, this brought F1 to the people when Gilles Villeneuve was breaking into F1. That Villeneuve won at his first attempt there for Ferrari, albeit after Lotus stand-in Jean-Pierre Jarier had his car break, was a dream result, brightening a cold October day for the *tifosi*. Subsequent races would be held earlier in the year.

Its greatest Grand Prix: A surprise result always stands out, so Sauber fans will never forget 2008 when not only did the Swiss team claim its first win, but a one-two, as Robert Kubica led Nick Heidfeld home.

A local hero: It's hard to imagine anyone topping Gilles Villeneuve in the hearts of Canadian F1 fans. His buccaneering style was a bright light in F1 as he not only won Grands Prix for Ferrari but did so in a tail-out style. He was never a world champion, dying at Zolder in 1982, but his memory remains.

RED BULL RING

On a summer's day, there isn't a more scenic F1 circuit as it rises and falls on a mountainside. However, its layout does appear to attract contact between the cars – and controversy.

INSIDE TRACK

AUSTRIAN GRAND PRIX

Date:	2 July
Circuit name:	Red Bull Ring
Circuit length:	2.688 miles/4.326km
Number of laps:	71
Email:	information@projekt-spielberg.at
Website:	www.projekt-spielberg.at

PREVIOUS WINNERS

2015	Nico Rosberg	MERCEDES
2016	Lewis Hamilton	MERCEDES
2017	Valtteri Bottas	MERCEDES
2018	Max Verstappen	RED BULL
2019	Max Verstappen	RED BULL
2020	Valtteri Bottas	MERCEDES
2020*	Lewis Hamilton	MERCEDES
2021	Max Verstappen	RED BULL
2021*	Max Verstappen	RED BULL
2022	Charles Leclerc	FERRARI

*In the Styrian GP

There are two main pinch points in the lap and neither can be seen when the drivers power away from the grid, as the climb to the first corner is so steep that this is all they can see.

On reaching the entry to turn 1, the slope flattens out and the drivers can finally see into the turn, with many a driver squeezed on to the outside line finding themselves edged out beyond the kerbs. They get away with this as there's a large expanse of run-off area, and some have been known to keep their foot flat to the floor and gain an advantage before rejoining. This is something that needs to be tackled, perhaps by the tarmac being replaced by a gravel trap at this 80-degree right.

The drivers accelerate hard from here, with the slope steepening through a kink at turn 2 to another corner entered over a brow: turn 3. It's a place where it's extremely tempting for a driver to attempt a move by diving at the apex of this tight right, but this usually leads to contact and is the most notorious pinch point on the circuit.

The track rises a little more as it traverses the face of the hillside before dropping to turn 4 where the fall from the turn-in point to the exit is marked, and many a driver tries a passing move here, some of which work.

The next stretch is a descent through turns 6 and 7, then a slight rise through an esse at turn 8 before the short straight to turn 9 takes the drivers to a dropping corner, and then the last corner on to the start/finish straight with a nasty compression at its apex.

Location: The Styrian Alps are towards the western end of Austria and the closest city, Graz, is 45 miles to the south-east.

How it started: The Österreichring was opened in 1969, as a sweeping 3.673-mile track. This was chopped back to 2.684 miles in 1996 and renamed the A1-Ring, but this changed in 2014 when it became the Red Bull Ring.

Its greatest Grand Prix: Everyone likes a surprise and the Austrian GP produced a run of first-time winners, with John Watson's victory in 1976 made memorable as he had to go ahead with a bet with team boss Roger Penske and shave off his beard if he won.

A local hero: Austria boxed above its weight by producing world champions Jochen Rindt and Niki Lauda as well as Grand Prix winner Gerhard Berger. Rindt was killed before he clinched the 1970 title, while Lauda survived a fiery accident and was champion in 1975, 1977 and 1984 to become Austria's greatest.

Rising national star: It continues to be a mystery how Austria is producing new great GT drivers but few single-seater stars, with Formula 4 racer Charlie Wurz – son of F1 racer Alex Wurz – the best of its young guns.

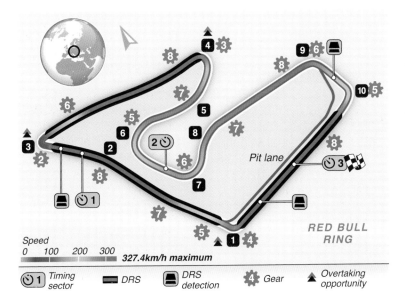

Pit lane

RED BULL RING

Speed
0   100   200   300
327.4km/h maximum

⏱ 1 Timing sector	▬ DRS	▣ DRS detection	⚙ Gear	▲ Overtaking opportunity

2022 POLE TIME: **NOT APPLICABLE AS SPRINT RACE USED INSTEAD**
2022 WINNER'S AVERAGE SPEED: **135.361MPH/217.843KPH**
2022 FASTEST LAP: **VERSTAPPEN (RED BULL), 1M07.275S, 143.576MPH/231.063KPH**
LAP RECORD: **SAINZ JR (MCLAREN), 1M05.619S, 147.199MPH/236.894KPH, 2020***

SILVERSTONE

The surge in support for F1 following its push on Netflix led to record crowds turning up at Silverstone last year and it never looks better than when rammed with fans across all three days of the meeting.

Silverstone was one of hundreds of airfields used in World War II. What saved it from falling into dereliction was the idea to use it for car racing and it's never looked back. However, it has also constantly reinvented itself, with a nip here and a tuck there, to make its flat landscape more interesting, and even the moving of the pit lane.

The lap starts with high-speed Abbey, where Guanyu Zhou got airborne last year and ended up squeezed into a tiny gap between the tyre wall and fencing. His survival was a miracle.

Ordinarily, though, it's a sweep of little consideration with more focus usually on what follows, because the drivers have to brake hard for Village as they feed into a loop where action is frantic on the opening lap, before accelerating hard on to the Wellington Straight. This isn't a

long straight, but a good exit from Aintree can give a driver a chance of passing a rival into Brooklands.

The two Luffield corners feed the cars past the old pits and then into Copse, one of the toughest corners of the lap, where Lewis Hamilton and Max Verstappen had their clash in 2021.

Trickier still is what happens next, with the Maggotts/Becketts esse combination one of the most difficult stretches of track that F1 drivers tackle all year.

Then comes the Hangar Straight where drivers can get a tow on the approach to Stowe, and either try a passing move there as they dive out of a rival's slipstream, or perhaps into the tight left at Vale, or even up the inside into the seemingly endless right-hander, Club, that returns them to the start straight.

80

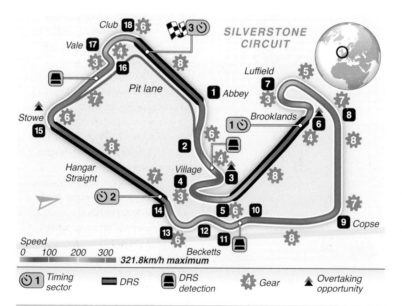

2022 POLE TIME: **SAINZ JR (FERRARI), 1M40.983S, 130.495MPH/210.011KPH**
2022 WINNER'S AVERAGE SPEED: **82.819MPH/133.285KPH**
2022 FASTEST LAP: **HAMILTON (MERCEDES), 1M30.510S, 145.594MPH/234.312KPH**
LAP RECORD: **VERSTAPPEN (RED BULL), 1M27.097S 151.300MPH/243.494KPH, 2020**

INSIDE TRACK

BRITISH GRAND PRIX

Date:	9 July
Circuit name:	Silverstone
Circuit length:	3.659 miles/5.900km
Number of laps:	52
Email:	sales@silverstone-circuit.co.uk
Website:	www.silverstone-circuit.co.uk

PREVIOUS WINNERS

2014	**Lewis Hamilton**	MERCEDES
2015	**Lewis Hamilton**	MERCEDES
2016	**Lewis Hamilton**	MERCEDES
2017	**Lewis Hamilton**	MERCEDES
2018	**Sebastian Vettel**	FERRARI
2019	**Lewis Hamilton**	MERCEDES
2020	**Lewis Hamilton**	MERCEDES
2020*	**Max Verstappen**	RED BULL
2021	**Lewis Hamilton**	MERCEDES
2022	**Charles Leclerc**	FERRARI

*In the 70th Anniversary GP

Location: Centrally located in England, the circuit straddles the Buckinghamshire/Northamptonshire border, being situated 40 miles to the north-east of Oxford.

How it started: Both the runways were used in its original layout in 1948, joined together by sections of the access roads. The first British GP held there was won by Luigi Villoresi for Maserati. Two years later, it hosted the first round of the inaugural World Championship with Giuseppe Farina leading home an Alfa Romeo one-two-three.

Its greatest Grand Prix: One of the greatest scraps was in 1969 when Jackie Stewart (Matra) and Jochen Rindt (Lotus) lapped all others by lap 56 of 84 before Rindt's rear wing came loose, finally leaving Stewart to win.

A local hero: British fans are spoiled for choice with Lewis Hamilton, George Russell and Lando Norris. However, the driver that previously ignited their passion most was Nigel Mansell, who won here three times between 1987 and 1992.

Rising national star: With no British drivers shining in F2, fans should look to 17-year-old Ollie Bearman, who starred in last year's FIA F3 series.

HUNGARORING

This is one of the circuits on which a good grid position is vital, as its tight and sinuous layout makes overtaking unusually difficult and therefore makes a good strategy extra important.

HUNGARIAN GRAND PRIX

Date:	**23 July**
Circuit name:	**Hungaroring**
Circuit length:	**2.722 miles/4.381km**
Number of laps:	**70**
Email:	**office@hungaroring.hu**
Website:	**www.hungaroring.hu**

PREVIOUS WINNERS

2013	**Lewis Hamilton** MERCEDES
2014	**Daniel Ricciardo** RED BULL
2015	**Sebastian Vettel** FERRARI
2016	**Lewis Hamilton** MERCEDES
2017	**Sebastian Vettel** FERRARI
2018	**Lewis Hamilton** MERCEDES
2019	**Lewis Hamilton** MERCEDES
2020	**Lewis Hamilton** MERCEDES
2021	**Esteban Ocon** ALPINE
2022	**Max Verstappen** RED BULL

The greatest shame when the Hungaroring was built was that its wonderful site, set in a valley between two hills, was not graced with a more flowing circuit with more high-speed corners, as the layout is too tight and twisty to offer much chance of overtaking.

The lap begins by dipping towards turn 1, a tight right that opens out on its downhill exit. The track continues to edge down the hillside behind the pits before doubling back on itself at turn 2, a place where many a passing move is attempted on the opening lap.

From here, the descent continues through the kink at turn 3 until reaching its lowest point halfway along the straight to turn 4. This is the most challenging corner as, although it's taken in only fourth gear, it is fairly blind on entry with the apex on a crest, or at least on a point where the ascent eases off.

Then comes the run across the far side of the valley, with the track level from the exit of turn 5 through a chicane and three sweepers.

At turn 11, the track drops again, with a short straight that takes the lap to its final combination of corners. Much tighter than it used to be, turn 12 is a 90-degree right, followed by the uphill hairpin at turn 13. Then comes a steep climb to the final corner, a wider right-hand hairpin. A good exit here is crucial as the run down the start/finish straight offers a rare chance to slipstream a rival through the lap's fastest point on the start/finish straight and then try to duck out of the tow to make a passing move into turn 1.

Location: The circuit is in rolling hills near the village of Mogyoród, a dozen miles to the north-east of capital city Budapest.

How it started: In the 1980s, F1 had a calendar that changed little, so it was a surprise in 1986 when Hungary, a country with little history of motor racing, especially as it was in communist Eastern Europe, was awarded a race on a brand new circuit.

Its greatest Grand Prix: Dogged determination in defence is not normally high on the list of things to look for in racing, but Thierry Boutsen's unflinching drive in 1990 stands out for the way that the Belgian driver kept his Williams in front of Ayrton Senna's McLaren from start to finish.

A local hero: Only one nation can claim the first-ever Grand Prix winner and it is Hungary. Back in 1906, Ferenc Szisz won the French GP on a road circuit centred on Le Mans for Renault. More than a century on, Hungary still awaits its second winner.

Rising national star: László Tóth remains the best of Hungary's slim crop of rising drivers, but his second year in the FIA Formula 3 Championship was no better than his first as he seldom even broke into the top 20.

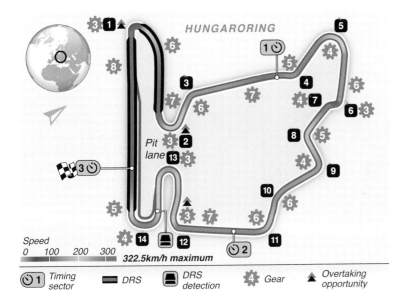

HUNGARORING

Pit lane

Speed
0   100   200   300
322.5km/h maximum

	Timing sector		DRS		DRS detection		Gear		Overtaking opportunity

2022 POLE TIME: RUSSELL (MERCEDES), 1M17.377S, 126.653MPH/203.828KPH
2022 WINNER'S AVERAGE SPEED: 114.779MPH/184.719KPH
2022 FASTEST LAP: HAMILTON (MERCEDES), 1M21.386S, 120.413MPH/193.787KPH
LAP RECORD: HAMILTON (MERCEDES), 1M16.627S, 127.892MPH/205.823KPH, 2020

SPA-FRANCORCHAMPS

Whether in rain or shine, and this circuit experiences equal measures of both, this remains one of the world's classic racing circuits thanks to its combination of history, topography and high-speed corners.

The short dash from the grid to La Source is as before, but overtaking into the right-hand hairpin is more difficult than it was before 2022 when drivers were greeted no longer by a tarmac run-off area if they ran wide, but by a gravel trap. They could escape from a slip-up before, but now face the race-wrecking peril of ending up bogged down there.

From here, the track drops steeply past the old pits to a more open and smoother Eau Rouge, at which point the track rears up and twists through Raidillon before feeding the cars on to the Kemmel Straight.

At the top of the long straight, the cars hit 200mph (322kph) before the drivers have to brake hard for probably the best potential passing point of the lap. This is the Les Combes esse, a right/left combination.

Then the track dips again, starting its descent at Malmedy and dropping through the Rivage hairpin, the newly named Jacky Ickx Curve, a tricky left-hander. The drivers head next towards the double-apex Pouhon, the gradient then reducing through the twisters at Fagnes and Campus before reaching Curve Paul Frère. This open right-hander is where it meets the return leg of the original circuit and starts to climb back towards the pits.

It's a flat-out charge through what is probably the most challenging corner, Blanchimont. The barriers have long been moved away from the edge of the circuit, but any corner taken at 195mph (314kph) still gets a driver's attention. If a driver can use a tow through here, then the tight right at the end of the Bus Stop is their next best chance to make a passing move.

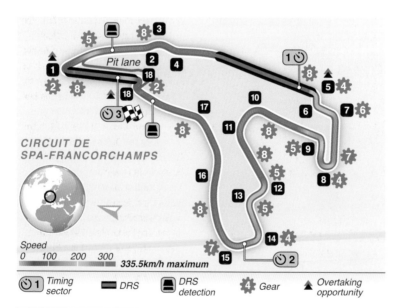

CIRCUIT DE SPA-FRANCORCHAMPS

Speed
0   100   200   300
335.5km/h maximum

| ⏱1 | Timing sector | ▬ DRS | ⬛ DRS detection | 4 Gear | ▲ Overtaking opportunity |

2022 POLE TIME: **SAINZ JR (FERRARI)**, 1M44.297S, 150.219MPH/241.755KPH
2022 WINNER'S AVERAGE SPEED: **133.729MPH/215.216KPH**
2022 FASTEST LAP: **VERSTAPPEN (RED BULL)**, 1M49.354S, 143.272MPH/230.575KPH
LAP RECORD: **BOTTAS (MERCEDES)**, 1M46.286S, 147.422MPH/237.290KPH, 2018

INSIDE TRACK

BELGIAN GRAND PRIX

Date:	**30 July**
Circuit name:	**Spa-Francorchamps**
Circuit length:	**4.352 miles/7.004km**
Number of laps:	**44**
Email:	secretariat@spa-francorchamps.be
Website:	www.spa-francorchamps.be

PREVIOUS WINNERS

2013	**Sebastian Vettel** RED BULL
2014	**Daniel Ricciardo** RED BULL
2015	**Lewis Hamilton** MERCEDES
2016	**Nico Rosberg** MERCEDES
2017	**Lewis Hamilton** MERCEDES
2018	**Sebastian Vettel** FERRARI
2019	**Charles Leclerc** FERRARI
2020	**Lewis Hamilton** MERCEDES
2021	**Max Verstappen** RED BULL
2022	**Max Verstappen** RED BULL

Location: The circuit is draped over a wooded valley ten miles to the south of Spa, the original spa town, starting just to the south of the village of Francorchamps.

How it started: The circuit was opened in 1924, running from La Source into the neighbouring valley and passing near the towns of Malmedy and Stavelot before climbing back to the hairpin in a nine-mile lap. This was used in the first Belgian GP in 1925 when Antonio Ascari won for Alfa Romeo.

Its greatest Grand Prix: Bruce McLaren will never forget 1968 as it was when his eponymous team recorded its first win in a race that he didn't even realise he had won. He had failed to notice that Jackie Stewart had needed to dive in for fuel in his Matra at the start of the final lap.

A local hero: Jacky Ickx remains the greatest Belgian driver. He was pipped in the F1 drivers' title for Ferrari in 1970, but his claim to fame is winning the Le Mans 24 Hours six times between 1969 and 1982.

Rising national star: Amaury Cordeel stepped up to Formula 2 and put in a solid first season in F1's feeder category, but failed to finish in the top ten in any of the races.

ZANDVOORT

If you want loud, colourful fans worshipping a home-grown driver in a carnival atmosphere, look no further than this track between the sand dunes on the Netherlands' North Sea coast.

INSIDE TRACK

DUTCH GRAND PRIX

Date:	27 August
Circuit name:	Zandvoort
Circuit length:	2.676miles/4.307km
Number of laps:	71
Email:	info@circuitzandvoort.nl
Website:	www.circuitzandvoort.nl

The start/finish straight is on the level and so the entry to the first turn, Tarzan, is simple enough, with mild banking helping the cars around this 180-degree right. Then the track begins to rise and fall as it twists its way through Gerlachbocht and into the compression at Hugenholtzbocht.

For most of the Grand Prix, the best place to try to pull off a passing manoeuvre is at the end of the pit straight. However, on the opening lap, it's at Hugenholtzbocht. This is the lap's third corner and since being not just wider but slightly banked too for 2021, it offers drivers a number of different lines both in and out of the left-hander and so gives an attacking driver more scope to get the jump on a rival.

From here, the track rises over a brow and drivers are still accelerating hard as they go over a slight crest at Slotemakerbocht. What comes next is the lap's most challenging corner, Scheivlak, where the drivers are largely unsighted as they arc right and down in sixth gear, diving between giant dunes.

The flow is broken at turn 8, now known as Mastersbocht, and only after accelerating out of turn 10 do the drivers get up to speed again.

The turn 11/12 complex is still a little tight, but then the drivers aim their cars into the penultimate corner and prepare themselves for getting a slingshot out of the lap's banked final corner, a corner named after the only Dutch winner of the Indianapolis 500, Arie Luyendyk Bocht.

The approach to Tarzan is where the cars hit their highest speed, touching 195mph (314kph), before having to brake for the lap's first corner.

PREVIOUS WINNERS

1978	**Mario Andretti**	LOTUS
1979	**Alan Jones**	WILLIAMS
1980	**Nelson Piquet**	BRABHAM
1981	**Alain Prost**	RENAULT
1982	**Didier Pironi**	FERRARI
1983	**Rene Arnoux**	FERRARI
1984	**Alain Prost**	McLAREN
1985	**Niki Lauda**	McLAREN
2021	**Max Verstappen**	RED BULL
2022	**Max Verstappen**	RED BULL

Location: Easy to reach from Amsterdam, the circuit is on the northern edge of the Zandvoort resort on the coast, eight miles west of Haarlem.

How it started: Opened in 1948, this seaside circuit held a World Championship round for the first time four years later when Alberto Ascari won for Ferrari.

Its greatest Grand Prix: The 1976 Dutch GP was a must-win for James Hunt while title rival Niki Lauda was sidelined with burns, so he was frustrated to have John Watson challenge his McLaren so hard before the Penske driver's gearbox failed after an epic tussle.

A local hero: Despite a love of F1, there have been few Dutch F1 drivers. Max Verstappen's father Jos was a podium visitor in 1994 with Benetton, but was seldom with a top team after that. Before him, Jan Lammers had even less chance, but proved his longevity by winning the Le Mans 24 Hours with Jaguar six years after leaving F1 and then making an F1 comeback four years after that aged 36.

Rising national star: Richard Verschoor has continued winning in F2 for a second season, while Rinus VeeKay has been a frontrunner in IndyCar racing on the other side of the Atlantic.

83

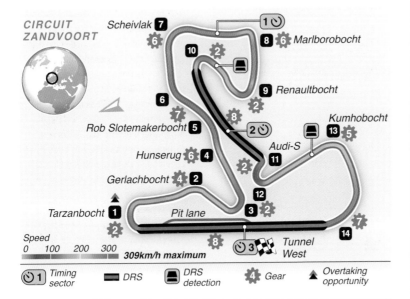

CIRCUIT ZANDVOORT

Scheivlak 7 — 1

8 6 Marlborobocht

10

9 Renaultbocht

Rob Slotemakerbocht 5

Kumhobocht

8 2

13 5

Audi-S

Hunserug 6 4

11

Gerlachbocht 4 2

12

Tarzanbocht 1

Pit lane

3 2

Speed
0 100 200 300
309km/h maximum

8 3 Tunnel West

14

🕐 1	Timing sector
▬ DRS	DRS
■ DRS detection	DRS detection
⚙ 4 Gear	Gear
▲ Overtaking opportunity	Overtaking opportunity

2022 POLE TIME: VERSTAPPEN (RED BULL), 1M10.342S, 135.439MPH/217.969KPH
2022 WINNER'S AVERAGE SPEED: 118.187MPH/190.204KPH
2022 FASTEST LAP: VERSTAPPEN (RED BULL), 1M13.652S, 129.352MPH/208.173KPH
LAP RECORD: HAMILTON (MERCEDES), 1M11.097S, 134.001MPH/215.654KPH, 2021

MONZA

Even if Monza didn't have a century of history behind it, this magnificent Italian venue is packed with the effervescent atmosphere you would expect of the venue for Ferrari's home Grand Prix.

INSIDE TRACK

ITALIAN GRAND PRIX

Date:	**3 September**
Circuit name:	**Autodromo Nazionale Monza**
Circuit length:	**3.600 miles/5.793km**
Number of laps:	**53**
Email:	**infoautodromo@monzanet.it**
Website:	**www.monzanet.it**

The feeling that Monza used to give drivers was one of racing flat-out everywhere, hunting in multi-car slipstreaming packs. However, that changed when three chicanes were inserted for 1972 and the lap has been more stop-start since then.

The first chicane, inserted to cut speeds through the long right-hander that follows, has been reprofiled many times. Its current hard right/hard left format certainly slows them down, but its ultra-tight nature leads to many a clash on the opening lap in particular.

The second chicane is a little more open and then comes the first of the tricky Lesmos, with the second of these right-handers remaining the trickiest corner of the lap. The kerbs on its exit unsettle many a car as they run wide when the drivers are trying their hardest to get the power down

to accelerate on to the kinked straight that takes them to Ascari.

Although the drivers then dip under a bridge carrying a section of the old banked circuit, going on to hit 205mph (330kph) before braking for the left/right/left Ascari chicane, this isn't the fastest point on the circuit. Neither is the approach to the lap's final corner, the long right of Curva Parabolica. The fastest stretch is the home straight, and on the approach to the corner that starts the following lap, drivers reach that first chicane at speeds nigh on 210mph (338kph).

This blast past the pits still offers the best opportunity for a driver to catch a tow and thus also to try a passing move. Not all work, as shown by Max Verstappen's Red Bull ending up on top of Lewis Hamilton's Mercedes there in 2021.

PREVIOUS WINNERS

2013	**Sebastian Vettel**	RED BULL
2014	**Lewis Hamilton**	MERCEDES
2015	**Lewis Hamilton**	MERCEDES
2016	**Nico Rosberg**	MERCEDES
2017	**Lewis Hamilton**	MERCEDES
2018	**Lewis Hamilton**	MERCEDES
2019	**Charles Leclerc**	FERRARI
2020	**Pierre Gasly**	ALPHATAURI
2021	**Daniel Ricciardo**	McLAREN
2022	**Max Verstappen**	RED BULL

Location: Ten miles north-west of Italy's industrial powerhouse, Milan, the town of Monza has a royal park and the circuit is within its walls.

How it started: Blessed with a powerful and burgeoning automotive industry, Italy wanted to showcase its wares and so it built this circuit a century ago, in 1922, using 3,500 people labouring for 110 days from start to finish. The second-ever Italian GP was held here that year and victory went to Pietro Bordino in a Fiat.

Its greatest Grand Prix: The 1971 Italian GP was special as the first five cars were covered by just 0.61 seconds until a surge out of the Parabolica on the final lap helped Peter Gethin to pull level then past Ronnie Peterson to win for BRM.

A local hero: Alberto Ascari won a non-championship F1 race at Monza in 1949 and then won the 1951 and 1952 Italian GPs, all for Ferrari.

Rising national star: There used to be promising Italian drivers at every turn, but it hasn't been like that for decades since its domestic single-seater scene dwindled. Last year, their best driver outside F1 was Gabriele Mini, then 17, who competed in the sport's fourth division, Formula Regional European.

AUTODROMO NAZIONALE MONZA

Curva di Lesmo
Curva del Serraglio
Variante della Roggia
Variante Ascari
Curva Biassono
Pit lane
Curva Parabolica

Speed
0   100   200   300
344.8km/h maximum

⏱1 Timing sector	▬ DRS	▣ DRS detection
⚙4 Gear	▲ Overtaking opportunity	

2022 POLE TIME: LECLERC (FERRARI), 1M20.161S, 161.656MPH/260.161KPH
2022 WINNER'S AVERAGE SPEED: 142.125MPH/228.729KPH
2022 FASTEST LAP: PEREZ (RED BULL), 1M24.030S, 154.213MPH/248.182KPH
LAP RECORD: M SCHUMACHER (FERRARI), 1M21.046S, 159.909KPH/257.349KPH, 2004

MARINA BAY

Expect more and more street circuits to be added to the F1 calendar in the years to come, and this track in the heart of Singapore is as good a template as you can get.

SINGAPORE GRAND PRIX

Date:	**17 September**
Circuit name:	**Marina Bay Circuit**
Circuit length:	**3.062 miles/4.928km**
Number of laps:	**63**
Email:	**info@singaporegp.sg**
Website:	**www.singaporegp.sg**

PREVIOUS WINNERS

2011	**Sebastian Vettel** RED BULL
2012	**Sebastian Vettel** RED BULL
2013	**Sebastian Vettel** RED BULL
2014	**Lewis Hamilton** MERCEDES
2015	**Sebastian Vettel** FERRARI
2016	**Daniel Ricciardo** RED BULL
2017	**Lewis Hamilton** MERCEDES
2018	**Lewis Hamilton** MERCEDES
2019	**Sebastian Vettel** FERRARI
2022	**Sergio Perez** RED BULL

In contrast to Monaco's tight and slow F1 street circuit, Singapore's Marina Bay track is largely open and fast.

The dash to the first corner isn't long and the field is inevitably packed tight as it approaches this left-hander on the opening lap. As it feeds directly into a right-hand swerve and then a hairpin, there is more than a little scope for overtaking, but also wing damage too.

The track then opens out as it ducks under more elevated sliproads from the East Coast Parkway, with a short straight followed by a long one. The fastest point of the lap is at the end of this kinked straight, at which point drivers have to brake hard to decelerate from 185mph (298kph) to be able to drop to third gear and around 70mph (113kph) to negotiate the 90-degree left at turn 7.

Two more 90-degree bends take the circuit on to another short straight around the back of the Singapore Cricket Club before a sweeping stretch that takes it over the Anderson Bridge down to turn 13.

This is probably the lap's trickiest corner as this second-gear hairpin feeds on to the lap's second longest straight over the Esplanade Bridge, and a good exit may just help a driver to be in position to make a passing move into turn 14.

The lap then heads towards a right/left, left/right, right/left complex of largely third-gear corners before drivers set themselves to accelerate flat out through the final two kinks. This leads them on to the start/finish straight, and a good tow past the pits can offer the drivers their best passing opportunity of the lap.

Location: Head to downtown Singapore when the Grand Prix isn't on and it is hard to pick out where the circuit is located, but it is right in the city centre, running around Esplanade Park, along Raffles Avenue and the Marina Promenade.

How it started: Famed for its efficient business manner, Singapore produced a street circuit that really impressed the F1 establishment when it made its debut in 2008. Everything about it was slick and it is a shame that its inaugural Grand Prix is remembered for Renault's underhand tactics that enabled Fernando Alonso to win thanks to his team-mate Nelson Piquet Jr being asked to spin to bring out the safety car.

Its greatest Grand Prix: Some race results mean more than the maximum points haul, and this was definitely the case in 2016 when Nico Rosberg not only held off a late-race charge from Red Bull's Daniel Ricciardo, but his win moved him ahead of Mercedes team-mate Lewis Hamilton for the first time and put him on course for his world title.

Rising national star: The decimation of the Asian racing scene by the COVID pandemic has not helped the latest crop of youngsters to show their skills, so Singapore continues its wait for a star of its own.

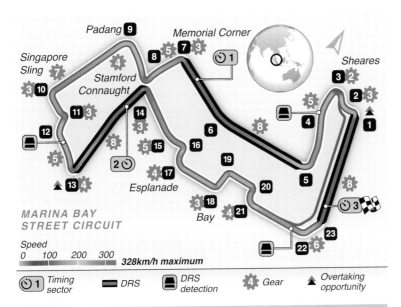

MARINA BAY STREET CIRCUIT

Speed
0   100   200   300
328km/h maximum

🕐 1 Timing sector   ▬ DRS   ◻ DRS detection   ⚙4 Gear   ▲ Overtaking opportunity

2022 POLE TIME: **LECLERC (FERRARI)**, 1M46.412S, 103.513MPH/166.588KPH
2022 WINNER'S AVERAGE SPEED: **90.992MPH/146.437KPH**
2022 FASTEST LAP: **RUSSELL (MERCEDES)**, 1M46.458S, 106.385MPH/171.211KPH
LAP RECORD: **MAGNUSSEN (HAAS)**, 1M41.905S, 109.900MPH/178.860KPH, 2018

SUZUKA

Opened for business in 1962 when it was cutting-edge, Suzuka's design is such a brilliant layout that it still cuts it today, challenging drivers and engineers like few others.

Gradient is one of the key components that makes Suzuka one of the world's most revered tracks.

It was designed by John Hugenholtz, previously the director of the Zandvoort circuit in the Netherlands for 25 years. It makes the most of the hillside it occupies as part of an entertainment complex that also includes a funfair with a giant Ferris wheel that overlooks the final corner.

The run from the grid to the first corner is downhill and a considered entry line into this sixth-gear right-hander is vital. A driver needs not only to be set up for the tighter turn 2 that follows, but be in a position to defend, as it is one of the main passing points and going in wide leaves the door ajar on the inside.

Turning uphill again, the incline increases as the drivers reach the trickiest section of the lap, the fifth-gear esses from turn 3 to turn 6.

The track then plateaus through Dunlop Curve and the next tricky turn is the second Degner, just before the track goes under a bridge carrying the lap's return leg.

The next regular passing place is at the hairpin, but a fumbled move here costs a driver big time, as they need to be quickly back on to the throttle for the arcing run through turns 12 and 13 before the track dips again into Spoon. This is another corner that demands a clean exit as the drivers are then fed on to the return leg – down a long straight, through the seventh-gear 130R kink and then on to heavy braking for the chicane.

This final right/left is probably the most frequent place for overtaking, albeit the line is very tight.

INSIDE TRACK

JAPANESE GRAND PRIX

Date:	24 September
Circuit name:	Suzuka Circuit
Circuit length:	3.608 miles/5.806km
Number of laps:	53
Email:	info@suzukacircuit.co.up
Website:	www.suzukacircuit.co.jp

PREVIOUS WINNERS

2011	**Jenson Button**	McLAREN
2012	**Sebastian Vettel**	RED BULL
2013	**Sebastian Vettel**	RED BULL
2014	**Lewis Hamilton**	MERCEDES
2015	**Lewis Hamilton**	MERCEDES
2016	**Nico Rosberg**	MERCEDES
2017	**Lewis Hamilton**	MERCEDES
2018	**Lewis Hamilton**	MERCEDES
2019	**Valtteri Bottas**	MERCEDES
2022	**Max Verstappen**	RED BULL

Location: Suzuka nestles in the gentle coastal hills 30 miles to the south-west of Nagoya, a city on Japan's main island, Honshu.

How it started: Suzuka's construction was financed by Honda, chiefly as a testing facility when it opened for racing in 1962 as the Japanese racing scene took off. It took 25 years, though, before F1 paid its first visit.

Its greatest Grand Prix: Mika Häkkinen's fans will never forget the climax of the 1998 season when the Finn was being pressed for the title by Michael Schumacher, but the German's comeback after stalling on the grid ended when his Benetton had a blowout.

A local hero: Two Japanese drivers have finished third in a Grand Prix, firstly Aguri Suzuki in 1990 and Takuma Sato in 2004. However, Suzuki's result with Larrousse was more meritorious, not just because it came at Suzuka, but because BAR driver Sato's came in a race at Indianapolis in which only eight cars finished.

Rising national star: Japan already has its next in line, with Ayumu Iwasa looking to follow in Yuki Tsunoda's footsteps by racing in F2. The 21-year-old became a race winner in his rookie campaign, doing so at Paul Ricard, the home race for his French team, DAMS.

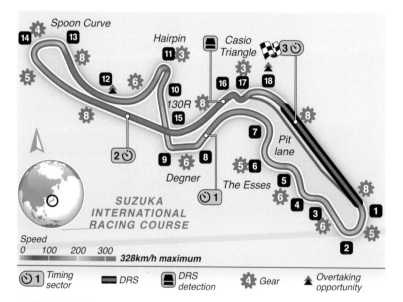

Spoon Curve
Hairpin
Casio Triangle
130R
Degner
The Esses
Pit lane

SUZUKA INTERNATIONAL RACING COURSE

Speed
0   100   200   300
328km/h maximum

⏱1 Timing sector   DRS   DRS detection   4 Gear   ▲ Overtaking opportunity

2022 POLE TIME: VERSTAPPEN (RED BULL), 1M29.304S, 145.457MPH/234.090KPH

2022 WINNER'S AVERAGE SPEED: 33.294MPH/53.582KPH

2022 FASTEST LAP: GUANYU (ALFA ROMEO), 1M44.411S, 124.411MPH/200.220KPH

LAP RECORD: HAMILTON (MERCEDES), 1M30.983S 142.772MPH/229.770KPH, 2019

LOSAIL

Qatar bankrolled the hosting of last year's Football World Cup and, anxious for further publicity, is now looking to remain permanently as part of the Formula 1 World Championship calendar.

QATAR GRAND PRIX

Date:	**8 October**
Circuit name:	**Losail International Circuit**
Circuit length:	**3.343 miles/5.380km**
Number of laps:	**57**
Email:	**info@lcsc.qa**
Website:	**www.lcsc.qa**

PREVIOUS WINNERS

2021   **Lewis Hamilton** MERCEDES

Losail, or Lusail, as it is sometimes known, made its World Championship debut in a trio of races held in the Middle East to bring the 2021 season to a close. Yet it's not a new circuit, having been operating since 2004, and only modification of the kerbs was required for F1's first visit.

The 16-turn lap starts with a 140-degree right-hander as its opening corner and then snakes through an equivalent left. Next comes a fast kink and then a short straight to turn 4, the first of two similar, rounded 90-degree right-handers.

Turn 5 is a hairpin that then leads to a more open right-hander at turn 7. From there, there are a couple of esses before heavier braking is required into turn 10.

The next part of the lap is more open as the drivers continue in a clockwise direction with an arcing run to turn 12, which is the first of three fast right-hand kinks, followed by one to the left.

This feeds the cars into the final straight down to the last corner of the lap, a broad right-hander on to the start/finish straight. As with so many circuits, a good exit on to a straight of notable length offers the best chance to pull off an overtaking move, in this case under braking for turn 1.

With its unremarkable desert setting, the circuit is made to look more attractive by the Grand Prix starting after nightfall, with the pit buildings illuminated and the track covered by huge floodlights.

With a ten-year contract in place, the Qatari race organisers are looking to drop Losail in the years ahead once it has built a new circuit.

Location: The Qatar peninsula juts out into the Persian Gulf and the circuit is on the east coast just to the north of capital Doha.

How it started: The Losail circuit opened for racing in 2004, but was very much a motorbike racing circuit in its early years, hosting MotoGP from the outset and later adding World Superbike events. Its first international-standard car race meeting was when the World Touring Car Championship visited in 2015, with a GP Masters series race there the following year, won by Nigel Mansell.

Its greatest Grand Prix: As there has been only one Qatar GP to date, it must be the one from 2021 won by Lewis Hamilton. It was a victory that enabled the Mercedes driver to close the points gap to series leader Max Verstappen to just eight points with two races still to run. The Red Bull Racing driver had been hampered by a five-place grid penalty for not respecting waved yellow flags when there was debris on the track in qualifying, but he was still good enough to come through to second. Fernando Alonso set a record in making a one-stop strategy work to finish third for Alpine, with his gap of 104 Grands Prix since his previous podium finish setting a new record.

A local hero: There are no local racing drivers of note and, as such, no rising stars, meaning that it's up to the Qatari sporting bodies to encourage young fans to try racing in the Middle Eastern single-seater series, perhaps after starting them in karting, and then work up from there.

87

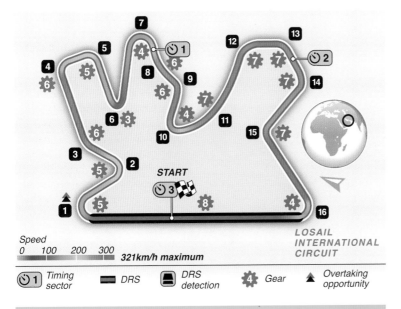

LOSAIL INTERNATIONAL CIRCUIT

Speed
0   100   200   300

321km/h maximum

🕐1 Timing sector   ▬ DRS   ◼ DRS detection   🔧4 Gear   ▲ Overtaking opportunity

2021 POLE TIME: **HAMILTON (MERCEDES), 1M20.827S, 148/894MPH/239.622KPH**
2021 WINNER'S AVERAGE SPEED: **135.342MPH/217.812KPH**
2021 FASTEST LAP: **VERSTAPPEN (RED BULL), 1M23.196S, 144.654MPH/232.799KPH**
LAP RECORD: **VERSTAPPEN (RED BULL), 1M23.196S, 144.654MPH/232.799KPH, 2021**

CIRCUIT OF THE AMERICAS

With competition for the affection of American F1 fans from the street circuits in Miami and Las Vegas, this established venue offers something for the traditionalist, with its classical layout.

INSIDE TRACK

UNITED STATES GRAND PRIX

Date:	**22 October**
Circuit name:	**Circuit of the Americas**
Circuit length:	**3.400 miles/5.472km**
Number of laps:	**56**
Email:	info@circuitoftheamericas.com
Website:	www.circuitoftheamericas.com

By the standards of the circuits that have hosted the itinerant United States GP, the Circuit of the Americas is something of a long-stayer, having been the venue since 2012.

The appeal of this Texan circuit is that it uses its hilly site to good advantage and the designers sought to mimic the best corners on the best tracks around the world in its 20-turn layout.

The run from the grid to the first corner rises almost as steeply as the equivalent incline at the Red Bull Ring. The hairpin at the top is a definite passing place on any lap, but especially on the opening one, as there is plenty of width both on the way in and on the way out.

The track then plunges back down the slope to the fifth-gear right-hander at its foot. The flow is then fabulous from here through a sinuous run of esses all the way through to turn 8. Then, after a tighter corner at turn 9, the track opens out again for a high-speed blast down to the hairpin at turn 11.

A good exit from here can give a driver a chance of catching a tow from a rival and then trying a move into the lap's best passing place, the braking zone for the tight left at turn 12, where drivers wrestle their cars down from over 190mph (306kph).

What follows, all seen from the top of the landmark observation tower, is a tight and twisting section through to turn 17, one of the most difficult points around the lap, where the track clears a crest at its apex before dropping down a slight incline to the last two corners, with the last one notably tight.

PREVIOUS WINNERS

2012	**Lewis Hamilton**	McLAREN
2013	**Sebastian Vettel**	RED BULL
2014	**Lewis Hamilton**	MERCEDES
2015	**Lewis Hamilton**	MERCEDES
2016	**Lewis Hamilton**	MERCEDES
2017	**Lewis Hamilton**	MERCEDES
2018	**Kimi Raikkonen**	FERRARI
2019	**Valtteri Bottas**	MERCEDES
2021	**Max Verstappen**	RED BULL
2022	**Max Verstappen**	RED BULL

Location: The circuit is a ten-mile ride south-east of Texas state capital Austin, set into a gentle rolling landscape.

How it started: The circuit was built in 2012 as the answer to the USA's decades-long desire to find a permanent home for its annual Grand Prix on a proper road circuit.

Its greatest Grand Prix: The title battle was bubbling when the teams arrived here in 2021. Max Verstappen and Red Bull Racing out-thought Mercedes by making him run a very long stint on worn tyres, which he just managed to do to resist Lewis Hamilton.

A local hero: Texas produced Carroll Shelby in the 1950s, but he was better known for winning Le Mans for Aston Martin in 1959. He was followed by Jim Hall, who raced to fifth in the 1963 German GP in a British Racing Partnership, but made his name with his Chaparral sports car marque.

Rising national star: Jak Crawford is next in line behind F2 star Logan Sargeant in the quest to reach F1. The 17-year-old shone in FIA F3 last year in his second season in the championship, winning at the Red Bull Ring and scoring strongly to rank seventh for the Prema Racing team that has produced so many stars.

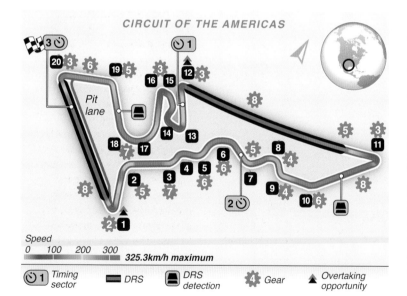

CIRCUIT OF THE AMERICAS

Speed
0   100   200   300
325.3km/h maximum

🕐1 Timing sector   ▬ DRS   ▣ DRS detection   ⚙4 Gear   ▲ Overtaking opportunity

2022 POLE TIME: SAINZ JR (FERRARI), 1M34.356S, 130.698MPH/210.339KPH
2022 WINNER'S AVERAGE SPEED: 112.510MPH/181.068KPH
2022 FASTEST LAP: RUSSELL (MERCEDES), 1M38.788S, 124.834MPH/200.902KPH
LAP RECORD: LECLERC (FERRARI), 1M36.169S, 128.235MPH/206.374KPH, 2019

MEXICO CITY

This high-altitude circuit with a lengthy history is packed with atmosphere and offers a fabulous first-corner complex at the end of a long straight that is made for overtaking.

INSIDE TRACK

MEXICAN GRAND PRIX

Date:	**29 October**
Circuit name:	**Autodromo Hermanos Rodriguez**
Circuit length:	**2.674 miles/4.303km**
Number of laps:	**71**
Email:	**Rosario@cie.com.mx**
Website:	www.autodromohermanosrodriguez.com.mx

One of the best things about the Autódromo Hermanos Rodríguez is its long, wide main straight. This helps drivers to catch a tow up to the first corner and then have a number of possible cornering lines through the right/left/right combination, making it a fabulous place to overtake. On the opening lap, it can often produce mayhem.

A straight then takes the cars down to a left/right combination before they reach a hairpin at the furthest point from the pits.

The return leg is markedly different in nature as there is a wonderful set of esses from turn 7 to turn 11. They don't provide any opportunities to pass, but the cars look brilliant through here.

After another short straight, the lap offers a sharp right and then a unique experience as this turns the cars into a curve of giant grandstands, into what is otherwise used as a baseball stadium. The track snakes in front of them before running through a gap to rejoin halfway around what was once the circuit's most feared corner. This is the Peraltada, a lightly banked 180-degree right-hander on to the start/finish straight. If that was still used in full, it would be the lap's most challenging corner. As it is, if a driver can get the power down early out of turn 16, it will find them an extra bit of speed to carry down the straight past the pits. Speeds then reach 195mph (314kph) before they have to hit the brakes hard for turn 1.

Being 6,000 feet above sea level, the air is thin and the engineers have to work out how to retain as much power as possible with the engines being starved of oxygen.

PREVIOUS WINNERS

1990	**Alain Prost**	FERRARI
1991	**Riccardo Patrese**	WILLIAMS
1992	**Nigel Mansell**	WILLIAMS
2015	**Nico Rosberg**	MERCEDES
2016	**Lewis Hamilton**	MERCEDES
2017	**Max Verstappen**	RED BULL
2018	**Max Verstappen**	RED BULL
2019	**Lewis Hamilton**	MERCEDES
2021	**Max Verstappen**	RED BULL
2022	**Max Verstappen**	RED BULL

Location: The circuit was built in the outer suburbs, but such has been the spread of Mexico City that the park in which it is located is now not far from the city's eastern edge.

How it started: The circuit was opened in 1962 as an appetite for circuit racing grew, alongside the national passion for road races.

Its greatest Grand Prix: The 1964 title decider was a three-horse race between three British drivers: Graham Hill, John Surtees and Jim Clark. Hill's BRM was hit and its exhausts were damaged, then Clark was heading for victory until his Lotus engine failed on the final lap, leaving Surtees to win for Ferrari.

A local hero: Sergio Perez has won more Grands Prix than any other Mexican driver, but Ricardo Rodriguez would have set the bar higher had he not been killed in practice for the 1962 Mexican GP while still just 20. He had qualified second on his Grand Prix debut for Ferrari at the 1961 Italian GP, so the promise was there to see.

Rising national star: Mexican fans will be hoping that race winner Patricio O'Ward crosses over from IndyCar racing at some point in the future.

89

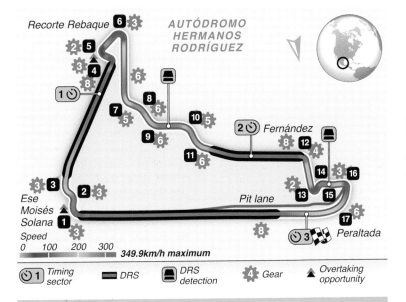

AUTÓDROMO HERMANOS RODRÍGUEZ

Recorte Rebaque

Ese Moisés Solana

Fernández

Pit lane

Peraltada

Speed
0 100 200 300
349.9km/h maximum

| ⏱1 | Timing sector | ▬ DRS | ◼ DRS detection | ⚙ Gear | ▲ Overtaking opportunity |

2022 POLE TIME: VERSTAPPEN (RED BULL), 1M17.775S, 123.789MPH/199.220KPH

2022 WINNER'S AVERAGE SPEED: 115.444MPH/185.790KPH

2022 FASTEST LAP: RUSSELL (MERCEDES), 1M20.153S, 120.117MPH/193.310KPH

LAP RECORD: BOTTAS (MERCEDES), 1M17.774S, 123.791MPH/199.223KPH, 2021

⟫ INTERLAGOS

This outstanding circuit is living proof that a circuit's facilities can be a bit tatty, but a classic layout will outweigh that and it has produced scintillating races over the decades.

Built on a hillside and snaking between lakes – the name Interlagos means 'between the lakes' – the circuit uses the topography superbly from the first corner all the way around to the 15th and last.

Sitting on the grid, drivers are dwarfed by a high pit wall to their left and the proximity of a lofty grandstand to their right. Visibility into the first corner is limited until the drivers turn in and get to see how the track drops sharply to the left, before turning almost immediately to the right at the Senna S, with the cars accelerating hard through the compression.

Then the lap opens out, with grandstands far away across a grass verge to the right beyond the banked original first corner as the track falls all the way down the slope until it reaches Descida do Lago. From the second of these open left-handers, the track begins to climb again. It rises through Ferradura before flattening out at turn 7, then dropping again out of turn 8, Laranja.

The flow is fabulous here as the track then drops to turn 9, Pinheirinho, rises again to turn 10 and then plunges back down the slope to turn 12, Juncao.

This is the point at which the drivers start their flat-out blast all the way back to the start/finish line, accelerating up and across the slope and into the gulley between pit wall and grandstand. Here they reach speeds approaching 200mph (322kph) before braking for the lap's most prolific overtaking spot. Get their exit from Juncao wrong, though, and they can easily be picked off by a rival, so it is undoubtedly the most important and challenging of all the lap's 15 corners.

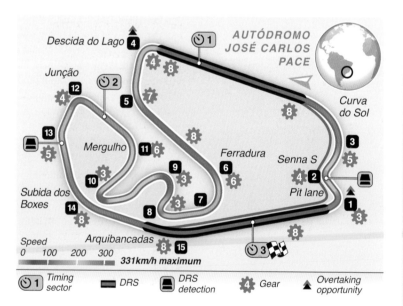

INSIDE TRACK

SAO PAOLO GRAND PRIX

Date:	5 November
Circuit name:	Autodromo Jose Carlos Pace Interlagos
Circuit length:	2.667 miles/4.292km
Number of laps:	71
Email:	info@gpbrazil.com
Website:	www.gpbrazil.com

PREVIOUS WINNERS

2012	**Jenson Button** McLAREN
2013	**Sebastian Vettel** RED BULL
2014	**Nico Rosberg** MERCEDES
2015	**Nico Rosberg** MERCEDES
2016	**Lewis Hamilton** MERCEDES
2017	**Sebastian Vettel** FERRARI
2018	**Lewis Hamilton** MERCEDES
2019	**Max Verstappen** RED BULL
2021	**Lewis Hamilton** MERCEDES
2022	**George Russell** MERCEDES

Location: Interlagos has been enveloped by São Paulo's urban sprawl, with the southern suburbs having edged out to and past this circuit that was once set in open fields nine miles south of the city centre.

How it started: Interlagos opened in 1940 and first hosted the World Championship in 1973. Jacarepaguá took over and when F1 returned in 1990, the track had been cut from 4.893 to 2.667 miles.

Its greatest Grand Prix: The 2007 title decider stands out, as McLaren's Fernando Alonso and Lewis Hamilton were outpaced by the Ferraris. However, Hamilton made an error and later had his engine left in neutral for 30 seconds, enabling title outsider Kimi Räikkönen to win both the race and the title for Ferrari.

A local hero: Emerson Fittipaldi became Brazil's first world champion in 1972 and Nelson Piquet went on to win three titles, but Ayrton Senna is the greatest because he seemed to perform on a level beyond his rivals as he too collected three F1 crowns between 1988 and 1991.

Rising national star: Felipe Drugovich is the first Brazilian since Bruno Junqueira in 2000 to win the title in F1's feeder formula, which was F3000 back then and is F2 now. The 22-year-old won five of last year's races.

Descida do Lago ⏱4 — ⏱1
Junção
⏱2
AUTÓDROMO JOSÉ CARLOS PACE
Curva do Sol
Mergulho
Ferradura
Senna S
Pit lane
Subida dos Boxes
Arquibancadas
⏱3 🏁

Speed 0 100 200 300
331km/h maximum

| ⏱1 Timing sector | ▬ DRS | DRS detection | 4 Gear | ▲ Overtaking opportunity |

2022 POLE TIME: **MAGNUSSEN (HAAS)**, 1M11.674S, 134.482MPH/216.429KPH
2022 WINNER'S AVERAGE SPEED: **115.695MPH/186.194KPH**
2022 FASTEST LAP: **RUSSELL (MERCEDES)**, 1M13.785S, 130.635MPH/210.237KPH
LAP RECORD: **BOTTAS (MERCEDES)**, 1M10.540S, 136.645MPH/219.909KPH, 2018

LAS VEGAS

The World Championship visited Las Vegas over 40 years ago, but this time, using a different venue, the intent is way more serious so it stands a chance of making an impact.

If the first Grand Prix circuit used in Las Vegas in 1981 and 1982 was uninspiring, that's because it was little more than a dull, tight and repetitive track laid out in the car park of the Caesars Palace Hotel. Gambling was the city's currency and F1 was little more than a sideshow.

This time around, with a new American audience excited by F1 because of Netflix's *Drive to Survive* series, the welcome should be way more receptive.

The second iteration of an F1 venue in Las Vegas is more of a traditional street circuit, its 17-turn layout offering the longer straights favoured by the designers of recent street circuits. Indeed, this one is so open that it is expected to have an average lap speed similar to Monza's. Thus it will be wholly unlike the two F1 races hosted by Caesars Palace, the faster of which only just topped a 100mph (161kph) average.

However, the start of the lap gives few clues to this as the first corner is a hairpin, followed by a long right-hander that feeds the cars on to a straight down to turn 5.

Mid-speed corners follow around the MSG Sphere before things tighten up at turn 9, but then the flow returns with a sweep down to turn 12, where the drivers have to negotiate a 90-degree left on to the Las Vegas Strip, thereafter powering past Caesars Palace, the Bellagio, the Venetian and other landmark venues. It's estimated that cars will top 210mph (338kph) on the straight down past this casino city's most extravagant buildings to turn 14.

The remainder of the lap is a left/right/left chicane and a fast kink on to the short start/finish straight.

INSIDE TRACK

LAS VEGAS GRAND PRIX

Date:	**18 November**
Circuit name:	Las Vegas F1 Circuit
Circuit length:	3.803 miles/6.120km
Number of laps:	50
Email:	tba
Website:	www.F1lasvegasgrandprix.com

PREVIOUS WINNERS

1981	**Alan Jones**	WILLIAMS
1982	**Michele Alboreto**	TYRRELL

Location: In the middle of Las Vegas.

How it started: The first racing circuit in the area was the Stardust Raceway in the mid-1960s, financed by the owners of the Stardust Hotel & Casino. Flat in nature, it offered little to excite and was soon redeveloped for housing. It then took until 1981 for the owners of the rival Caesars Palace Hotel & Casino to open a circuit to attract the World Championship. Unfortunately, the layout around its car park was unexciting in the extreme, failing to show American fans F1 cars at speed, and so lasted just two years.

Its greatest Grand Prix: Its second Grand Prix, in 1982, was its most exciting and it looked set to be a Renault race, with both Alain Prost and René Arnoux leading, but Michele Alboreto delighted the Tyrrell mechanics who took odds of 20-1 for him to win, and he did as title challenger John Watson fell just short with second, meaning fifth was enough for Keke Rosberg to be crowned champion.

Its worst Grand Prix: 1981. It had a title battle between Williams' Carlos Reutemann and Brabham's Nelson Piquet, with Jacques Laffite an outside shot. None finished on the podium, but Reutemann wilted under the pressure and Piquet's fifth place was enough for the title.

What Caesars Palace did next: In a word, nothing. However, race promoter Bruton Smith opened a banked oval on the edge of town which proved a hit as it filled the giant grandstands with capacity crowds, while a twisting road course was used for sports car racing.

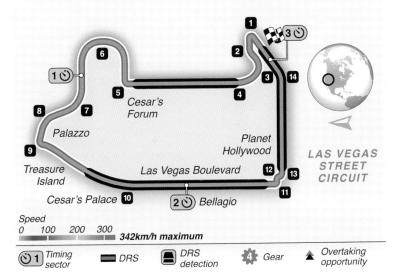

Cesar's Forum

Palazzo

Treasure Island

Cesar's Palace

Las Vegas Boulevard

Planet Hollywood

Bellagio

LAS VEGAS STREET CIRCUIT

Speed
0 100 200 300
342km/h maximum

🕐1 Timing sector   ▬ DRS   DRS detection   4 Gear   ▲ Overtaking opportunity

THIS TEMPORARY CIRCUIT WILL LOOK SPECTACULAR AS ITS RACE WILL BE HELD ON SATURDAY NIGHT RATHER THAN ON THE MORE TYPICAL SUNDAY AFTERNOON, WITH THE LIGHTS OF THE HOTELS AND CASINOS LINING THE LAS VEGAS STRIP PROVIDING A STUNNING BACKDROP. THE PITS AND PADDOCK WILL BE LAID OUT IN WHAT IS CURRENTLY A DISUSED PLOT.

YAS MARINA

The recent tweaking of the circuit layout has made this top-end circuit a better place to go racing than before, something that is vital as it frequently hosts the championship-deciding race.

INSIDE TRACK

ABU DHABI GRAND PRIX

Date:	**26 November**
Circuit name:	**Yas Marina Circuit**
Circuit length:	**3.281 miles/5.281km**
Number of laps:	**58**
Email:	customerservice@yasmarinacircuit.com
Website:	**www.yasmarinacircuit.com**

The start of the lap of the Yas Marina Circuit is fast and flowing once the field of cars has negotiated the relatively open 90-degree first corner. The sweeping run towards the first hairpin was made far simpler in 2021 by the removal of what had been the tight turn 5/6 complex.

Although the old turn 5 had been an overtaking place, so is the hairpin now. However, any fumbled passing move that puts a driver off line has consequences, as the exit of what is now turn 5 leads on to the circuit's longest straight. If a driver is a second slower getting on to the throttle out of here, it can wreck their hopes whether they are attacking or in defensive mode. The cars hit 200mph (322kph) down the straight before having to brake hard and position themselves for the tight left-hander that is followed immediately by a more open right.

This format used to be repeated with another long straight down to a sequence of tight turns. However, this too was modified for 2021, with the corner at the end of the second long straight now a long, arcing left-hander. It's a great improvement.

Then comes the run around the marina, with the majority of the corners having been made less acute in angle and so giving the drivers a better flow. One of the most spectacular images from the Yas Marina Circuit is the short straight between turns 13 and 14 where the track runs under a bridge between the two parts of the Yas Viceroy Hotel, something that looks spectacular as day turns to night through the course of the Grand Prix.

PREVIOUS WINNERS

2013	**Sebastian Vettel**	RED BULL
2014	**Lewis Hamilton**	MERCEDES
2015	**Nico Rosberg**	MERCEDES
2016	**Lewis Hamilton**	MERCEDES
2017	**Valtteri Bottas**	MERCEDES
2018	**Lewis Hamilton**	MERCEDES
2019	**Lewis Hamilton**	MERCEDES
2020	**Max Verstappen**	RED BULL
2021	**Max Verstappen**	RED BULL
2022	**Max Verstappen**	RED BULL

Location: Part of the Yas Marina sports complex, the circuit is on Yas Island to the east of the sheikhdom's capital.

How it started: The circuit was built to make Abu Dhabi an upmarket tourist destination in 2009, alongside a marina, a golf course and the Ferrari World theme park.

Its first Grand Prix: The 2009 Abu Dhabi GP was an eye-opener both for the exquisite circuit infrastructure and for its long straights into tight corners. Red Bull Racing liked it best as it dominated, with Sebastian Vettel leading home Mark Webber in a one-two ahead of the Brawns that had dominated the first half of the season.

Its greatest Grand Prix: The 2016 title shoot-out between Mercedes' drivers was a cliffhanger, with race leader Lewis Hamilton trying to slow Nico Rosberg enough so that Sebastian Vettel could pass him. It didn't work and Rosberg took the title.

Rising national star: With no national racing hero to follow other than her father Khaled, who raced in the GT class of the World Endurance Championship, 20-year-old Hamda Al Qubaisi is the best of the UAE's young racers, racing in last year's Formula Regional European championship.

Pit lane

YAS MARINA CIRCUIT

Speed
0 100 200 300
325km/h maximum

⏱ 1 Timing sector	▬ DRS	DRS detection	▲ Overtaking opportunity
		4 Gear	

2022 POLE TIME: **VERSTAPPEN (RED BULL), 1M23.824S, 140.929MPH/226.803KPH**
2022 WINNER'S AVERAGE SPEED: **130.065MPH/209.319KPH**
2022 FASTEST LAP: **NORRIS (MCLAREN), 1M28.391S, 133.647MPH/215.085KPH**
LAP RECORD: **VERSTAPPEN (RED BULL), 1M26.103S, 137.198MPH/220.800KPH, 2021**

One of the most unusual sections in
any F1 circuit is where the track ducks
beneath Yas Marina's Viceroy Hotel.

REVIEW OF THE 2022 SEASON

If the 2021 World Championship was as close as can be, last year's series was anything but. Ferrari started with a bang, its cars the best interpretation of the new regulations. However, Red Bull Racing gave chase and Max Verstappen overhauled them, with the Italian team executing awful race strategies that harmed Charles Leclerc's chances. Mercedes, for so long so dominant, spent the year playing catch-up.

New regulations gave the designers plenty to consider and it was soon apparent that the FIA-developed concept was less than brilliant as many teams found their cars porpoising, making handling tricky as the cars' bottoms hit the track and the ride uncomfortable. Aware of the dangers, the FIA discovered that some teams had used flexible floors to try to reduce the wear on the floors of their cars. These were banned from the Belgian GP onwards.

Red Bull started the year behind Ferrari, with both cars retiring. The speed was there for Verstappen to bounce back to win in Jeddah but he retired from the third, before he won five of the next six races

in a car that was both aero-efficient and light on its tyres as Ferrari began to fumble. Perez got in on the winning act too, at Monaco, when Ferrari wrecked Leclerc's chances again. The second half of the season resulted in another run of wins, increasingly backed up by Perez who won in Singapore and proved the best Red Bull number two in years, helping Verstappen to be champion again with four rounds to run. The season ended under a cloud, though, as Red Bull was adjudged to have exceeded the budget cap in 2021.

Leclerc had an amazing ability to set pole laps, but Ferrari have to shoulder the blame for him failing to convert many of these into

wins. Ferrari started the year with the car that worked best to the new regulations, as shown by the Leclerc/Sainz Jr one-two at Sakhir. However, Leclerc spun at Imola and spun off again at Paul Ricard. Like many, Sainz had to develop a new style of driving, but then atoned for errors to take his first F1 win, at Silverstone.

Mercedes started on the back foot, with the cars' porpoising making the drivers uncomfortable. Indeed, it was new signing Russell who adapted better, finishing between second and fifth before winning in Brazil. Hamilton took longer to feel confident but showed his class from mid-season onwards.

Alpine had a season-long scrap with McLaren to rank fourth. Whenever conditions were poor, Alonso showed why he is a double world champion, such as qualifying second in Canada. Ocon claimed the team's best finish, though, fourth at Suzuka. Alpine was unsettled, though when Alonso announced that he was joining Aston Martin and reserve driver Piastri elected not to step up.

McLaren's programme was effectively a one-driver attack, led by Norris, as Ricciardo was out of sorts and seemingly unable to get his head around how to rediscover his mojo. The MCL36 worked all right at some tracks, like at Marina Bay where the pair finished fourth and fifth, but then performed poorly next time out, and in the end Norris's best result was third place at Imola.

Alfa Romeo started with a great result in Bahrain, as Bottas finished sixth and rookie team-mate Guanyu tenth. Three races later, Bottas took fifth at Imola and clearly enjoyed battling with his former team-mate Hamilton as Mercedes struggled. As ever with this Swiss team, the second half of the year was a story of competitive decline.

Aston Martin took until the fourth round to score any points, then remained on the cusp of points for the rest of the year, advancing up the rankings with Vettel showing flashes of brilliance.

Haas went in the opposite direction after starting with a bang with fifth for Magnussen. However, Schumacher showed improved form after two major shunts in the first half of the year.

AlphaTauri's form fluctuated, starting with an eighth for Tsunoda then peaking with fifth for Gasly in Baku, but the cars normally finished outside the points.

Williams was back to where it had been in 2020, at the tail of the field. Its rare point-scoring drives were hard-earned, with Albon proving a master of preserving his tyres, as was stand-in de Vries at Monza and Latifi at Suzuka.

BAHRAIN GP

The first race run under new technical regulations showed that Mercedes' pre-race fears about their lack of pace proved to be correct as Ferrari and Red Bull dominated from the outset. Charles Leclerc won, with Ferrari also picking up second place as the Red Bulls failed late on.

Leclerc felt the omens for his 2022 season must be good when he not only qualified on pole but resisted Max Verstappen on the run to Sakhir's first corner. Carlos Sainz slotted into third, but Sergio Perez lost fourth to Lewis Hamilton, with the Mercedes driver anxious to gain track position with a car that wasn't really up to speed.

The driver who was soon having trouble, though, was Verstappen, with his brakes starting to overheat. However, any ground lost was regained when Leclerc's pit stop was a little long. Then, having been told that he would have just one shot at passing Leclerc before his brake problem would slow him, Verstappen dived past on lap 17, only to be repassed almost immediately. Typically, Verstappen decided to have another go but the outcome was the same.

A safety car deployment while Pierre Gasly's AlphaTauri was recovered gave Verstappen a final shot, but he was squeezed at the restart by Leclerc and this not only allowed the Ferrari driver to make a break, but left him suddenly vulnerable as Sainz closed in. Then, Verstappen's mechanical problems became worse when, with three laps to go, he slowed and retired with a fuel pump malfunction. Two laps later, team-mate Perez suffered a similar failure, giving Red Bull Racing an awful end to what had been a promising outing.

These failures promoted the Mercedes drivers to third and fourth, with Hamilton surprised to have achieved a podium finish despite never having been on the pace.

Having qualified a hugely impressive seventh after his last-minute call-up to Haas F1 – after sanctions against Russia ruled out Nikita Mazepin – Kevin Magnussen performed better still in the race and his fifth place finish netted the team its best finish since the 2018.

SAKHIR ROUND 1

DATE: **20 MARCH 2022**

Laps: **57** · Distance: **191.536 miles/308.238km** · Weather: **Warm & dry**

Pos	Driver	Team	Result	Stops	Qualifying Time	Grid
1	**Charles Leclerc**	Ferrari	1h37m33.584s	3	1m30.558s	1
2	**Carlos Sainz Jr**	Ferrari	1h37m39.182s	3	1m30.687s	3
3	**Lewis Hamilton**	Mercedes	1h37m43.259s	3	1m31.238s	5
4	**George Russell**	Mercedes	1h37m44.795s	3	1m31.216s	9
5	**Kevin Magnussen**	Haas	1h37m48.338s	3	1m31.808s	7
6	**Valtteri Bottas**	Alfa Romeo	1h37m49.703s	3	1m31.560s	6
7	**Esteban Ocon**	Alpine	1h37m53.007s	3	1m31.782s	11
8	**Yuki Tsunoda**	AlphaTauri	1h37m53.970s	3	1m32.750s	16
9	**Fernando Alonso**	Alpine	1h37m55.974s	3	1m32.195s	8
10	**Guanyu Zhou**	Alfa Romeo	1h37m56.648s	3	1m33.543s	15
11	**Mick Schumacher**	Haas	1h38m06.158s	2	1m31.998s	12
12	**Lance Stroll**	Aston Martin	1h38m19.457s	3	1m33.032s	19
13	**Alexander Albon**	Williams	1h38m27.516s	3	1m32.664s	14
14	**Daniel Ricciardo**	McLaren	1h38m28.559s	3	1m32.945s	18
15	**Lando Norris**	McLaren	1h38m29.919s	3	1m32.008s	13
16	**Nicholas Latifi**	Williams	1h38m35.379s	3	1m33.634s	20
17	**Nico Hulkenberg**	Aston Martin	1h38m37.413s	3	1m32.777s	17
R	**Sergio Perez**	Red Bull	56 laps/fuel pump	3	1m30.921s	4
R	**Max Verstappen**	Red Bull	54 laps/fuel pump	3	1m30.681s	2
R	**Pierre Gasly**	AlphaTauri	44 laps/power unit	2	1m32.338s	10

FASTEST LAP: LECLERC, 1M34.570S, 128.108MPH/206.018KPH ON LAP 51
RACE LEADERS: LECLERC 1-31 & 34-57, SAINZ JR 32-33

Carlos Sainz and Charles Leclerc celebrate a winning start for Ferrari, with Mercedes in their wake.

SAUDI ARABIAN GP

Max Verstappen bounced back from his first-round retirement by triumphing on F1's second visit to Jeddah's bumpy street circuit. Second place was enough, though, for Charles Leclerc to hold a 20-point lead over him, while tenth for Lewis Hamilton emphasised Mercedes' struggles.

It felt strange to be back at the circuit so soon after its dramatic inaugural race less than four months before, and then stranger still when there was a missile attack on a nearby oil depot.

Sergio Perez claimed pole for Red Bull and pulled away in front of Leclerc, while Red Bull team-mate Verstappen forced his way into third place when Carlos Sainz got slightly baulked by Leclerc into the first corner.

They ran in this order up to their one planned pit stop and this is where Perez's race came undone. Nicholas Latifi crashed his Williams just after the Mexican pitted and this brought out the safety car, enabling his rivals to pit and return without losing as much time. This promoted Leclerc into the lead – with Verstappen second and Sainz third – and dropped Perez to fourth, which was very frustrating for him.

Nothing appeared set to change, with Leclerc controlling the race from Verstappen, but then there was a virtual safety car deployment after Fernando Alonso and Daniel Ricciardo both coasted to a halt. When the VSC period ended, Verstappen's Red Bull appeared to get heat into its tyres better than Leclerc's Ferrari, and this enabled him to get close enough to make a pass in the DRS zone. Leclerc showed his ability to box clever and got back in front twice in a great cat-and-mouse battle before Verstappen made his move stick.

Behind the Red Bull and Ferrari pairings, George Russell was Mercedes' better-placed driver in finishing fifth, while Lewis Hamilton could only come home tenth after starting from 15th on the grid. He had battled his way up to sixth, but then there was some confusion about entering the pits around Ricciardo's limping McLaren, which led to him staying out and losing the places he'd gained.

Max Verstappen came through to win from fourth on the grid for his first points of the year.

JEDDAH ROUND 2

DATE: **27 MARCH 2021**

Laps: **50** · Distance: **191.668 miles/308.450km** · Weather: **Hot & dry**

Pos	Driver	Team	Result	Stops	Qualifying Time	Grid
1	**Max Verstappen**	Red Bull	1h24m19.293s	1	1m28.461s	4
2	**Charles Leclerc**	Ferrari	1h24m19.842s	1	1m28.225s	2
3	**Carlos Sainz Jr**	Ferrari	1h24m27.390s	1	1m28.402s	3
4	**Sergio Perez**	Red Bull	1h24m30.093s	1	1m28.200s	1
5	**George Russell**	Mercedes	1h24m52.025s	1	1m29.104s	6
6	**Esteban Ocon**	Alpine	1h25m15.310s	1	1m29.068s	5
7	**Lando Norris**	McLaren	1h25m15.417s	1	1m29.651s	11
8	**Pierre Gasly**	AlphaTauri	1h25m22.239s	1	1m29.254s	9
9	**Kevin Magnussen**	Haas	1h25m23.601s	1	1m29.588s	10
10	**Lewis Hamilton**	Mercedes	1h25m33.241s	1	1m30.343s	15
11	**Guanyu Zhou**	Alfa Romeo	1h25m41.508s	2	1m29.819s	12
12	**Nico Hulkenberg**	Aston Martin	1h25m51.035s	1	1m30.543s	17
13	**Lance Stroll**	Aston Martin	49 laps	1	1m31.009s	13
R	**Alexander Albon**	Williams	47 laps/collision	1	1m30.492s	16
R	**Valtteri Bottas**	Alfa Romeo	36 laps/overheating	2	1m29.183s	8
R	**Fernando Alonso**	Alpine	35 laps/power unit	1	1m29.147s	7
R	**Daniel Ricciardo ***	McLaren	35 laps/power unit	1	1m29.773s	14
R	**Nicholas Latifi**	Williams	14 laps/spun off	0	1m31.817s	18
NS	**Yuki Tsunoda**	AlphaTauri	0 laps/drivetrains	-	no time	19
W	**Mick Schumacher**	Haas	0 laps/driver injury	-	-	

FASTEST LAP: LECLERC, 1M31.634S, 150.722MPH/242.556KPH ON LAP 48
RACE LEADERS: PEREZ 1-14, LECLERC 15-41 & 43-45, VERSTAPPEN 42 & 46-50
* 3-PLACE GRID PENALTY FOR IMPEDING ANOTHER DRIVER

AUSTRALIAN GP

It was great for F1 to be back in Melbourne for the first time since the start of 2020, and this time the drivers got to race rather than be turned home by Covid. It was Ferrari all the way, with Charles Leclerc winning as he pleased.

The Mercedes domination of the previous eight seasons was clearly not something that the team in silver was capable of adding to on its 2022 form, as its drivers continued to be held back and indeed made nauseous by their cars' porpoising. Conversely, it was all smiles at Ferrari as their cars were far less of a handful. Thus, Charles Leclerc not only grabbed his second pole of the year but did so by the healthy margin of 0.286s over Max Verstappen's Red Bull.

Leclerc's team-mate Carlos Sainz might have had an inkling that this wasn't going to be his meeting when his final run in qualifying was compromised. Then, from ninth on the grid, he fell back further because of a steering wheel glitch at the start, before spinning out on lap 2 as he tried to regain places. This ruined his chances of staying close to Leclerc on points, especially knowing that it was unlikely he would be helped by the team later in the year if Leclerc needed letting by.

As it was, Leclerc needed no help as he led every lap of the race and won by 20 seconds. This wasn't ahead of leading rival Max Verstappen, as the 2021 world champion retired for the second time in three races, this time with a fuel leak, but ahead of his team-mate Sergio Perez, who had to pass both Mercedes to get there. Lewis Hamilton might have finished third, but the deployment of a safety car just after he pitted dropped him back one place, so team-mate George Russell took his first F1 podium. McLaren wasn't really in the hunt, but Lando Norris and Daniel Ricciardo finished fifth and sixth.

One of the outstanding performances was Alexander Albon's drive to tenth place, managing to get his generally uncompetitive Williams up to take the final point, thanks to saving his only pit stop until the penultimate lap.

98

MELBOURNE ROUND 3

DATE: **10 APRIL 2022**

Laps: **58** • Distance: **190.216 miles/306.124km** • Weather: **Hot & dry**

Pos	Driver	Team	Result	Stops	Qualifying Time	Grid
1	Charles Leclerc	Ferrari	1h27m46.548s	1	1m17.868s	1
2	Sergio Perez	Red Bull	1h28m07.072s	1	1m18.240s	3
3	George Russell	Mercedes	1h28m12.141s	1	1m18.933s	6
4	Lewis Hamilton	Mercedes	1h28m15.091s	1	1m18.825s	5
5	Lando Norris	McLaren	1h28m39.851s	1	1m18.703s	4
6	Daniel Ricciardo	McLaren	1h28m40.285s	1	1m19.032s	7
7	Esteban Ocon	Alpine	1h28m28.231s	1	1m19.061s	8
8	Valtteri Bottas	Alfa Romeo	1h28m54.987s	1	1m19.410s	12
9	Pierre Gasly	AlphaTauri	1h29m02.769s	1	1m19.226s	11
10	Alexander Albon *!	Williams	1h29m05.930s	1	no time	20
11	Guanyu Zhou	Alfa Romeo	1h29m08.243s	1	1m20.155s	14
12	Lance Stroll *	Aston Martin	1h29m15.146s	2	no time	19
13	Mick Schumacher	Haas	57 laps	1	1m20.465s	15
14	Kevin Magnussen	Haas	57 laps	1	1m20.254s	16
15	Yuki Tsunoda	AlphaTauri	57 laps	1	1m19.424s	13
16	Nicholas Latifi	Williams	57 laps	2	1m21.372s	18
17	Fernando Alonso	Alpine	57 laps	2	no time	10
R	Max Verstappen	Red Bull	38 laps/fuel leak	1	1m18.154s	2
R	Sebastian Vettel	Aston Martin	22 laps/spun off	1	1m21.149s	17
R	Carlos Sainz Jr	Ferrari	1 lap/spun off	0	1m19.408s	9

FASTEST LAP: LECLERC, 1M20.260S, 147.103MPH/236.740KPH ON LAP 58 • RACE LEADERS: LECLERC 1-58
* 3-PLACE GRID PENALTY FOR CAUSING A COLLISION • *! EXCLUDED FROM QUALIFYING FOR INABILITY TO PROVIDE A FUEL SAMPLE

Leclerc blasts away from pole and he went on to lead every lap for his second win from three.

EMILIA ROMAGNA GP

Despite enjoying strong form, Ferrari fumbled when it mattered and was unable to give the *tifosi* the win they desired. Carlos Sainz Jr didn't finish lap 1 and then Charles Leclerc slid off when contesting third, ultimately finishing sixth as Max Verstappen motored on to victory.

This was one of the rounds at which there was a sprint race and Charles Leclerc rocketed into the lead of that as Max Verstappen made a poor start. However, the Monegasque driver was always in his sights and Verstappen found a way to win, giving him pole for the main race.

With rain sweeping through three hours before the start, the track was still damp enough for all of the cars to go out on intermediate rubber. The *tifosi* then had to endure both Ferraris making poor starts, allowing Verstappen to take the lead, followed by Red Bull team-mate Sergio Perez and McLaren's Lando Norris. Moments later, bad turned to worse as Daniel Ricciardo's McLaren pivoted on a wet kerb and clipped Carlos Sainz Jr, firing the Spaniard's Ferrari off into a gravel trap. An enforced pit stop for repairs also wrecked the Australian's hopes.

This was a bonus for Red Bull. Their cars had proved marginally faster than the Ferraris in practice, but this gift of track position was not one to be squandered and Verstappen and Sergio Perez raced to a one-two finish, something that helped to make up the ground lost at the first round when neither finished. Nine laps before the finish, Leclerc got on to Perez's tail and fancied relieving him of second place, but slid off and did light damage to his car. After an enforced pit stop for a new front wing, this dropped him to sixth.

A surprised Norris was thus promoted to the final place on the podium, showing how rapidly McLaren was making progress. Behind him, George Russell leapt from 11th to sixth on lap 1 and then fought on with back and chest pains caused by his car's porpoising, but managed to finish fourth, while team-mate Lewis Hamilton trailed home 13th to an apology from team boss Toto Wolff for 'not providing a car worthy of a world champion'.

Sainz keeps his helmet on to hide his embarrassment after crashing out on the opening lap.

IMOLA ROUND 4

DATE: **24 APRIL 2022**

Laps: **63** · Distance: **192.034 miles/309.049km** · Weather: **Overcast & damp**

Pos	Driver	Team	Result	Stops	Qualifying Time	Grid
1	**Max Verstappen**	Red Bull	1h32m07.986s	2	-	1
2	**Sergio Perez**	Red Bull	1h32m24.513s	2	-	3
3	**Lando Norris**	McLaren	1h32m42.820s	1	-	5
4	**George Russell**	Mercedes	1h32m50.492s	1	-	11
5	**Valtteri Bottas**	Alfa Romeo	1h32m51.167s	1	-	7
6	**Charles Leclerc**	Ferrari	1h33m04.058s	3	-	2
7	**Yuki Tsunoda**	AlphaTauri	1h33m09.096s	1	-	12
8	**Sebastian Vettel**	Aston Martin	1h33m18.878s	1	-	13
9	**Kevin Magnussen**	Haas	1h33m23.246s	1	-	8
10	**Lance Stroll**	Aston Martin	62 laps	1	-	15
11	**Alexander Albon**	Williams	62 laps	1	-	18
12	**Pierre Gasly**	AlphaTauri	62 laps	1	-	17
13	**Lewis Hamilton**	Mercedes	62 laps	1	-	14
14	**Esteban Ocon**	Alpine	62 laps	1	-	16
15	**Guanyu Zhou !**	Alfa Romeo	62 laps	1	-	20
16	**Nicholas Latifi**	Williams	62 laps	1	-	19
17	**Mick Schumacher**	Haas	62 laps	2	-	10
18	**Daniel Ricciardo**	McLaren	62 laps	3	-	6
R	**Fernando Alonso**	Alpine	6 laps/crash damage	0	-	9
R	**Carlos Sainz Jr**	Ferrari	0 laps/crash damage	0	-	4

FASTEST LAP: VERSTAPPEN, 1M18.446S, 139.983MPH/225.281KPH ON LAP 55 · RACE LEADERS: VERSTAPPEN 1-63
! STARTED FROM PIT LANE AS CAR MODIFIED UNDER PARC FERMÉ CONDITIONS. · NB GRID DETERMINED BY FINISHING ORDER IN SPRINT RACE

MIAMI GP

The track wasn't up to much, but the atmosphere was electric. When the A-, B- and C-list celebrities had been cleared from the grid, Max Verstappen hunted down Charles Leclerc and passed him for a lead he would keep, despite late race safety car chaos.

When making your first visit to a circuit, track time is everything. This is why Max Verstappen was less than happy as mechanical problems restricted him to limited running on the first day. What he did discover, though, was that the track surface was poor and, not surprisingly, the drivers were critical. Sure, the circuit next to the Hard Rock Stadium had been dressed to look like a marina rather than a car park, but they wanted something up to the task.

Ferrari locked out the front row, with Verstappen third. However, once the ridiculously packed grid was cleared, the Dutchman demoted Carlos Sainz Jr at the first corner. He then tracked Charles Leclerc and passed him on lap 9, the Ferrari driver struggling for grip. And that was that, his only scare coming on lap 40 when Lando Norris collided with Pierre Gasly's AlphaTauri and lost a wheel, with the clear-up operation requiring the safety car to be deployed, compressing Verstappen's lead. However, Verstappen was still in control when it withdrew and was able to win by four seconds.

Valtteri Bottas shone by qualifying fifth for Alfa Romeo, but he slid wide, having lost concentration on lap 49, and this let both Mercedes drivers through. George Russell, who had fallen to 15th, was on rubber that was 18 laps fresher than Lewis Hamilton's and simply picked him off to claim fifth.

One of the star drives came from Alexander Albon, who showed again that he can nurse his tyres better than anyone as he advanced from 18th to tenth in his Williams. Then, when Fernando Alonso was hit with a pair of five-second penalties, that became ninth. Although he claimed a pair of third-place finishes when he raced for Red Bull in 2020, his 2022 tyre-saving runs were earning him just as much respect.

MIAMI ROUND 5   DATE: **8 MAY 2022**

Laps: **57** • Distance: **191.585 miles/308.326km** • Weather: **Hot & bright**

Pos	Driver	Team	Result	Stops	Qualifying Time	Grid
1	**Max Verstappen**	Red Bull	1h34m24.258s	1	1m28.991s	3
2	**Charles Leclerc**	Ferrari	1h34m28.044s	1	1m28.796s	1
3	**Carlos Sainz Jr**	Ferrari	1h34m32.487s	1	1m28.986s	2
4	**Sergio Perez**	Red Bull	1h34m34.896s	2	1m29.036s	4
5	**George Russell**	Mercedes	1h34m42.840s	1	1m30.173s	12
6	**Lewis Hamilton**	Mercedes	1h34m45.626s	1	1m29.625s	6
7	**Valtteri Bottas**	Alfa Romeo	1h34m49.331s	1	1m29.475s	5
8	**Esteban Ocon**	Alpine	1h34m52.644s	1	no time	20
9	**Alexander Albon**	Williams	1h34m56.623s	1	1m31.266s	18
10	**Lance Stroll !**	Aston Martin	1h35m01.284s	1	1m30.676s	10
11	**Fernando Alonso *!!**	Alpine	1h35m01.386s	1	1m30.160s	11
12	**Yuki Tsunoda**	AlphaTauri	1h35m04.404s	2	1m29.932s	9
13	**Daniel Ricciardo !!**	McLaren	1h35m05.160s	2	1m30.310s	14
14	**Nicholas Latifi**	Williams	1h35m14.194s	1	1m31.325s	19
15	**Mick Schumacher**	Haas	1h35m37.563s	2	1m30.423s	15
16	**Kevin Magnussen ***	Haas	56 laps/crash damage	2	1m30.975s	16
R	**Sebastian Vettel !**	Aston Martin	54 laps/crash damage	1	1m30.214s	13
R	**Pierre Gasly**	AlphaTauri	45 laps/crash damage	2	1m29.690s	7
R	**Lando Norris**	McLaren	39 laps/accident	1	1m29.750s	8
R	**Guanyu Zhou**	Alfa Romeo	6 laps/water pump	0	1m31.020s	17

FASTEST LAP: VERSTAPPEN, 1M31.361S, 132.510MPH/213.255KPH ON LAP 54 •
RACE LEADERS: LECLERC 1-8, VERSTAPPEN 9-26 & 28-57, SAINZ JR 27 • ! STARTED FROM PIT LANE • * 5S PENALTY FOR CAUSING A COLLISION
!! 5S PENALTY FOR LEAVING TRACK AND GAINING AN ADVANTAGE

Leclerc, Verstappen and Sainz look confused by their American Football helmets on the podium.

SPANISH GP

When Charles Leclerc retired before halfway, this race was put on a plate for Max Verstappen and he made the most of it, although possibly the best drive was Lewis Hamilton's recovery to fifth after a first-lap tangle with Kevin Magnussen.

Ferrari continued to ride high on F1's second race of the year in Europe. Temperatures were sky high but the Ferraris looked just as good as at cooler venues. Pole was secured with ease by Leclerc, his fourth in sixth rounds, and he then led away with ease, keeping clear of Max Verstappen through the Circuit de Catalunya's tricky first two corners.

Behind them, George Russell had demoted the second Ferrari to run third, but then team-mate Lewis Hamilton was almost immediately in the wars, colliding with the Haas of Kevin Magnussen, who had tried to go around the outside at turn 4. Both had to pit for repairs.

The race then settled down, with Verstappen unable to overthrow Leclerc as Hamilton began his long climb back through the order. Fortunately for the seven-time world champion, modifications to the Mercedes W13 had reduced its propensity to porpoise and so he was able to keep on charging.

All was fine up front for Leclerc, but Carlos Sainz compounded his poor start, which dropped him two places, when, on lap 7, he spun and dropped from fifth to 11th. He wasn't the only spinner, though, as Verstappen also looped around at turn 4 two laps later and fell to fourth.

Perez was comfortable in second place and Russell likewise with third, having enjoyed a good defensive drive ahead of Verstappen for fully 19 laps after the Dutchman had spun. Indeed, Red Bull elected to alter Verstappen's strategy to ensure that he found a way past, something that he did but was exceedingly unhappy about.

Leclerc was forced to retire on lap 27 with engine issues and, by lap 49, Verstappen had just Sergio Perez in front of him and the Mexican was encouraged to let Verstappen past.

Perez leads Verstappen, but Red Bull Racing soon sent him a message to move aside.

BARCELONA ROUND 6   DATE: **22 MAY 2022**
Laps: **66** · Distance: **191.645 miles/308.424km** · Weather: **Very hot & sunny**

Pos	Driver	Team	Result	Stops	Qualifying Time	Grid
1	**Max Verstappen**	Red Bull	1h37m20.475s	3	1m19.073s	2
2	**Sergio Perez**	Red Bull	1h37m33.547s	3	1m19.420s	5
3	**George Russell**	Mercedes	1h37m53.402s	3	1m19.393s	4
4	**Carlos Sainz Jr**	Ferrari	1h38m05.683s	3	1m19.166s	3
5	**Lewis Hamilton**	Mercedes	1h38m15.009s	3	1m19.512s	6
6	**Valtteri Bottas**	Alfa Romeo	1h38m20.451s	2	1m19.608s	7
7	**Esteban Ocon**	Alpine	1h38m35.872s	3	1m20.638s	12
8	**Lando Norris**	McLaren	1h38m43.710s	3	1m20.471s	11
9	**Fernando Alonso ***	Alpine	65 laps	3	1m21.043s	20
10	**Yuki Tsunoda**	AlphaTauri	65 laps	3	1m20.639s	13
11	**Sebastian Vettel**	Aston Martin	65 laps	2	1m20.954s	16
12	**Daniel Ricciardo**	McLaren	65 laps	3	1m20.297s	9
13	**Pierre Gasly**	AlphaTauri	65 laps	3	1m20.861s	14
14	**Mick Schumacher**	Haas	65 laps	2	1m20.368s	10
15	**Lance Stroll**	Aston Martin	65 laps	3	1m21.418s	17
16	**Nicholas Latifi**	Williams	64 laps	3	1m21.915s	19
17	**Kevin Magnussen**	Haas	64 laps	2	1m19.682s	8
18	**Alexander Albon**	Williams	64 laps	4	1m21.645s	18
R	**Guanyu Zhou**	Alfa Romeo	28 laps/power unit	1	1m21.094s	15
R	**Charles Leclerc**	Ferrari	27 laps/power unit	1	1m18.750s	1

FASTEST LAP: PEREZ, 1M24.108S, 124.336MPH/200.099KPH ON LAP 55
RACE LEADERS: LECLERC 1-26, RUSSELL 27-30, PEREZ 31-37 & 45-48, VERSTAPPEN 38-44 & 49-66
* MADE TO START FROM BACK OF GRID FOR USING ADDITIONAL POWER UNIT ELEMENTS

MONACO GP

While there were many people delighted that Sergio Perez came through to win, there was equal disappointment for Charles Leclerc, who started from pole and was in control of the race until Ferrari's weak tactics on a changing track turned that into a fourth-place finish.

Rain delayed the start of the race when it fell with increasing intensity. Then, an attempt to get going was called off after two laps behind the safety car.

Finally, 75 minutes after the planned start, racing got underway and, as is almost always the case at Monaco, grid order was maintained, with no passing achieved at Sainte Devote, Leclerc still leading team-mate Carlos Sainz, ahead of Perez and Max Verstappen. The track was drying gradually and the question was going to be when the teams opted to change their cars from full wets to intermediate tyres.

Red Bull Racing went first, bringing in Perez on lap 16. Ferrari took two laps to respond, before calling Leclerc in to do the same. This was poor thinking, since the Mexican's first two laps on intermediates were faster than the Monegasque's last two on full wets, and so their positions were reversed, leaving Leclerc aghast at how his lead had been lost so unnecessarily.

Worse was to follow as Ferrari didn't bring in Sainz for a change of tyres until lap 21, when the Spaniard decided that he would go straight from full wets to slicks. However, the team also called in Leclerc for slicks at the same time, and the fumble ended Leclerc's hopes of winning on home soil as he emerged in fourth through no fault of his own. The post-race debrief can't have been much fun.

Then Mick Schumacher had a huge shunt at the exit of Piscine on lap 25, hitting the barriers hard enough for the rear end to be ripped off his Haas. This brought out the red flag.

Perez then controlled the restart and all that followed, revelling in a lead he would never lose to the chasing Sainz. Verstappen might have hoped that Red Bull could find a way to get him ahead of Perez, as they had in Spain, but it wasn't to be.

MONTE CARLO ROUND 7

DATE: 29 MAY 2022

Laps: **64** · Distance: **132.705 miles/213.568km** · Weather: **Warm & overcast**

Pos	Driver	Team	Result	Stops	Qualifying Time	Grid
1	**Sergio Perez**	Red Bull	1h56m30.265s	3	1m11.629s	3
2	**Carlos Sainz Jr**	Ferrari	1h56m31.419s	2	1m11.601s	2
3	**Max Verstappen**	Red Bull	1h56m31.756s	3	1m11.666s	4
4	**Charles Leclerc**	Ferrari	1h56m33.187s	3	1m11.376s	1
5	**George Russell**	Mercedes	1h56m42.233s	2	1m12.112s	6
6	**Lando Norris**	McLaren	1h56m42.496s	4	1m11.849s	5
7	**Fernando Alonso**	Alpine	1h57m16.623s	2	1m12.247s	7
8	**Lewis Hamilton**	Mercedes	1h57m20.653s	3	1m12.560s	8
9	**Valtteri Bottas**	Alfa Romeo	1h57m22.790s	2	1m12.909s	12
10	**Sebastian Vettel**	Aston Martin	1h57m23.80s	3	1m12.732s	9
11	**Pierre Gasly**	AlphaTauri	1h57m24.554s	3	1m13.660s	17
12	**Esteban Ocon !**	Alpine	1h57m25.909s	2	1m13.047s	10
13	**Daniel Ricciardo**	McLaren	1h57m27.900s	2	1m12.964s	14
14	**Lance Stroll**	Aston Martin	1h57m31.067s	4	1m13.678s	18
15	**Nicholas Latifi**	Williams	63 laps	4	1m14.403s	19
16	**Guanyu Zhou**	Alfa Romeo	63 laps	2	1m15.606s	20
17	**Yuki Tsunoda**	AlphaTauri	63 laps	4	1m12.797s	11
R	**Alexander Albon !!**	Williams	48 laps/handling	3	1m13.611s	16
R	**Mick Schumacher**	Haas	24 laps/accident	2	1m13.081s	15
R	**Kevin Magnussen**	Haas	19 laps/power unit	0	1m12.921s	13

FASTEST LAP: NORRIS, 1M14.693S, 99.937MPH/160.834KPH ON LAP 55 · RACE LEADERS: LECLERC 1-17, SAINZ JR 18-20, PEREZ 21-64
! 5 SECOND PENALTY FOR CAUSING A COLLISION · !! 5 SECOND PENALTY FOR LEAVING TRACK AND GAINING AN ADVANTAGE

Perez was delighted to triumph for Red Bull on a day when Ferrari's tactics cost Leclerc victory.

AZERBAIJAN GP

Max Verstappen stormed to a fifth win in six finishes to extend his lead, while Ferrari had a terrible time, with both its cars retiring. Red Bull even picked up a one-two, being joined on the podium by George Russell, who continued his run of points finishes.

When Charles Leclerc bagged his fourth pole position in succession, things looked rosy again in the Ferrari camp. He and team-mate Carlos Sainz were separated on the grid by the Red Bulls, with Sergio Perez ahead of Verstappen, all appreciably faster than the best of the rest, followed by Russell in his porpoising Mercedes.

However, it wasn't to be Ferrari's day, with Leclerc getting wheelspin as he accelerated off the grid and Perez pulled alongside. Then, going into the first corner, Leclerc locked up and Perez was through into the lead.

Worse was to follow for Ferrari as Sainz became the race's first retirement, dropping out after eight laps with hydraulic failure. This brought out the yellow flags and then a virtual safety car period as the Spaniard had parked up an escape road. Ferrari pounced to bring Leclerc in for a 'cheap' stop, but they messed up the stop and any notional gain was lost. Red Bull had their own problems as Perez failed to understand a call to pit at the same time. After that, with Leclerc starting to fly, Verstappen closed in on Perez and shot into the lead. His too was a slow one. Verstappen's was better, but both were behind Leclerc when they rejoined, although it mattered not as Leclerc's engine blew.

This left the Red Bulls in control, Verstappen four seconds clear of Perez, and so they remained in that order to the finish, although Verstappen extended the gap before it was closed by a second virtual safety car period. This was caused by the unusual reason that Kevin Magnussen's Haas had begun to roll downhill after he had parked it with engine failure, therefore needing to be rescued and moved to a safe place.

Russell persevered, even as his back suffered from his W13's porpoising, and collected his third third-place finish.

Wheelspin wasted Leclerc's pole position and Perez was able to take the lead into Turn 1.

BAKU ROUND 8

DATE: 12 JUNE 2022

Laps: **51** • Distance: **190.170 miles/306.049km** • Weather: **Hot & sunny**

Pos	Driver	Team	Result	Stops	Qualifying Time	Grid
1	Max Verstappen	Red Bull	1h34m05.941s	2	1m41.706s	3
2	Sergio Perez	Red Bull	1h34m26.764s	2	1m41.641s	2
3	George Russell	Mercedes	1h34m51.936s	2	1m42.712s	5
4	Lewis Hamilton	Mercedes	1h35m17.620s	2	1m42.924s	7
5	Pierre Gasly	AlphaTauri	1h35m23.240s	1	1m42.845s	6
6	Sebastian Vettel	Aston Martin	1h35m30.040s	1	1m43.091s	9
7	Fernando Alonso	Alpine	1h35m34.537s	1	1m43.173s	10
8	Daniel Ricciardo	McLaren	1h35m38.148s	1	1m43.574s	12
9	Lando Norris	McLaren	1h35m38.497s	1	1m43.398s	11
10	Esteban Ocon	Alpine	1h35m54.125s	1	1m43.585s	13
11	Valtteri Bottas	Alfa Romeo	50 laps	1	1m44.444s	15
12	Alexander Albon	Williams	50 laps	2	1m44.719s	17
13	Yuki Tsunoda	AlphaTauri	50 laps	2	1m43.056s	8
14	Mick Schumacher	Haas	50 laps	2	1m45.775s	20
15	Nicholas Latifi	Williams	50 laps	2	1m45.367s	18
16	Lance Stroll	Aston Martin	46 laps/vibration	1	1m45.371s	19
R	Kevin Magnussen	Haas	31 laps/engine	1	1m44.643s	16
R	Guanyu Zhou	Alfa Romeo	23 laps/hydraulics	1	1m43.790s	14
R	Charles Leclerc	Ferrari	21 laps/power unit	1	1m41.359s	1
R	Carlos Sainz Jr	Ferrari	8 laps/hydraulics	0	1m41.814s	4

FASTEST LAP: **PEREZ, 1M46.046S, 126.627MPH/203.787KPH ON LAP 36**
RACE LEADERS: **PEREZ 1-14, VERSTAPPEN 15-18 & 20-51, LECLERC 19**

CANADIAN GP

A full helping of 25 points for Max Verstappen and an early-race retirement for Red Bull team-mate Sergio Perez meant that the reigning world champion left Canada with a 46-point lead, something that had seemed unlikely when he retired from two of the first three races.

Things were looking good for Max Verstappen when he grabbed pole position in a wet session – in which former world champion Fernando Alonso showed his class to qualify second for Alpine – as the Circuit Gilles Villeneuve is a tricky one on which to pass. His fortune was made to look better still after Charles Leclerc was told that he would have to start from the back of the grid for having to have a third power unit change.

Verstappen duly led away at the start, followed by Alonso, who was passed a few laps later by Carlos Sainz. The Spaniard attempted to take the battle to Red Bull, with Lewis Hamilton holding a watching brief in a car that had improved from the Friday sessions when he described it as 'the worst car ever'.

After just seven laps, sitting comfortably in the lead, Verstappen's closest challenger in the championship, team-mate Sergio Perez, parked up with an engine problem.

There were a couple of virtual safety car periods, first while Perez's Mercedes was moved to safety and then for the same reason while Mick Schumacher's Haas was cleared away. The timing of pit stops enabled Alonso to return to second, but fellow Spaniard Sainz was soon back up to second and Alonso would in turn be overtaken by both Mercedes drivers and his own team-mate Esteban Ocon.

There was a wonderful moment when Verstappen emerged from his second pit stop to find his 2021 nemesis Hamilton alongside him, but the Dutchman was soon back in the lead.

Then Yuki Tsunoda brought the safety car out when he crashed his AlphaTauri, with the pack closing on to the leader's tail accordingly. However, Verstappen controlled the restart as he went on to beat Sainz by just one second, with Hamilton happy to have made it to the podium.

MONTREAL ROUND 9

DATE: **19 JUNE 2022**

Laps: **70** • Distance: **189.686 miles/305.270km** • Weather: **Warm & sunny**

Pos	Driver	Team	Result	Stops	Qualifying Time	Grid
1	**Max Verstappen**	Red Bull	1h36m21.757s	2	1m21.299s	1
2	**Carlos Sainz Jr**	Ferrari	1h36m22.750s	2	1m22.096s	3
3	**Lewis Hamilton**	Mercedes	1h36m28.763s	2	1m22.891s	4
4	**George Russell**	Mercedes	1h36m34.070s	2	1m23.557s	8
5	**Charles Leclerc !**	Ferrari	1h36m36.925s	1	no time	19
6	**Esteban Ocon**	Alpine	1h36m45.647s	2	1m23.529s	7
7	**Valtteri Bottas**	Alfa Romeo	1h36m47.004s	1	1m26.788s	11
8	**Guanyu Zhou**	Alfa Romeo	1h36m48.709s	2	1m24.030s	10
9	**Fernando Alonso ***	Alpine	1h36m51.702s	2	1m21.944s	2
10	**Lance Stroll**	Aston Martin	1h36m59.979s	1	1m35.532s	17
11	**Daniel Ricciardo**	McLaren	1h37m04.804s	2	1m23.749s	9
12	**Sebastian Vettel**	Aston Martin	1h37m06.002s	2	1m34.512s	16
13	**Alexander Albon**	Williams	1h37m06.650s	2	1m26.858s	12
14	**Pierre Gasly**	AlphaTauri	1h37m06.940s	2	1m34.492s	15
15	**Lando Norris ****	McLaren	1h37m13.902s	2	no time	14
16	**Nicholas Latifi**	Williams	1h21.735s	2	1m35.660s	18
17	**Kevin Magnussen**	Haas	1h37m29.937s	1	1m22.960s	5
R	**Yuki Tsunoda !**	AlphaTauri	47 laps/spun off	2	1m36.575s	20
R	**Mick Schumacher**	Haas	18 laps/hydraulics	0	1m23.356s	6
R	**Sergio Perez**	Red Bull	7 laps/hydraulics	0	1m33.127s	13

FASTEST LAP: SAINZ, 1M15.749S, 128.784MPH/207.258KPH ON LAP 63 • RACE LEADERS: VERSTAPPEN 1-8, 20-42, 49-70, SAINZ JR 9-19, 43-48
! REQUIRED TO START FROM BACK OF GRID FOR USING ADDITIONAL POWER UNIT ELEMENTS
* 5S PENALTY FOR MORE THAN ONE CHANGE OF DIRECTION • ** 5S PENALTY FOR SPEEDING IN THE PIT LANE

A sensational getaway gave Verstappen a clear lead over Alonso as they turned into Turn 1.

BRITISH GP

Ferrari's Carlos Sainz Jr finally landed his first F1 win midway through his eighth F1 campaign, but this achievement was overshadowed by Guanyu Zhou being saved from serious injury by the halo on his Alfa Romeo, which protected him during a violent first-corner accident.

Carlos Sainz had given himself his best opportunity of victory by qualifying on pole for the first time, and he was thus upset when Max Verstappen blasted past him at the start. However, moments later the red flags were flown as there had been a monumental accident behind him.

There was side-to-side contact between George Russell's Williams and Guanyu Zhou's Alfa Romeo, with Alex Albon's Williams spearing into the pit wall in avoidance as the Chinese driver's Alfa Romeo inverted, skidded through the gravel trap, hit the tyre wall and flipped into a tiny gap between the back of that and the grandstand beyond. Miraculously, and clearly due to the halo in front of his head, he was extracted, alive.

As the red flags were flown to mark the cessation of the race, the drivers were faced with their second shock of the day when they drove past seven protesters sitting on the track in a dangerous protest for the Just Stop Oil campaign.

After an hour's delay, the drivers set off again and this time Sainz stayed in the lead, resisting another push from Verstappen. He didn't resist it for long, though, as Verstappen moved into the lead on lap 10 with a move into Chapel when Sainz ran wide. Three laps later, Sainz was back in front when Verstappen suffered a puncture. On rejoining though, his RB19 was a handful and was later found to have a piece of debris jammed beneath it.

By pitting later than his rivals, Lewis Hamilton led for the first time in 2022 but then there was a safety car deployment for Esteban Ocon's Alpine to be moved to safety. On release, the front runners had a fabulous scrap, with Hamilton doing the best overtaking as he fought with Leclerc and Perez. As this happened, however, Sainz edged clear and so, at his 150th attempt, Sainz became an F1 winner.

Guanyu Zhou's Alfa Romeo arrived at Abbey upside down and then flipped over the tyre barrier.

SILVERSTONE ROUND 10

DATE: **3 JULY 2022**

Laps: **52** · Distance: **190.262 miles/306.198km** · Weather: **Warm & bright**

Pos	Driver	Team	Result	Stops	Qualifying Time	Grid
1	Carlos Sainz Jr	Ferrari	1h21m20.440s	2	1m40.983s	1
2	Sergio Perez	Red Bull	1h21m24.219s	2	1m41.616s	4
3	Lewis Hamilton	Mercedes	1h21m26.665s	2	1m41.995s	5
4	Charles Leclerc	Ferrari	1h21m28.986ms	1	1m41.298s	3
5	Fernando Alonso	Alpine	1h21m30.011s	2	1m42.116s	7
6	Lando Norris	McLaren	1h21m32.383s	2	1m42.084s	6
7	Max Verstappen	Red Bull	1h21m39.217s	3	1m41.055s	2
8	Mick Schumacher	Haas	1h21m39.435s	2	1m42.708s	19
9	Sebastian Vettel	Aston Martin	1h21m42.796s	2	1m42.666s	18
10	Kevin Magnussen	Haas	1h21m45.030s	1	1m42.159s	17
11	Lance Stroll	Aston Martin	1h21m46.587s	2	1m43.430s	20
12	Nicholas Latifi	Williams	1h21m52.951s	2	2m03.095s	10
13	Daniel Ricciardo	McLaren	1h21m53.257s	3	1m44.355s	14
14	Yuki Tsunoda	AlphaTauri	1h22m01.350s	2	1m44.311s	13
R	Esteban Ocon	Alpine	37 laps/fuel pump	1	1m45.190s	15
R	Pierre Gasly	AlphaTauri	26 laps/crash damage	1	1m43.702s	11
R	Valtteri Bottas	Alfa Romeo	20 laps/gearbox	0	1m44.232s	12
R	George Russell	Mercedes	0 laps/outside assistance	0	1m42.161s	8
R	Guanyu Zhou	Alfa Romeo	0 laps/accident	0	1m42.719s	9
R	Alexander Albon	Williams	0 laps/accident	0	1m42.078s	16

FASTEST LAP: HAMILTON, 1M30.510S, 145.594MPH/234.312KPH ON LAP 52
RACE LEADERS: SAINZ JR 1-9 & 13-20 & 39 & 43-52, VERSTAPPEN 10-12, LECLERC 21-25 & 34-38 & 40-42, HAMILTON 26-33

AUSTRIAN GP

Charles Leclerc's season got back on track with a dominant win that moved him back to second in the title chase, although the Monegasque had a mechanical scare before leading Max Verstappen home on a day when neither Perez nor Sainz Jr scored.

Max Verstappen won the sprint race and so started the Grand Prix from pole position. He duly led the first 11 laps before Charles Leclerc took the lead for Ferrari in a fashion that left the Dutchman crestfallen since the pass into turn 4 was made so easily, such was the Ferrari's extra speed and his own car's lack of grip as its tyres wore.

His Red Bull team-mate Sergio Perez found his race hampered as early as the first lap when he clashed with George Russell's Mercedes and had to recover from a spin before pitting for repairs. Russell nursed his car around with a damaged front wing until lap 12 but was hit with a five-second penalty as he was blamed for the collision. At least he got to finish, though, coming home fourth, whereas the Mexican didn't go the distance.

Ferrari was in control and Verstappen had no answers. However, the Italian team didn't get to achieve a maximum points haul as its dream of a one-two finish went up in smoke with 14 laps to go when Sainz Jr's engine failed in a fiery manner. Then, Leclerc had a late-race scare when his car began to suffer from its throttle sticking at low speeds. Even with the safety car being deployed to remove Sainz Jr's car, thus allowing Verstappen to close up a comfortable gap, Leclerc was never going to be passed. He nursed the problem to collect his third win of 2022 and so moved into second in the points table ahead of Perez, who retired because of crash damage.

The only thing that Lewis Hamilton enjoyed about the meeting was rising from eighth to third for his third podium finish in a row. Before that, he was rightly upset when he was jeered by sections of the crowd after crashing in qualifying, and it was only right that Leclerc and others came out in support.

RED BULL RING ROUND 11 — DATE: 11 JULY 2022

Laps: 71 · Distance: **190.420 miles/306.452km** · Weather: **Hot & sunny**

Pos	Driver	Team	Result	Stops	Qualifying Time	Grid
1	Charles Leclerc	Ferrari	1h24m24.312s	3	-	2
2	Max Verstappen	Red Bull	1h24m25.844s	3	-	1
3	Lewis Hamilton	Mercedes	1h25m05.529s	2	-	8
4	George Russell	Mercedes	1h25m23.284s	2	-	4
5	Esteban Ocon	Alpine	1h25m32.748s	2	-	6
6	Mick Schumacher	Haas	70 laps	2	-	9
7	Lando Norris	McLaren	70 laps	2	-	10
8	Kevin Magnussen	Haas	70 laps	2	-	7
9	Daniel Ricciardo	McLaren	70 laps	2	-	11
10	Fernando Alonso !	Alpine	70 laps	3	-	19
11	Valtteri Bottas !	Alfa Romeo	70 laps	2	-	20
12	Alexander Albon	Williams	70 laps	2	-	15
13	Lance Stroll	Aston Martin	70 laps	2	-	12
14	Guanyu Zhou	Alfa Romeo	70 laps	2	-	13
15	Pierre Gasly *	AlphaTauri	70 laps	2	-	14
16	Yuki Tsunoda	AlphaTauri	70 laps	2	-	16
17	Sebastian Vettel **	Aston Martin	70 laps	2	-	18
R	Carlos Sainz Jr	Ferrari	56 laps/engine	2	-	3
R	Nicholas Latifi	Williams	48 laps/floor	2	-	17
R	Sergio Perez	Red Bull	24 laps/crash damage	1	-	5

FASTEST LAP: VERSTAPPEN, 1M07.275S, 143.576MPH/231.063KPH ON LAP 62 · RACE LEADERS: VERSTAPPEN 1-11 & 28-32 & 51-52, LECLERC 12-26 & 33-49 & 53-71, SAINZ JR 27 & 50 · * 5S PENALTY FOR CAUSING A COLLISION · ** 5S PENALTY FOR EXCEEDING TRACK LIMITS ! REQUIRED TO START FROM BACK OF GRID FOR USING ADDITIONAL POWER UNIT ELEMENTS · NB GRID DETERMINED BY FINISHING ORDER IN SPRINT RACE

Leclerc even had time to enjoy the view as he dominated, until a safety car closed things up.

FRENCH GP

Max Verstappen looked to have done enough in the early stages of the race to win in France, but then title rival Charles Leclerc made a mistake and crashed on his own to make life very easy for Red Bull's Dutchman to win as he pleased.

Charles Leclerc rediscovered his ability to set pole positions after three races away from the premier position on the grid. With a margin of 0.3 seconds over Max Verstappen, things looked good. Team-mate Carlos Sainz Jr was not so fortunate, as a change of control electronic parts took him past his season's allowance which left him confined to the back of the pack. With Mercedes' form dropping away in qualifying, things looked good for Leclerc to regain some of the ground that he'd lost in recent rounds.

Leading away at the start was what he wanted and got, with Verstappen just doing enough to hold off a fast-starting Lewis Hamilton.

However, Verstappen had closed in before pitting on lap 16 and was looking well placed when he was gifted the win on a plate as Leclerc ran wide at turn 11, Le Beausset, and spun off into the tyre wall. Leclerc was beside himself with frustration afterwards, saying that he didn't deserve to win the title if he carried on making mistakes like this.

Verstappen duly stretched his points margin to 63 over Leclerc, with Perez now just seven points further back.

Hamilton came home an exhausted second on a day when the drivers really suffered in Europe's heat spike. He reckoned that he had lost 3kg and took a while to recover in order to enjoy his best result of the season so far.

Team-mate George Russell fought to the finish and moved past Perez with a few laps to go to claim the final position on the podium, albeit only after resisting a stern attempt by the Mexican to take the place back. The double podium for Mercedes moved them to within 44 points of Ferrari, highlighting how the Italian team and its drivers were squandering their cars' performance.

Leclerc was upset after his slip-up handed victory to Verstappen, who moved 63 points clear.

PAUL RICARD ROUND 12   DATE:**24 JULY 2022**
Laps: **53** · Distance: **192.392 miles/309.626km** · Weather: **Very hot & sunny**

Pos	Driver	Team	Result	Stops	Qualifying Time	Grid
1	**Max Verstappen**	Red Bull	1h30m02.112s	1	1m31.176s	2
2	**Lewis Hamilton**	Mercedes	1h30m12.699s	1	1m31.765s	4
3	**George Russell**	Mercedes	1h30m18.607s	1	1m32.131s	6
4	**Sergio Perez**	Red Bull	1h30m19.422s	1	1m31.335s	3
5	**Carlos Sainz Jr ***	Ferrari	1h30m30.984s	2	no time	19
6	**Fernando Alonso**	Alpine	1h30m44.991s	1	1m32.552s	7
7	**Lando Norris**	McLaren	1h30m54.138s	1	1m32.032s	5
8	**Esteban Ocon**	Alpine	1h30m59.071s	1	1m33.048s	10
9	**Daniel Ricciardo**	McLaren	1h31m02.484s	1	1m32.922s	9
10	**Lance Stroll**	Aston Martin	1h31m04.661s	1	1m33.439s	15
11	**Sebastian Vettel**	Aston Martin	1h31m06.606s	1	1m33.276s	12
12	**Pierre Gasly**	AlphaTauri	1h31m07.560s	1	1m33.439s	14
13	**Alexander Albon**	Williams	1h31m10.677s	1	1m33.307s	13
14	**Valtteri Bottas**	Alfa Romeo	1h31m18.778s	2	1m33.052s	11
15	**Mick Schumacher**	Haas	1h31m22.508s	2	1m33.701s	17
16	**Guanyu Zhou**	Alfa Romeo	47 laps/power unit	2	1m33.674s	16
R	**Nicholas Latifi**	Williams	40 laps/crash damage	2	1m33.794s	18
R	**Kevin Magnussen ***	Haas	37 laps/crash damage	2	no time	20
R	**Charles Leclerc**	Ferrari	17 laps/spun off	0	1m30.872s	1
R	**Yuki Tsunoda**	AlphaTauri	17 laps/crash damage	1	1m32.780s	8

FASTEST LAP: **SAINZ JR, 1M35.781S, 136.437MPH/219.575KPH ON LAP 51** · RACE LEADERS: **LECLERC 1-17, HAMILTON 18, VERSTAPPEN 19-53**
* REQUIRED TO START FROM BACK OF GRID AS ADDITIONAL POWER UNIT ELEMENTS HAD BEEN USED

HUNGARIAN GP

This was a remarkable performance from Max Verstappen as he survived a spin to advance from tenth on the grid to victory in a wet/dry race. Title rival Charles Leclerc was in a position to win, but again suffered from Ferrari's poor race strategy.

Ferrari were surprised not to be fastest in qualifying after dominating practice, but Carlos Sainz Jr and Charles Leclerc were pipped to pole by a sensational lap from George Russell. The Englishman then led for the first 15 laps before pitting for medium tyres. This allowed Carlos Sainz Jr into the lead, albeit only for a lap before his team-mate took over when the Spaniard was called into the pits.

Leclerc stayed out until lap 21 before making his first pit visit, five laps after Red Bull had called in Verstappen to change tyres, and the Dutchman managed to be in front of Lewis Hamilton when the Mercedes driver emerged from his first pit stop three laps later. This put Verstappen into fourth, behind Russell, Leclerc and Sainz Jr, with Leclerc reeling in the Mercedes driver before passing him for the lead on lap 31.

On lap 38, Verstappen made a second stop and Ferrari, already known for poor race strategy in 2022, brought Leclerc in a lap later and changed his car on to hard compound tyres. This was a disaster as he would have been better served by being allowed to stay out longer, as he wanted to, and thus have the scope to make a later second stop and so end the race on the softer tyre. It was an extraordinary gaffe.

As it was, Verstappen caught and passed him with ease. However, on the very next lap, Verstappen spun at turn 13 and so had to do it all again. Once all the drivers had made their second stops, Verstappen was in front and Lewis Hamilton was able to make a better go of things as Mercedes left him out until lap 51 before bringing him in for soft compound tyres. This was the way to do things and Hamilton passed team-mate Russell to claim his second second-place finish in succession, with Russell holding on to finish third, just ahead of Sainz Jr, Sergio Perez and Leclerc.

HUNGARORING ROUND 13
DATE: 31 JULY 2022
Laps: **70** · Distance: **190.531 miles/306.630km** · Weather: **Hot & overcast**

Pos	Driver	Team	Result	Stops	Qualifying Time	Grid
1	**Max Verstappen**	Red Bull	1h39m35.912s	2	1m18.823s	10
2	**Lewis Hamilton**	Mercedes	1h39m43.746s	2	1m18.142s	7
3	**George Russell**	Mercedes	1h39m48.249s	2	1m17.377s	1
4	**Carlos Sainz Jr**	Ferrari	1h39m50.491s	2	1m17.421s	2
5	**Sergio Perez**	Red Bull	1h39m51.600s	2	1m18.516s	11
6	**Charles Leclerc**	Ferrari	1h39m51.959s	3	1m17.567s	3
7	**Lando Norris**	McLaren	1h40m54.212s	2	1m17.769s	4
8	**Fernando Alonso**	Alpine	69 laps	1	1m18.078s	6
9	**Esteban Ocon**	Alpine	69 laps	1	1m18.018s	5
10	**Sebastian Vettel**	Aston Martin	69 laps	2	1m19.273s	18
11	**Lance Stroll**	Aston Martin	69 laps	2	1m19.137s	14
12	**Pierre Gasly !**	AlphaTauri	69 laps	2	1m19.527s	20
13	**Guanyu Zhou**	Alfa Romeo	69 laps	2	1m18.573s	12
14	**Mick Schumacher**	Haas	69 laps	2	1m19.202s	15
15	**Daniel Ricciardo ***	McLaren	69 laps	2	1m18.379s	9
16	**Kevin Magnussen**	Haas	69 laps	3	1m18.825s	13
17	**Alexander Albon**	Williams	69 laps	3	1m19.256s	17
18	**Nicholas Latifi**	Williams	69 laps	3	1m19.570s	19
19	**Yuki Tsunoda**	AlphaTauri	68 laps	3	1m19.240s	16
R	**Valtteri Bottas**	Alfa Romeo	65 laps/power loss	1	1m18.157s	8

FASTEST LAP: HAMILTON, 1M21.386S, 120.413MPH/193.787KPH ON LAP 57 · RACE LEADERS: RUSSELL 1-15 & 22-30, SAINZ JR 16 & 40-46, LECLERC 17-21 & 31-39, HAMILTON 47-50, VERSTAPPEN 51-70 · * 5S PENALTY FOR CAUSING A COLLISION
! REQUIRED TO START FROM PIT LANE FOR CAR BEING MODIFIED UNDER PARC FERMÉ CONDITIONS & USING ADDITIONAL POWER UNIT ELEMENTS

Leclerc leads Verstappen, but Ferrari's tactics were poor and he was five places back by the end.

BELGIAN GP

Max Verstappen hit extraordinary form at a race where rival teams hoped that performance might be more balanced. However, he found so much pace that he was able to recover from a grid penalty – which had relegated him to start back in 14th on the grid – to win with ease.

Max Verstappen and title rival Charles Leclerc were both made to start from the rear of the grid as their cars had used extra power unit elements. Fortunately for them, so too were Esteban Ocon, Lando Norris, Guanyu Zhou, Mick Schumacher and Yuki Tsunoda, meaning that they lined up 14th and 15th respectively, with Verstappen empowered by the fact that his 'pole' lap had been 0.61 seconds clear of his closest rival, Carlos Sainz Jr. For the record, the Mercedes duo, although seventh (Lewis Hamilton) and eighth (George Russell), were fully 1.7 seconds and 2 seconds off his pace.

Sainz Jr was able to lead away from his adopted pole position, but there was soon trouble behind him as both Hamilton and Fernando Alonso shot past Sergio Perez and then fought over second as they entered Les Combes. Hamilton did not see Alonso's Alpine in his blind spot and turned across its nose, tipping his Mercedes off the ground, which was too damaged to continue.

This brought out the safety car for three laps and then the field was released, with Verstappen immediately attacking from eighth place, passing Alexander Albon and Daniel Ricciardo within a lap, then hunting down Sebastian Vettel. In turn, Alonso, Russell and Perez were overtaken, putting him into the lead by the 12th lap after Sainz Jr had pitted.

Any hopes for Ferrari fans that Leclerc might also have rocketed up the order were dashed when he pitted on lap 3 because, oddly, a tear-off strip from his visor had lodged in a brake duct.

Verstappen made his first pit stop four laps after Sainz Jr had and was in control thereafter, with Perez claiming second to make it a doubly dominant day for Red Bull Racing. Leclerc could only finish fifth, which became sixth with a penalty.

Hamilton's race was dramatic and short as he hit and rode over Alonso's Alpine at the first corner.

SPA-FRANCORCHAMPS ROUND 14 DATE:**28 AUGUST 2022**
Laps: **44** • Distance: **191.414 miles/308.052km** • Weather: **Hot & sunny**

Pos	Driver	Team	Result	Stops	Qualifying Time	Grid
1	**Max Verstappen !**	Red Bull	1h25m52.894s	2	1m43.665s	14
2	**Sergio Perez**	Red Bull	1h26m10.735s	2	1m44.462s	2
3	**Carlos Sainz Jr**	Ferrari	1h26m19.780s	2	1m44.297s	1
4	**George Russell**	Mercedes	1h26m22.034s	2	1m45.776s	5
5	**Fernando Alonso**	Alpine	1h27m06.150s	2	1m45.368s	3
6	**Charles Leclerc !, ***	Ferrari	1h27m07.830s	3	1m44.553s	15
7	**Esteban Ocon !**	Alpine	1h27m08.534s	2	1m45.180s	16
8	**Sebastian Vettel**	Aston Martin	1h27m11.001s	2	1m46.344s	10
9	**Pierre Gasly !!**	AlphaTauri	1h27m25.075s	2	1m45.827s	8
10	**Alexander Albon**	Williams	1h27m34.794s	2	1m45.837s	6
11	**Lance Stroll**	Aston Martin	1h27m35.972s	2	1m46.611s	9
12	**Lando Norris !**	McLaren	1h27m37.633s	2	1m46.178s	17
13	**Yuki Tsunoda !**	AlphaTauri	1h27m38.111s	2	1m46.692s	20
14	**Guanyu Zhou !**	Alfa Romeo	1h27m39.146s	2	1m46.085s	18
15	**Daniel Ricciardo**	McLaren	1h27m40.057s	2	1m45.767s	7
16	**Kevin Magnussen**	Haas	43 laps	2	1m46.557s	12
17	**Mick Schumacher !**	Haas	43 laps	2	1m47.718s	19
18	**Nicholas Latifi**	Williams	43 laps	3	1m46.401s	11
R	**Valtteri Bottas !**	Alfa Romeo	1 lap/accident	0	1m47.866s	13
R	**Lewis Hamilton**	Mercedes	0 laps/collision	0	1m45.503s	4

FASTEST LAP: VERSTAPPEN, 1M49.354S, 143.265MPH/230.575KPH ON LAP 32 • RACE LEADERS: SAINZ JR 1-10 & 16-17, PEREZ 11, VERSTAPPEN 12-15 & 18-44 • ! MADE TO START FROM BACK OF GRID FOR USING ADDITIONAL POWER UNIT ELEMENTS • !! STARTED FROM PIT LANE
* 5S PENALTY FOR SPEEDING IN THE PIT LANE

DUTCH GP

Lewis Hamilton went ballistic at the end of this race, furious that his team's race strategy had not only cost him victory but even a podium finish when a safety car was deployed late on. Max Verstappen thus took the win that his raucous home fans demanded.

The first job was to take pole position, as Zandvoort is not a circuit on which it is easy to overtake. The Ferrari drivers looked to be best placed to do this, but vociferous home support spurred Max Verstappen on and he just managed to outstrip them.

At the start, Verstappen led away, with Charles Leclerc tucking in behind as the field negotiated the first corner, Tarzan, without any incident other than Lewis Hamilton having minor contact with Carlos Sainz Jr.

The Mercedes drivers had started on the harder tyre compound and both managed to lap at a competitive pace, so their rivals reacted to this. When Ferrari brought Sainz Jr in, his tyres weren't all ready and the delay dropped him seven places. Being hit later on with a five-second penalty for an unsafe release in the pits added insult to injury.

Hamilton took the lead as Verstappen and the others pitted, staying out 11 laps longer before pitting and putting Verstappen back into the lead.

Yuki Tsunoda changed the course of the race when he pulled his AlphaTauri to the side of the track, convinced that something was amiss on his out lap. He pitted again then rejoined, before the team told him something was definitely wrong and to pull off. This triggered a virtual safety car period and, ten laps later, there was a real safety car deployment when Valtteri Bottas parked his Alfa Romeo.

Verstappen dived in for a set of soft tyres, but Hamilton stayed out and so took the lead. However, Russell and Leclerc followed Verstappen's example and also asked for a set of soft tyres. This left Hamilton as a sitting duck and he was picked off by all three of them in consecutive laps on their fresher rubber. And, as Verstappen eased away to make it four wins in a row, Hamilton was furious.

ZANDVOORT ROUND 15

DATE: 4 SEPTEMBER 2022

Laps: 72 · Distance: 190.504 miles/306.587km · Weather: Warm & bright

Pos	Driver	Team	Result	Stops	Qualifying Time	Grid
1	Max Verstappen	Red Bull	1h36m42.773s	3	1m10.342s	1
2	George Russell	Mercedes	1h36m46.844s	3	1m11.147s	6
3	Charles Leclerc	Ferrari	1h36m53.702s	3	1m10.363s	2
4	Lewis Hamilton	Mercedes	1h36m55.789s	2	1m10.648s	4
5	Sergio Perez	Red Bull	1h37m00.941s	3	1m11.077s	5
6	Fernando Alonso	Alpine	1h37m01.527s	2	1m11.613s	13
7	Lando Norris	McLaren	1h37m02.079s	3	1m11.174s	7
8	Carlos Sainz Jr *	Ferrari	1h37m03.689s	3	1m10.434s	3
9	Esteban Ocon	Alpine	1h37m03.890s	2	1m11.605s	12
10	Lance Stroll	Aston Martin	1h37m05.232s	3	no time	10
11	Pierre Gasly	AlphaTauri	1h37m09.782s	3	1m11.512s	11
12	Alexander Albon	Williams	1h37m13.163s	3	1m11.802s	15
13	Mick Schumacher	Haas	1h37m15.768s	3	1m11.442s	8
14	Sebastian Vettel **	Aston Martin	1h37m18.780s	3	1m12.391s	19
15	Kevin Magnussen	Haas	1h37m19.642s	3	1m12.319s	18
16	Guanyu Zhou	Alfa Romeo	1h37m20.093s	3	1m11.704s	14
17	Daniel Ricciardo	McLaren	1h37m20.537s	4	1m12.081s	17
18	Nicholas Latifi	Williams	71 laps	3	1m13.353s	20
R	Valtteri Bottas	Alfa Romeo	53 laps/fuel system	2	1m11.961s	16
R	Yuki Tsunoda	AlphaTauri	43 laps/differential	3	1m12.556s	9

FASTEST LAP: VERSTAPPEN, 1M13.652S, 129.352MPH/208.173KPH ON LAP 62 · RACE LEADERS: VERSTAPPEN 1-18, 29-56 & 61-72, HAMILTON 19-28 & 57-60 · * 5S PENALTY FOR UNSAFE RELEASE · ** 5S PENALTY FOR IGNORING BLUE FLAGS

The home fans turn the air orange in celebration of Max Verstappen's home win at Zandvoort.

ITALIAN GP

This was a race with an unsatisfactory start as the number of drivers moved back on the grid made the shape of the race odd. Then, finishing behind the safety car brought back memories of the 2021 finale. Max Verstappen still made it five in a row.

The charge to the first corner had a funny look to it. Charles Leclerc led the way followed by George Russell, but many of the regular front runners were starting further back due to grid penalties. You had to look back to seventh for Max Verstappen, 13th for Sergio Perez, 18th for Carlos Sainz Jr and 19th for Lewis Hamilton, all choosing this race to take engine-change penalties as it's a circuit on which overtaking is relatively possible.

With Verstappen in such strong form – arriving at Monza with a four-race winning streak – no one doubted that he had the speed to make it towards the front, but surely his six-place initial deficit to the Ferrari team leader was going to be too much to make up?.

However, when the race settled down and Leclerc led with ease, surely it was going to be Ferrari's day at the perfect place to restore the team's reputation? But this was 2022 and so, of course, that didn't happen. Although there was another fumble by Ferrari, it was the pace of Verstappen's Red Bull that was simply irresistible and he advanced through the field relentlessly.

Verstappen's early laps were very impressive as he charged up to second by lap 5. Helping him apply the pressure on Sainz was the fact that his car was wearing its tyres less. This made Ferrari gamble on going on to a two-stop strategy in the hope of having fresher rubber late in the race. Yet even this was not enough and Verstappen won regardless, with Leclerc coming through to second as the race ended behind the safety car while Daniel Ricciardo's McLaren was moved. This was a cack-handed process, as it emerged in front of Russell instead of leader Verstappen, delaying the process and meaning that there was no race to the finish.

Charles Leclerc holds off George Russell at the start, but it wasn't to be Ferrari's day.

MONZA ROUND 16

DATE: **11 SEPTEMBER 2022**

Laps: **53** · Distance: **190.587 miles/306.720km** · Weather: **Warm & bright**

Pos	Driver	Team	Result	Stops	Qualifying Time	Grid
1	**Max Verstappen !**	Red Bull	1h20m27.511s	2	1m20.306s	7
2	**Charles Leclerc**	Ferrari	1h20m29.957s	3	1m20.161s	1
3	**George Russell**	Mercedes	1h20m30.916s	2	1m21.542s	2
4	**Carlos Sainz Jr ^**	Ferrari	1h20m32.572s	2	1m20.429s	18
5	**Lewis Hamilton ^**	Mercedes	1h20m32.891s	1	1m21.524s	19
6	**Sergio Perez !!**	Red Bull	1h20m33.602s	2	1m21.206s	13
7	**Lando Norris**	McLaren	1h20m33.718s	2	1m21.584s	3
8	**Pierre Gasly**	AlphaTauri	1h20m33.907s	1	1m22.648s	5
9	**Nyck de Vries**	Williams	1h20m34.633s	1	1m22.471s	8
10	**Guanyu Zhou**	Alfa Romeo	1h20m35.421s	1	1m22.577s	9
11	**Esteban Ocon !**	Alpine	1h20m35.834s	1	1m22.130s	14
12	**Mick Schumacher !!!**	Haas	1h20m36.060s	1	1m23.005s	17
13	**Valtteri Bottas !!!**	Alfa Romeo	52 laps	1	1m33.235s	15
14	**Yuki Tsunoda ^**	AlphaTauri	52 laps	2	no time	20
15	**Nicholas Latifi**	Williams	52 laps	2	1m22.587s	10
16	**Kevin Magnussen */!!!**	Haas	52 laps	2	1m22.908s	16
R	**Daniel Ricciardo**	McLaren	45 laps/oil leak	1	1m21.925s	4
R	**Lance Stroll**	Aston Martin	39 laps/withdrawn	1	1m22.748s	12
R	**Fernando Alonso**	Alpine	31 laps/water pump	0	1m22.089s	6
R	**Sebastian Vettel**	Aston Martin	10 laps/power unit	0	1m22.636s	11

FASTEST LAP: PEREZ, 1M24.030S, 154.213MPH/248.182KPH ON LAP 46 · RACE LEADERS: LECLERC 1-11 & 26-33, VERSTAPPEN 12-25 & 34-53
* 5S PENALTY FOR LEAVING TRACK & GAINING AN ADVANTAGE · ! 5-PLACE GRID PENALTY FOR USING ADDITIONAL POWER UNIT ELEMENTS
!! 10-PLACE GRID PENALTY · !!! 15-PLACE GRID PENALTY · ^ REQUIRED TO START FROM BACK OF GRID FOR USING ADDITIONAL POWER UNIT ELEMENTS

SINGAPORE GP

Delayed by over an hour after torrential rain, the race had action from the very first turn. Yet, after taking the lead from pole man Charles Leclerc with a brilliant start, Sergio Perez absorbed race-long pressure from the Ferrari driver to take his second win of the year.

It's always hot and humid in Singapore and it was even more so than usual, with heavy rain falling an hour and a half before the start. Unfortunately, it then took an age to dry. Eventually, with the start delayed by more than an hour, the drivers set off on an extremely slippery track.

While Sergio Perez nailed his getaway and accelerated past Charles Leclerc's Ferrari, Lewis Hamilton got it wrong at the first corner complex, his Mercedes running wide and falling to fourth. Worse was to follow when he bent his car's nose against a wall, forcing an extra stop that dropped him down the order. Then, late on, while heading Max Verstappen, he ran wide again as he pressured Sebastian Vettel's Aston Martin and dropped two places.

Verstappen had been hampered by his car not having enough fuel in it at the end of qualifying, costing him the chance to go for a final run. He was livid and had to start eighth, but was able to reach only seventh after falling to 12th at the start and spending the rest of the race trapped behind slower cars.

Regular points gatherer George Russell failed to get into Q3 and then had to start from the tail of the grid, so had little chance of making it up to the top ten on this track that is so hard to pass on. Eventually, after experimenting with slicks, he finished last.

Benefiting from this and from other slip-ups, including Fernando Alonso's Alpine retiring with engine trouble, McLaren claimed fourth and fifth, thus moving them ahead of Alpine in the constructors' championship.

Perez was still under investigation when the chequered flag fell for not remaining within ten car lengths of the safety car at the second restart. However, Red Bull had anticipated a five-second penalty and urged Perez to increase the gap to Leclerc to more than that, which he did, so kept his win.

MARINA BAY ROUND 17
DATE: 2 OCTOBER 2022

Laps: 59 • Distance: 185.614 miles/298.717km • Weather: Hot & humid

Pos	Driver	Team	Result	Stops	Qualifying Time	Grid
1	Sergio Perez	Red Bull	2h02m15.238s	1	1m49.434s	2
2	Charles Leclerc	Ferrari	2h02m22.833s	1	1m49.412s	1
3	Carlos Sainz Jr	Ferrari	2h02m30.543s	1	1m49.583s	4
4	Lando Norris	McLaren	2h02m41.371s	1	1m50.584s	6
5	Daniel Ricciardo	McLaren	2h03m13.520s	1	1m56.226s	16
6	Lance Stroll	Aston Martin	2h03m16.568s	1	1m54.211s	11
7	Max Verstappen	Red Bull	2h03m19.063s	2	1m51.395s	8
8	Sebastian Vettel	Aston Martin	2h03m20.270s	1	1m54.380s	13
9	Lewis Hamilton	Mercedes	2h03m21.748s	1	1m49.466s	3
10	Pierre Gasly	AlphaTauri	2h03m29.994s	1	1m51.211s	7
11	Valtteri Bottas	Alfa Romeo	2h03m49.082s	1	1m56.083s	15
12	Kevin Magnussen	Haas	2h03m52.848s	2	1m51.573s	9
13	Mick Schumacher	Haas	58 laps	2	1m54.370s	12
14	George Russell !	Mercedes	57 laps	4	1m54.012s	20
R	Yuki Tsunoda	AlphaTauri	34 laps/accident	1	1m51.983s	10
R	Esteban Ocon	Alpine	26 laps/power unit	0	1m56.337s	17
R	Alexander Albon	Williams	25 laps/crash damage	0	1m56.985s	18
R	Fernando Alonso	Alpine	20 laps/power unit	0	1m49.966s	5
R	Nicholas Latifi	Williams	7 laps/crash damage	0	1m57.532s	19
R	Guanyu Zhou	Alfa Romeo	6 laps/collision	0	1m55.518s	14

FASTEST LAP: RUSSELL, 1M46.458S, 106.385MPH/171.211KPH ON LAP 54 • RACE LEADERS: PEREZ 1-59
! HAD TO START FROM BACK OF GRID FOR CAR BEING WORKED ON IN PARC FERME

Sergio Perez leads Charles Leclerc's pole-starting Ferrari into turn 1. He went on to win.

Max Verstappen landed his second F1 title but, such was the confusion over whether full points would be awarded after a rain-delayed and shortened race, he hadn't a clue if he had done it or not as he waited to step up on to the podium.

Weather conditions, as they can be in Japan's typhoon season, were awful. The first attempt at getting the race under way was a short one, as Carlos Sainz Jr aquaplaned off after the hairpin. This brought out the safety car so that his Ferrari could be removed safely. However, Pierre Gasly, whose AlphaTauri had been damaged by an advertising hoarding the Ferrari had knocked on to the track, emerged from the pits just as the red flag was waved to stop the race.

There was then very nearly a hideous postscript, as a recovery vehicle had moved on to the track and Gasly had no warning of it as he came blasting past. This would have been shocking on any track, but it was unforgivable on the one on which Jules Bianchi suffered fatal injuries in 2014 when his Marussia hit a recovery vehicle.

After a wait of two hours, the race got going again and Verstappen stretched his lead to half a minute, no doubt enjoying reports of team-mate Sergio Perez harrying Charles Leclerc for second. This came to a head on the final lap when Leclerc cut the chicane in his quest to keep ahead. However, a five-second penalty for the move dropped him to third.

The teams understood that a reduced points scale would be used for the race having lasted for more than half the planned distance but less than 75 per cent, so just 19 points for a win. However, this would have been the case if the race hadn't been able to resume, but it had, so full points were awarded. The confusion was not a good look.

Esteban Ocon scored a brilliant fourth for Alpine, with Fernando Alonso gambling on an extra pit stop, after which he flew on his fresh rubber past an inspired Nicholas Latifi, George Russell and very nearly Sebastian Vettel, failing to catch the Aston Martin by just 0.011 seconds.

Max Verstappen waves to the fans after claiming his 12th win and becoming champion again.

SUZUKA ROUND 18

DATE: **9 OCTOBER 2022**

Laps: 28 · Distance: **100.846 miles/162.296km** · Weather: **Warm & wet**

Pos	Driver	Team	Result	Stops	Qualifying Time	Grid
1	Max Verstappen	Red Bull	3h01m44.004s	2	1m29.304s	1
2	Sergio Perez	Red Bull	3h02m11.070s	2	1m29.709s	4
3	Charles Leclerc *	Ferrari	3h02m15.767s	2	1m29.314s	2
4	Esteban Ocon	Alpine	3h02m23.689s	2	1m30.165s	5
5	Lewis Hamilton	Mercedes	3h02m24.330s	2	1m30.261s	6
6	Sebastian Vettel	Aston Martin	3h02m30.362s	2	1m30.554s	9
7	Fernando Alonso	Alpine	3h02m30.373s	3	1m30.322s	7
8	George Russell	Mercedes	3h02m31.665s	2	1m30.389s	8
9	Nicholas Latifi !	Williams	3h02m54.147s	2	1m31.511s	19
10	Lando Norris	McLaren	3h02m54.786s	2	1m31.003s	10
11	Daniel Ricciardo	McLaren	3h02m56.881s	2	1m30.659s	11
12	Lance Stroll	Aston Martin	3h02m57.908s	3	1m31.419s	18
13	Yuki Tsunoda	AlphaTauri	3h02m59.603s	3	1m30.808s	13
14	Kevin Magnussen	Haas	3h03m10.020s	2	1m31.352s	17
15	Valtteri Bottas	Alfa Romeo	3h03m10.500s	2	1m30.709s	12
16	Guanyu Zhou	Alfa Romeo	3h03m11.047s	3	1m30.953s	14
17	Mick Schumacher	Haas	3h03m16.527s	2	1m31.439s	15
18	Pierre Gasly **/!!	AlphaTauri	3h03m32.095s	4	1m31.322s	20
R	Carlos Sainz Jr	Ferrari	0 laps/accident	0	1m29.361s	3
R	Alexander Albon	Williams	0 laps/accident	0	1m31.311s	16

FASTEST LAP: GUANYU, 1M44.411S, 124.411MPH/200.220KPH ON LAP 20 · RACE LEADERS: VERSTAPPEN 1-7 & 9-28, ALONSO 8
* 5S PENALTY FOR LEAVING TRACK & GAINING AN ADVANTAGE · ** 20S PENALTY FOR SPEEDING UNDER RED FLAG · ! 5-PLACE GRID PENALTY FOR CAUSING A COLLISION · !! REQUIRED TO START FROM BACK OF GRID

UNITED STATES GP

This was a race full of incident, starting with Carlos Sainz Jr wasting pole position and being spun out of the race. There followed a scary collision between Fernando Alonso and Lance Stroll, then a slow pit stop for Max Verstappen dropped him behind Lewis Hamilton before fighting back.

Carlos Sainz Jr was delighted to pip his Ferrari team-mate Charles Leclerc to pole. The later it is in the season, the more likely drivers are to be hit with grid penalties for using excess power unit elements. And so it was at COTA, with Leclerc then being dropped back ten places and Sergio Perez back five from fourth. This put Max Verstappen up to second and he made a better start than Sainz, who then found himself the meat in a Mercedes sandwich in which his car was spun around by George Russell who had dived up the inside into the first corner. The damage would put him out and a five-second penalty served in the pits would dent Russell's day as well.

Verstappen then controlled the race, easing clear of Hamilton before his lead was cut back by Valtteri Bottas until he spun his Alfa Romeo at the penultimate corner and the safety car was deployed.

When the safety car withdrew, there was immediately a far more eye-opening moment when Lance Stroll moved across into Fernando Alonso, launching his Alpine in dramatic fashion. The Aston Martin was out on the spot, but Alonso pitted for repairs and pressed on, eventually reaching seventh, which he only got to keep when a post-race penalty was rescinded.

It should have been easy for Verstappen when the field was again released to go racing, but a slow pit stop brought him back out behind Hamilton and Leclerc. However, he then passed the two of them after some of the year's best scrapping. In winning, he equalled the record tally of 13 wins in a season set by Michael Schumacher in 2004 and then equalled by Vettel in 2013.

The victory and fourth place for Perez was enough to clinch Red Bull the constructors' title, something that was notably poignant just a day after the death of Red Bull co-founder and massive racing fan Dietrich Mateschitz.

CIRCUIT OF THE AMERICAS ROUND 19 DATE: 23 OCTOBER 2022

Laps: **56** • Distance: **191.634 miles/308.405km** • Weather: **Warm & sunny**

Pos	Driver	Team	Result	Stops	Qualifying Time	Grid
1	Max Verstappen	Red Bull	1h42m11.687s	2	1m34.448s	2
2	Lewis Hamilton	Mercedes	1h42m16.710s	2	1m34.947s	3
3	Charles Leclerc !!	Ferrari	1h42m19.188s	2	1m34.421s	12
4	Sergio Perez !	Red Bull	1h42m19.980s	2	1m34.645s	9
5	George Russell	Mercedes	1h42m56.502s	3	1m34.988s	4
6	Lando Norris	McLaren	1h43m05.472s	2	1m35.690s	6
7	Fernando Alonso !	Alpine	1h43m36.765s	2	1m35.876s	14
8	Sebastian Vettel	Aston Martin	1h43m17.041s	2	1m36.298s	10
9	Kevin Magnussen	Haas	1h43m17.521s	1	1m36.949s	13
10	Yuki Tsunoda !	AlphaTauri	1h43m22.606s	2	1m37.147s	19
11	Esteban Ocon !!!	Alpine	1h43m24.562s	2	1m37.068s	20
12	Guanyu Zhou !	Alfa Romeo	1h43m27.851s	2	1m36.970s	18
13	Alex Albon *	Williams	1h43m31.744s	2	1m36.368s	8
14	Pierre Gasly **	AlphaTauri	1h43m33.450s	2	1m36.740s	11
15	Mick Schumacher *	Haas	1h43m36.177s	2	1m37.111s	16
16	Daniel Ricciardo	McLaren	1h43m42.174s	2	1m37.046s	15
17	Nicholas Latifi *	Williams	1h43m55.275s	2	1m37.244s	17
R	Lance Stroll	Aston Martin	21 laps/collision	1	1m35.598s	5
R	Valtteri Bottas	Alfa Romeo	16 laps/spun off	1	1m36.319s	7
R	Carlos Sainz Jr	Ferrari	1 lap/collision damage	0	1m34.356s	1

FASTEST LAP: RUSSELL, 1M38.788S, 124.834MPH/200.902KPH ON LAP 56 • RACE LEADERS: VERSTAPPEN 1-13, 15-17, 19-35 & 50-56, PEREZ 14 & 36-38, LECLERC 18, VETTEL 39-40, HAMILTON 41-49 • *5S PENALTY FOR LEAVING THE TRACK AND GAINING AN ADVANTAGE • ** 10S PENALTY FOR NOT SERVING SAFETY CAR INFRINGEMENT PENALTY CORRECTLY • ! 5-PLACE GRID PENALTY FOR USING ADDITIONAL POWER UNIT ELEMENTS !! 10-PLACE GRID PENALTY FOR USING ADDITIONAL POWER UNIT ELEMENTS • !!! STARTED FROM PIT LANE FOR CAR BEING MODIFIED IN PARC FERME

Carlos Sainz Jr was spun at the first corner by George Russell, leaving the Ferrari on the sidelines.

MEXICAN GP

Max Verstappen controlled a processional race and became the first driver to claim 14 wins in a year. Happier than the Dutchman at the end, though, was the driver in seventh, Daniel Ricciardo, who was one of the few to gain places and so arrest his slump in form.

All the talk on arrival was of the investigation into Red Bull Racing's breaching of the cost cap.

Firstly, Max Verstappen claimed pole, with George Russell and Lewis Hamilton next on the grid for Mercedes. This proved vital, as this was a track that many had said might represent Mercedes' best opportunity of taking a win in 2022, since the circuit's lofty altitude was going to reduce Red Bull's power advantage.

Any hopes that Russell might have had of snatching the lead were thwarted by a poor start that not only let Verstappen lead easily into the first corner complex, but also allowed Lewis Hamilton to attack. His Mercedes team-mate found extra momentum to go around the outside into second, while Sergio Perez sent the home crowd wild when he too got past.

Although the long main straight down to the first corner ought to make overtaking easier than at most circuits, this wasn't the case and Verstappen was untroubled at the front. So all eyes turned to how their tyres were working for them, with Mercedes opting for the harder compound, hoping that their resultant one-stop strategy would get their drivers into the hunt. Red Bull's softer compound, on the other hand, would mean a second pit stop that ought to bring the Dutchman out behind Hamilton in particular. The teams watched and waited and Verstappen complained about his tyres' behaviour. However, it was noted that their overall performance looked to be satisfactory and it soon became clear that no second stop would be needed for the Red Bulls. And that was that, with Mercedes suddenly realising that they simply weren't at the races.

Verstappen duly coasted around without stopping again, to beat Hamilton by 15 seconds. This win meant a record 14th win in the season.

Max Verstappen leads George Russell and Lewis Hamilton into turn 1 on the first lap of the race.

MEXICO CITY ROUND 20

DATE: 30 OCTOBER 2022

Laps: **71** · Distance: **189.738 miles/305.354km** · Weather: **Dry**

Pos	Driver	Team	Result	Stops	Qualifying Time	Grid
1	Max Verstappen	Red Bull	1h38m36.729s	1	1m17.775s	1
2	Lewis Hamilton	Mercedes	1h38m51.915s	1	1m19.084s	3
3	Sergio Perez	Red Bull	1h38m54.826s	1	1m18.128s	4
4	George Russell	Mercedes	1h39m26.160s	2	1m18.079s	2
5	Carlos Sainz Jr	Ferrari	1h39m34.852s	1	1m18.351s	5
6	Charles Leclerc	Ferrari	1h39m45.503s	1	1m18.555s	7
7	Daniel Ricciardo *	McLaren	70 laps	1	1m19.325s	11
8	Esteban Ocon	Alpine	70 laps	1	1m19.010s	10
9	Lando Norris	McLaren	70 laps	1	1m18.721s	8
10	Valtteri Bottas	Alfa Romeo	70 laps	1	1m18.401s	6
11	Pierre Gasly	AlphaTauri	70 laps	1	1m19.672s	14
12	Alex Albon	Williams	70 laps	1	1m20.859s	17
13	Guanyu Zhou	Alfa Romeo	70 laps	1	1m19.476s	12
14	Sebastian Vettel	Aston Martin	70 laps	1	1m20.419s	16
15	Lance Stroll !	Aston Martin	70 laps	2	1m20.520s	20
16	Mick Schumacher	Haas	70 laps	1	1m20.419s	15
17	Kevin Magnussen !!	Haas	70 laps	1	1m19.833s	19
18	Nicholas Latifi	Williams	69 laps	2	1m21.167s	18
R	Fernando Alonso	Alpine	63 laps/power unit	1	1m18.939s	9
R	Yuki Tsunoda	AlphaTauri	50 laps/crash damage	1	1m19.589s	13

FASTEST LAP: RUSSELL, 1M20.153S, 120.117MPH/193.310KPH ON LAP 71 · RACE LEADERS: VERSTAPPEN 1-24 & 35-71, HAMILTON 25-29, RUSSELL 30-34 · * 10S PENALTY FOR COLLIDING WITH TSUNODA · ! 3-PLACE GRID PENALTY FOR CAUSING A COLLISION IN PREVIOUS RACE !! 5-PLACE GRID PENALTY FOR USING ADDITIONAL POWER UNIT ELEMENT

George Russell won the sprint race and then took a long-awaited first grand prix win in a race that saw Max Verstappen clash with Lewis Hamilton, and then later not allow team-mate Sergio Perez through when he wanted help to end the year second overall.

Kevin Magnussen put in the perfect lap in changing conditions in qualifying to secure both his and Haas F1's first poles. In the sprint race, though, he was soon deposed from the lead as Max Verstappen hit the front. However, Mercedes' late-season chassis developments were clearly working, as George Russell achieved a confidence-boosting win.

In the grand prix itself, Russell led away from the front of the grid but there was almost immediate trouble as Daniel Ricciardo clipped Magnussen's Haas, which then spun and took both out. This triggered the safety car and Russell controlled the restart well to stay in front.

Again, there was trouble behind, this time with Verstappen diving down the inside of Lewis Hamilton into the second corner, pulling almost level but being left with nowhere to go, so clattering over the kerbs and into the side of the Mercedes. He came off the worse, as his Red Bull's nose was damaged. It got worse still when the stewards hit him with a 5s penalty.

Mercedes ran a two-stop strategy, while Ferrari's drivers were going for three, but they didn't find enough of a performance advantage from fresher rubber to topple the Mercedes. Then there was another safety car period after Lando Norris's McLaren retired, but Russell held on at the restart and raced to a famous first victory. Mercedes was even happier that its first win of the year was a one-two result. The Ferraris followed them home and Fernando Alonso made it fifth, despite having started his Alpine from 17th on the grid.

After the race, there was a lot of friction at Red Bull Racing and the drivers had to be briefed in a hastily convened meeting before speaking to the press, with Verstappen saying that 'he had his reasons' for not pulling over and Perez stating that 'this really showed who Max was'.

116

INTERLAGOS ROUND 21

DATE: **13 NOVEMBER 2022**

Laps: **71** · Distance: **190.064 miles/305.879km** · Weather: **Warm & sunny**

Pos	Driver	Team	Result	Stops	Qualifying Time	Grid
1	**George Russell**	Mercedes	1h38m34.044s	2	-	1
2	**Lewis Hamilton**	Mercedes	1h38m35.573s	2	-	2
3	**Carlos Sainz Jr !**	Ferrari	1h38m38.095s	3	-	7
4	**Charles Leclerc**	Ferrari	1h38m42.485s	3	-	5
5	**Fernando Alonso**	Alpine	1h38m43.605s	3	-	17
6	**Max Verstappen**	Red Bull	1h38m44.100s	3	-	3
7	**Sergio Perez**	Red Bull	1h38m48.124s	2	-	4
8	**Esteban Ocon**	Alpine	1h38m52.734s	2	-	16
9	**Valtteri Bottas**	Alfa Romeo	1h38m56.596s	2	-	14
10	**Lance Stroll**	Aston Martin	1h38m57.596s	2	-	15
11	**Sebastian Vettel**	Aston Martin	1h39m00.227s	2	-	9
12	**Guanyu Zhou**	Alfa Romeo	1h39m03.369s	2	-	13
13	**Mick Schumacher**	Haas	1h39m03.943s	2	-	12
14	**Pierre Gasly ***	AlphaTauri	1h39m05.911s	3	-	10
15	**Alex Albon**	Williams	1h39m10.060s	3	-	19
16	**Nicholas Latifi**	Williams	1h39m11.082s	3	-	18
17	**Yuki Tsunoda !!**	AlphaTauri	70 laps	3	-	20
R	**Lando Norris**	McLaren	50 laps/electrics	2	-	6
R	**Kevin Magnussen**	Haas	0 laps/collision	0	-	8
R	**Daniel Ricciardo**	McLaren	0 laps/collision	0	-	11

FASTEST LAP: RUSSELL, 1M13.785S, 130.635MPH/210.237KPH ON LAP 61 · RACE LEADERS: RUSSELL 1-24 & 30-71, HAMILTON 25-29
! 5-PLACE GRID PENALTY FOR USING ADDITIONAL POWER UNIT ELEMENTS · !! REQUIRED TO START FROM PITLANE AS CAR MODIFIED IN PARC FERME, * 5S PENALTY FOR SPEEDING IN THE PITLANE. NB. GRID DETERMINED BY FINISHING ORDER IN SPRINT RACE

It's celebration time as George Russell and his Mercedes' crew take delight in his first win.

ABU DHABI GP

Max Verstappen finished his second title-winning year in a far more relaxed manner than he had the first, scoring a record 15th win in a season. And Ferrari's Charles Leclerc did enough to beat Max's team-mate Sergio Perez to end the year as runner-up.

There was still rancour in the air when the teams arrived for the final round, with social media having had a field day following the Red Bull drivers' spat at the end of the Brazilian GP. For this final round, said their team, Verstappen would try to help Perez to score enough points to beat Leclerc and finish the year as runner-up.

When the Red Bulls qualified first and second, the stage was set. Except the race didn't go to plan for the Mexican. It was expected that he would pit twice but then it transpired that Leclerc, like Verstappen, would be stopping just once. Add to this a slow first stop and Perez was left with a mountain to climb as he needed to catch Leclerc by 1s per lap over the final 24 laps to get back into second place. Try as he might, it was too much of a challenge.

For Leclerc, ending the year as runner-up was a pleasing result, but the fact that he had enjoyed a large points lead over Verstappen early in the season was not lost on him. Ferrari will have spent the winter trying to work out on how they failed to capitalise on a competitive advantage that was, in time, exceeded by Red Bull Racing, with some poor race strategies holding their drivers back.

Then, with three laps to go, Hamilton retired from fourth place in what had been an underwhelming race for Mercedes. Sainz Jr was elevated to that position, which was enough to move him above Hamilton in the final points table. Russell finished 11s further back.

There were minor point scores for Ricciardo and Vettel, marking perhaps the final F1 outing for the Australian and certainly the last one for the German, who admitted to being disappointed with the one-stop strategy that Aston Martin put him on. The two-stop plan carried out by team-mate Lance Stroll enabled him to move past Vettel and finish eighth.

Max Verstappen marks his record 15th win in a year with some donuts in Abu Dhabi.

YAS MARINA ROUND 22   DATE: **20 NOVEMBER 2022**
Laps: **58** • Distance: **190.253 miles/306.193km** • Weather: **Warm & dry**

Pos	Driver	Team	Result	Stops	Qualifying Time	Grid
1	**Max Verstappen**	Red Bull	1h27m45.914s	1	1m23.824s	1
2	**Charles Leclerc**	Ferrari	1h27m54.685s	1	1m24.092s	3
3	**Sergio Perez**	Red Bull	1h27m56.007s	2	1m24.052s	2
4	**Carlos Sainz Jr**	Ferrari	1h28m10.806s	2	1m24.242s	4
5	**George Russell**	Mercedes	1h28m21.802s	2	1m24.511s	6
6	**Lando Norris**	McLaren	1h28m42.148s	2	1m24.769s	7
7	**Esteban Ocon**	Alpine	1h28m43.154s	2	1m24.830s	8
8	**Lance Stroll**	Aston Martin	1h29m02.845s	2	1m25.359s	14
9	**Daniel Ricciardo !**	McLaren	1h29m09.182s	1	1m25.045s	13
10	**Sebastian Vettel**	Aston Martin	1h29m09.812s	1	1m24.961s	9
11	**Yuki Tsunoda**	AlphaTauri	1h29m15.285s	2	1m25.219s	11
12	**Guanyu Zhou**	Alfa Romeo	57 laps	2	1m25.408s	15
13	**Alex Albon**	Williams	57 laps	2	1m26.028s	19
14	**Pierre Gasly**	AlphaTauri	57 laps	2	1m25.859s	17
15	**Valtteri Bottas**	Alfa Romeo	57 laps	1	1m25.892s	18
16	**Mick Schumacher ***	Haas	57 laps	2	1m25.225s	12
17	**Kevin Magnussen**	Haas	57 laps	1	1m25.834s	16
R	**Lewis Hamilton**	Mercedes	55 laps/hydraulics	2	1m24.508s	5
R	**Nicholas Latifi**	Williams	55 laps/electrical	3	1m26.054s	20
R	**Fernando Alonso**	Alpine	27 laps/water leak	2	1m25.096s	10

FASTEST LAP: NORRIS, 1M28.391S, 133.647MPH/215.085KPH ON LAP 44 • RACE LEADERS: VERSTAPPEN 1-20 & 22-58, LECLERC 21
* 5S PENALTY FOR CAUSING A COLLISION WITH LATIFI • ! 3-PLACE GRID PENALTY FOR CAUSING A COLLISION WITH MAGNUSSEN IN PREVIOUS RACE

POS	DRIVER	NAT		CAR-ENGINE	R1	R2	R3	R4	R5	R6
1	MAX VERSTAPPEN	NED		RED BULL-HONDA RB18	R	1	R	1PF	1F	1
2	CHARLES LECLERC	MON		FERRARI F1-75	1PF	2F	1PF	6	2P	RP
3	SERGIO PEREZ	MEX		RED BULL-HONDA RB18	R	4P	2	2	4	2F
4	GEORGE RUSSELL	GBR		MERCEDES F1 W13	4	5	3	4	5	3
5	CARLOS SAINZ JR	ESP		FERRARI F1-75	2	3	R	R	3	4
6	LEWIS HAMILTON	GBR		MERCEDES F1 W13	3	10	4	13	6	5
7	LANDO NORRIS	GBR		McLAREN-MERCEDES MCL36	16	7	5	3	R	8
8	ESTEBAN OCON	FRA		ALPINE-RENAULT A522	7	6	7	14	8	7
9	FERNANDO ALONSO	ESP		ALPINE-RENAULT A522	9	R	17	R	11	9
10	VALTTERI BOTTAS	FIN		ALFA ROMEO-FERRARI C42	6	R	8	5	7	6
11	DANIEL RICCIARDO	AUS		McLAREN-MERCEDES MCL36	14	R	6	18	13	12
12	SEBASTIAN VETTEL	GER		ASTON MARTIN-MERCEDES AMR22	-	-	R	8	R	11
13	KEVIN MAGNUSSEN	DEN		HAAS-FERRARI VF-22	5	9	14	9	16	17
14	PIERRE GASLY	FRA		ALPHATAURI-HONDA AT03	R	8	9	12	R	13
15	LANCE STROLL	CDN		ASTON MARTIN-MERCEDES AMR22	12	13	12	10	10	15
16	MICK SCHUMACHER	GER		HAAS-FERRARI VF-22	11	W	13	17	15	14
17	YUKI TSUNODA	JPN		ALPHATAURI-HONDA AT03	8	R	15	7	12	10
18	GUANYU ZHOU	PRC		ALFA ROMEO-FERRARI C42	10	11	11	15	R	R
19	ALEX ALBON	GBR/THA		WILLIAMS-MERCEDES FW44	13	14	10	11	9	18
20	NICHOLAS LATIFI	CDN		WILLIAMS-MERCEDES FW44	16	R	16	16	14	16
21	NYCK DE VRIES	NED		WILLIAMS-MERCEDES FW44	-	-	-	-	-	-
22	NICO HULKENBERG	GER		ASTON MARTIN-MERCEDES AMR22	17	12	-	-	-	-

118

SCORING

1st	25 points
2nd	18 points
3rd	15 points
4th	12 points
5th	10 points
6th	8 points
7th	6 points
8th	4 points
9th	2 points
10th	1 point
Fastest lap	1 point (if in top 10 finishers)

POS	TEAM-ENGINE	R1	R2	R3	R4	R5	R6
1	RED BULL-RBPT	R/R	1/4	2/R	1/2	1/4	1/2
2	FERRARI	1/2	2/3	1/R	6/R	2/3	4/R
3	MERCEDES	3/4	5/10	3/4	4/13	5/6	3/5
4	ALPINE-RENAULT	7/9	6/R	7/17	14/R	8/11	7/9
5	McLAREN-MERCEDES	4/15	7/R	5/6	3/18	13/R	8/12
6	ALFA ROMEO-FERRARI	6/10	11/R	8/11	5/15	7/R	6/R
7	ASTON MARTIN-MERCEDES	12/17	12/13	12/R	8/10	10/R	11/15
8	HAAS-FERRARI	5/11	9/W	13/14	9/17	15/16	14/17
9	ALPHATAURI-RBPT	8/R	8/R	9/15	7/12	12/R	10/13
10	WILLIAMS-MERCEDES	13/16	14/R	10/16	11/16	9/14	16/18

SYMBOLS AND GRAND PRIX KEY

ROUND 1	BAHRAIN GP	ROUND 7	MONACO GP	ROUND 13	HUNGARIAN GP	ROUND 19	UNITED STATES GP
ROUND 2	SAUDI ARABIAN GP	ROUND 8	AZERBAIJAN GP	ROUND 14	BELGIAN GP	ROUND 20	MEXICAN GP
ROUND 3	AUSTRALIAN GP	ROUND 9	CANADIAN GP	ROUND 15	DUTCH GP	ROUND 21	BRAZILIAN GP
ROUND 4	EMILIA ROMAGNA GP	ROUND 10	BRITISH GP	ROUND 16	ITALIAN GP	ROUND 22	ABU DHABI GP
ROUND 5	MIAMI GP	ROUND 11	AUSTRIAN GP	ROUND 17	SINGAPORE GP		
ROUND 6	SPANISH GP	ROUND 12	FRENCH GP	ROUND 18	JAPANESE GP		

D DISQUALIFIED   **F** FASTEST LAP   **NC** NOT CLASSIFIED   **NS** NON-STARTER   **P** POLE POSITION   **R** RETIRED   **W** WITHDRAWN

R7	R8	R9	R10	R11	R12	R13	R14	R15	R16	R17	R18	R19	R20	R21	R22	TOTAL
3	1	1P	7	2PF	1	1	1F	1PF	1	7	1P	1	1P	6	1P	454
4P	RP	5	4	1	RP	6	6	3	2P	2P	3	3	6	4	2	308
1	2	R	2	R	4	5	23	5	6F	1	2	4	3	7	3	305
5	3	4	R	4	3	3P	4	2	3	14F	8	5F	4P	1F	5	275
2	R	2F	1P	R	5F	4	3P	8	4	3	R	RP	5	3	4	246
8	4	3	3F	3	2	2F	R	4	5	9	5	2	2	2	R	240
6F	9	15	6	7	7	7	12	7	7	4	10	6	9	R	6F	122
12	10	6	R	5	8	9	7	9	11	R	4	11	8	8	7	92
7	7	9	5	10	6	8	5	6	R	R	7	7	R	5	R	81
9	11	7	R	11	14	R	R	13	11	15	R	10	R	9	15	49
13	8	11	13	9	9	15	15	17	R	5	11	16	7	R	9	37
10	6	12	9	17	11	10	8	14	R	8	6	8	14	11	10	37
R	R	17	10	8	R	16	16	15	16	12	14	9	17	RP	17	25
11	5	14	R	15	12	12	9	11	8	10	18	14	11	14	14	23
14	16	10	11	13	10	11	11	10	R	6	12	R	15	10	8	18
R	14	R	8	6	15	14	17	13	12	13	17	15	16	13	16	12
17	13	R	14	16	R	19	13	R	14	R	13	10	R	17	11	12
16	R	8	R	14	16	13	14	16	10	R	16F	12	13	12	12	6
R	12	13	R	12	13	17	10	12	-	R	R	13	12	15	13	4
15	15	16	12	R	R	18	18	18	15	R	9	17	18	16	R	2
-	-	-	-	-	-	-	-	9	-	-	-	-	-	-	-	2
-	-	-	-	-	-	-	-	-	-	-	-	-	-	-	-	0

R7	R8	R9	R10	R11	R12	R13	R14	R15	R16	R17	R18	R19	R20	R21	R22	TOTAL
1/3	1/2	1/R	2/7	2/R	1/4	1/5	1/2	1/5	1/6	1/7	1/2	1/4	1/3	6/7	1/3	759
2/4	R/R	2/5	1/4	1/R	5/R	4/6	3/6	3/8	2/4	2/3	3/R	3/R	5/6	3/4	2/4	554
5/8	3/4	3/4	3/R	3/4	2/3	2/3	4/R	2/4	3/5	9/14	5/8	2/5	2/4	1/2	5/R	515
7/12	7/10	6/9	5/R	5/10	6/8	8/9	5/7	6/9	11/R	R/R	4/7	7/11	8/R	5/8	7/R	173
6/13	8/9	11/15	6/13	7/9	7/9	7/15	12/15	7/17	7/R	4/5	10/11	6/16	7/9	R/R	6/9	159
9/16	11/R	7/8	R/R	11/14	14/16	13/R	14/R	16/R	10/13	11/R	15/16	12/R	10/13	9/12	12/15	55
10/14	6/16	10/12	9/11	13/17	10/11	10/11	8/11	10/14	R/R	6/8	6/12	8/R	14/15	10/11	8/10	55
R/R	14/R	17/R	8/10	6/8	15/R	14/16	16/17	13/15	12/16	12/13	14/17	9/15	16/17	13/R	16/17	37
11/17	5/13	14/R	14/R	15/16	12/R	12/19	9/13	11/R	8/14	10/R	13/18	10/14	11/R	14/17	11/14	35
15/R	12/15	13/16	12/R	12/R	13/R	17/18	10/18	12/18	9/15	R/R	9/R	13/17	12/18	15/16	13/R	8

STARTS

DRIVERS

358	Fernando Alonso	(SPA)	181	Romain Grosjean	(FRA)		Adrian Sutil	(GER)
349	Kimi Raikkonen	(FIN)	180	Ralf Schumacher	(GER)	126	Jack Brabham	(AUS)
325	Rubens Barrichello	(BRA)	176	Graham Hill	(GBR)	123	Ronnie Peterson	(SWE)
310	Lewis Hamilton	(GBR)	175	Jacques Laffite	(FRA)	122	Lance Stroll	(CDN)
308	Michael Schumacher	(GER)	171	Niki Lauda	(AUT)	119	Pierluigi Martini	(ITA)
307	Jenson Button	(GBR)	165	Jacques Villeneuve	(CDN)	116	Damon Hill	(GBR)
300	Sebastian Vettel	(GER)	163	Thierry Boutsen	(BEL)		Jacky Ickx	(BEL)
270	Felipe Massa	(BRA)		Carlos Sainz Jr	(SPA)		Alan Jones	(AUS)
256	Riccardo Patrese	(ITA)		Max Verstappen	(NED)	114	Keke Rosberg	(FIN)
	Jarno Trulli	(ITA)	162	Mika Hakkinen	(FIN)		Patrick Tambay	(FRA)
247	David Coulthard	(GBR)		Johnny Herbert	(GBR)	112	Denny Hulme	(NZL)
235	Sergio Perez	(MEX)	161	Ayrton Senna	(BRA)		Daniil Kvyat	(RUS)
232	Daniel Ricciardo	(AUS)	159	Heinz-Harald Frentzen	(GER)		Jody Scheckter	(RSA)
230	Giancarlo Fisichella	(ITA)	158	Martin Brundle	(GBR)	111	Heikki Kovalainen	(FIN)
216	Mark Webber	(AUS)		Olivier Panis	(FRA)		Esteban Ocon	(GBR)
210	Gerhard Berger	(AUT)	152	John Watson	(GBR)		John Surtees	(GBR)
208	Andrea de Cesaris	(ITA)	149	Rene Arnoux	(FRA)	109	Philippe Alliot	(FRA)
206	Nico Rosberg	(GER)	147	Eddie Irvine	(GBR)		Mika Salo	(FIN)
204	Nelson Piquet	(BRA)		Derek Warwick	(GBR)	108	Elio de Angelis	(ITA)
201	Jean Alesi	(FRA)	146	Carlos Reutemann	(ARG)		Pierre Gasly	(FRA)
200	Valtteri Bottas	(FIN)	144	Emerson Fittipaldi	(BRA)	106	Jos Verstappen	(NED)
199	Alain Prost	(FRA)	142	Kevin Magnussen	(DEN)	104	Jo Bonnier	(SWE)
194	Michele Alboreto	(ITA)	135	Jean-Pierre Jarier	(FRA)		Pedro de la Rosa	(SPA)
187	Nigel Mansell	(GBR)	132	Eddie Cheever	(USA)		Jochen Mass	(GER)
184	Nico Hulkenberg	(GER)		Clay Regazzoni	(SWI)	100	Bruce McLaren	(NZL)
183	Nick Heidfeld	(GER)	128	Mario Andretti	(USA)			

CONSTRUCTORS

1,052	Ferrari	546	Alfa Romeo II (*nee* Sauber including BMW Sauber)	230	March
925	McLaren			197	BRM
844	Williams	492	Lotus	144	Haas
716	Alpine (*nee* Toleman then Benetton then Renault II, Lotus II & Renault III)	482	Red Bull (*nee* Stewart then Jaguar Racing)	132	Osella
				129	Renault
670	AlphaTauri (*nee* Minardi then Toro Rosso)	447	Mercedes GP (*nee* BAR then Honda Racing then Brawn GP)		
579	Aston Martin II (*nee* Jordan then Midland then Spyker then Force India then Racing Point)	418	Tyrrell		
		409	Prost (*nee* Ligier)		
		394	Brabham		
		383	Arrows		

DRIVERS

103	Lewis Hamilton	(GBR)	16	Stirling Moss	(GBR)		Jody Scheckter	(RSA)
91	Michael Schumacher	(GER)	15	Jenson Button	(GBR)	9	Mark Webber	(AUS)
53	Sebastian Vettel	(GER)	14	Jack Brabham	(AUS)	8	Denny Hulme	(NZL)
51	Alain Prost	(FRA)		Emerson Fittipaldi	(BRA)		Jacky Ickx	(BEL)
41	Ayrton Senna	(BRA)		Graham Hill	(GBR)		Daniel Ricciardo	(AUS)
35	Max Verstappen	(NED)	13	Alberto Ascari	(ITA)	7	Rene Arnoux	(FRA)
32	Fernando Alonso	(SPA)		David Coulthard	(GBR)		Juan Pablo Montoya	(COL)
31	Nigel Mansell	(GBR)	12	Mario Andretti	(USA)	6	Tony Brooks	(GBR)
27	Jackie Stewart	(GBR)		Alan Jones	(AUS)		Jacques Laffite	(FRA)
25	Jim Clark	(GBR)		Carlos Reutemann	(ARG)		Riccardo Patrese	(ITA)
	Niki Lauda	(AUT)	11	Rubens Barrichello	(BRA)		Jochen Rindt	(AUT)
24	Juan Manuel Fangio	(ARG)		Felipe Massa	(BRA)		Ralf Schumacher	(GER)
23	Nelson Piquet	(BRA)		Jacques Villeneuve	(CDN)		John Surtees	(GBR)
	Nico Rosberg	(GER)	10	Gerhard Berger	(AUT)		Gilles Villeneuve	(CDN)
22	Damon Hill	(GBR)		Valtteri Bottas	(FIN)			
21	Kimi Raikkonen	(FIN)		James Hunt	(GBR)			
20	Mika Hakkinen	(FIN)		Ronnie Peterson	(SWE)			

CONSTRUCTORS

241	Ferrari	16	Cooper		Wolf	
182	McLaren	15	Renault	2	AlphaTauri (including Toro Rosso)	
125	Mercedes GP (including Honda Racing, Brawn GP)	10	Alfa Romeo		Honda	
114	Williams	9	Ligier	1	BMW Sauber	
92	Red Bull (including Stewart)		Maserati		Eagle	
79	Lotus		Matra		Hesketh	
49	Alpine (including Benetton, Renault II, Lotus II & Renault III)		Mercedes		Penske	
35	Brabham		Vanwall		Porsche	
23	Tyrrell	5	Aston Martin (including Jordan & Racing Point)		Shadow	
17	BRM	4	Jordan			
		3	March			

Lewis Hamilton pumps his fist as he is first to the chequered flag for the first time, taking victory for McLaren in the 2007 Canadian GP.

MOST WINS IN ONE SEASON

DRIVERS

15	Max Verstappen	2022		Michael Schumacher	2000	6	Mario Andretti	1978
13	Michael Schumacher	2004		Michael Schumacher	2001		Alberto Ascari	1952
	Sebastian Vettel	2013	8	Mika Hakkinen	1998		Jim Clark	1965
11	Lewis Hamilton	2014		Lewis Hamilton	2021		Juan Manuel Fangio	1954
	Lewis Hamilton	2018		Damon Hill	1996		Damon Hill	1994
	Lewis Hamilton	2019		Michael Schumacher	1994		James Hunt	1976
	Lewis Hamilton	2020		Ayrton Senna	1988		Nigel Mansell	1987
	Michael Schumacher	2002	7	Fernando Alonso	2005		Kimi Raikkonen	2007
	Sebastian Vettel	2011		Fernando Alonso	2006		Nico Rosberg	2015
10	Lewis Hamilton	2015		Jim Clark	1963		Michael Schumacher	1998
	Lewis Hamilton	2016		Alain Prost	1984		Michael Schumacher	2003
	Max Verstappen	2021		Alain Prost	1988		Michael Schumacher	2006
9	Lewis Hamilton	2017		Alain Prost	1993		Ayrton Senna	1989
	Nigel Mansell	1992		Kimi Raikkonen	2005		Ayrton Senna	1990
	Nico Rosberg	2016		Ayrton Senna	1991			
	Michael Schumacher	1995		Jacques Villeneuve	1997			

CONSTRUCTORS

19	Mercedes GP	2016		McLaren	2005		McLaren	2007
17	Red Bull	2022		McLaren	1989		Renault	2005
16	Mercedes GP	2014		Williams	1992		Renault	2006
	Mercedes GP	2015		Williams	1993		Williams	1997
15	Ferrari	2002	9	Ferrari	2001	7	Ferrari	1952
	Ferrari	2004		Ferrari	2006		Ferrari	1953
	McLaren	1988		Ferrari	2007		Ferrari	2008
	Mercedes GP	2019		McLaren	1998		Lotus	1963
13	Mercedes GP	2020		Mercedes GP	2021		Lotus	1973
12	McLaren	1984		Red Bull	2010		McLaren	1999
	Mercedes GP	2017		Williams	1986		McLaren	2000
	Red Bull	2011		Williams	1987		McLaren	2012
	Williams	1996	8	Benetton	1994		Red Bull	2012
11	Benetton	1995		Brawn GP	2009		Tyrrell	1971
	Red Bull	2021		Ferrari	2003		Williams	1991
	Mercedes GP	2018		Lotus	1978		Williams	1994
10	Ferrari	2000		McLaren	1991			

MOST POLE POSITIONS

DRIVERS

103	Lewis Hamilton	(GBR)	22	Fernando Alonso	(SPA)		James Hunt	(GBR)
68	Michael Schumacher	(GER)	20	Valtteri Bottas	(FIN)		Ronnie Peterson	(SWE)
65	Ayrton Senna	(BRA)		Damon Hill	(GBR)	13	Jack Brabham	(AUS)
57	Sebastian Vettel	(GER)	18	Mario Andretti	(USA)		Graham Hill	(GBR)
33	Jim Clark	(GBR)		Rene Arnoux	(FRA)		Jacky Ickx	(BEL)
	Alain Prost	(FRA)		Kimi Raikkonen	(FIN)		Juan Pablo Montoya	(COL)
32	Nigel Mansell	(GBR)		Max Verstappen	(NED)		Jacques Villeneuve	(CDN)
30	Nico Rosberg	(GER)	17	Jackie Stewart	(GBR)	12	Gerhard Berger	(AUT)
29	Juan Manuel Fangio	(ARG)	16	Felipe Massa	(BRA)		David Coulthard	(GBR)
26	Mika Hakkinen	(FIN)		Stirling Moss	(GBR)	11	Mark Webber	(AUS)
24	Niki Lauda	(AUT)	14	Alberto Ascari	(ITA)	10	Jochen Rindt	(AUT)
	Nelson Piquet	(BRA)		Rubens Barrichello	(BRA)			

CONSTRUCTORS

242	Ferrari	14	Tyrrell		Matra	
156	McLaren	12	Alfa Romeo	3	Shadow	
136	Mercedes GP (including Brawn GP, Honda Racing, BAR)	11	BRM		Toyota	
			Cooper	2	Lancia	
128	Williams	10	Maserati	1	AlphaTauri (including Toro Rosso)	
107	Lotus	9	Ligier		BMW Sauber	
81	Red Bull Racing	8	Mercedes		Haas	
39	Brabham	7	Vanwall			
34	Alpine (including Toleman, Benetton, Renault II, Lotus II & Renault III)	5	March			
31	Renault	4	Aston Martin (including Jordan, Force India & Racing Point)			

Above: Ferrari dominated 1961, as shown by this front row at Zandvoort of Hill, von Trips and Ginther.

Opposite: Two Schumachers and Jenson Button, in 2004, the fifth of Michael's Ferrari title years.

Jack Brabham charges to the second of four wins in a row, this one at Brands Hatch, as he races towards his third title in 1966.

MOST FASTEST LAPS

DRIVERS

76	Michael Schumacher	(GER)		Max Verstappen	(NED)	14	Jacky Ickx	(BEL)
61	Lewis Hamilton	(GBR)	20	Nico Rosberg	(GER)	13	Alberto Ascari	(ITA)
46	Kimi Raikkonen	(FIN)	19	Valtteri Bottas	(FIN)		Alan Jones	(AUS)
41	Alain Prost	(FRA)		Damon Hill	(GBR)		Riccardo Patrese	(ITA)
38	Sebastian Vettel	(GER)		Stirling Moss	(GBR)	12	Rene Arnoux	(FRA)
30	Nigel Mansell	(GBR)		Ayrton Senna	(BRA)		Jack Brabham	(AUS)
28	Jim Clark	(GBR)		Mark Webber	(AUS)		Juan Pablo Montoya	(COL)
25	Mika Hakkinen	(FIN)	18	David Coulthard	(GBR)	11	John Surtees	(GBR)
24	Niki Lauda	(AUT)	17	Rubens Barrichello	(BRA)	10	Mario Andretti	(USA)
23	Juan Manuel Fangio	(ARG)	16	Felipe Massa	(BRA)		Graham Hill	(GBR)
	Nelson Piquet	(BRA)		Daniel Ricciardo	(AUS)			
22	Fernando Alonso	(SPA)	15	Clay Regazzoni	(SWI)			
21	Gerhard Berger	(AUT)		Jackie Stewart	(GBR)			

CONSTRUCTORS

258	Ferrari		Renault, Lotus II & Renault III)	12	Matra
161	McLaren	40	Brabham	11	Prost (including Ligier)
133	Williams	22	Tyrrell	9	Mercedes
100	Mercedes GP (including BAR,	18	Renault	7	March
	Honda Racing & Brawn GP)	15	BRM	6	Alfa Romeo II (including Sauber)
84	Red Bull Racing		Maserati		Vanwall
71	Lotus	14	Alfa Romeo		
56	Alpine (including Toleman, Benetton,	13	Cooper		

MOST POINTS (this figure is gross tally, ie. including scores that were later dropped)

DRIVERS

4,405.5	Lewis Hamilton	(GBR)	658	Rubens Barrichello	(BRA)	310	Carlos Reutemann	(ARG)
3,098	Sebastian Vettel	(GER)	614	Ayrton Senna	(BRA)	307	Juan Pablo Montoya	(COL)
2,061	Fernando Alonso	(SPA)	535	David Coulthard	(GBR)	294	George Russell	(GBR)
2,011.5	Max Verstappen	(NED)	521	Nico Hulkenberg	(GER)	289	Graham Hill	(GBR)
1,873	Kimi Raikkonen	(FIN)	485.5	Nelson Piquet	(BRA)	281	Emerson Fittipaldi	(BRA)
1,787	Valtteri Bottas	(FIN)	482	Nigel Mansell	(GBR)		Riccardo Patrese	(ITA)
1,594.5	Nico Rosberg	(GER)	428	Lando Norris	(GBR)	277.5	Juan Manuel Fangio	(ARG)
1,566	Michael Schumacher	(GER)	420.5	Niki Lauda	(AUT)	275	Giancarlo Fisichella	(ITA)
1,274	Daniel Ricciardo	(AUS)	420	Mika Hakkinen	(FIN)	274	Jim Clark	(GBR)
1,235	Jenson Button	(GBR)	391	Romain Grosjean	(FRA)		Robert Kubica	(POL)
1,201	Sergio Perez	(MEX)	385	Gerhard Berger	(AUT)	261	Jack Brabham	(AUS)
1,167	Felipe Massa	(BRA)	364	Esteban Ocon	(FRA)	259	Nick Heidfeld	(GER)
1,047.5	Mark Webber	(AUS)	360	Damon Hill	(GBR)	255	Jody Scheckter	(RSA)
868	Charles Leclerc	(MON)		Jackie Stewart	(GBR)	248	Denny Hulme	(NZL)
798.5	Alain Prost	(FRA)	332	Pierre Gasly	(FRA)			
782.5	Carlos Sainz Jr	(SPA)	329	Ralf Schumacher	(GER)			

CONSTRUCTORS

9,238	Ferrari	1,691	Aston Martin (including Jordan, Midland, Spyker, Force India & Racing Point)	424	Prost (including Ligier)
7,301.5	Mercedes GP (including BAR, Honda Racing, Brawn GP)			333	Cooper
6,467	Red Bull Racing (including Stewart, Jaguar Racing)	1,514	Lotus	312	Renault
5,965.5	McLaren	983	Alfa Romeo II (including Sauber)	278.5	Toyota
3,598	Williams	854	Brabham	237	Haas
3332.5	Alpine (including Toleman, Benetton, Renault II, Lotus II & Renault III)	820	AlphaTauri (including Minardi & Toro Rosso)	171.5	March
		617	Tyrrell	167	Arrows
		439	BRM	155	Matra

CHAMPIONSHIP TITLES

DRIVERS

7	Lewis Hamilton	(GBR)		Jenson Button	(GBR)
	Michael Schumacher	(GER)		Giuseppe Farina	(ITA)
5	Juan Manuel Fangio	(ARG)		Mike Hawthorn	(GBR)
4	Alain Prost	(FRA)		Damon Hill	(GBR)
	Sebastian Vettel	(GER)		Phil Hill	(USA)
3	Jack Brabham	(AUS)		Denis Hulme	(NZL)
	Niki Lauda	(AUT)		James Hunt	(GBR)
	Nelson Piquet	(BRA)		Alan Jones	(AUS)
	Ayrton Senna	(BRA)		Nigel Mansell	(GBR)
	Jackie Stewart	(GBR)		Kimi Raikkonen	(FIN)
2	Fernando Alonso	(SPA)		Jochen Rindt	(AUT)
	Alberto Ascari	(ITA)		Keke Rosberg	(FIN)
	Jim Clark	(GBR)		Nico Rosberg	(GER)
	Emerson Fittipaldi	(BRA)		Jody Scheckter	(RSA)
	Mika Hakkinen	(FIN)		John Surtees	(GBR)
	Graham Hill	(GBR)		Jacques Villeneuve	(CDN)
	Max Verstappen	(NED)			
1	Mario Andretti	(USA)			

CONSTRUCTORS

16	Ferrari		Renault
9	Williams	1	Benetton
8	McLaren		Brawn
	Mercedes GP		BRM
7	Lotus		Matra
5	Red Bull		Tyrrell
2	Brabham		Vanwall
	Cooper		

NB. The Lotus stats listed are based on the team that ran from 1958-1994, whereas those listed as Lotus II are for the team that ran from 2012-2015. Those marked as Alpine are for the team based at Enstone that started as Toleman in 1981, became Benetton in 1986, then Renault II in 2002, Lotus II in 2012 and Renault III in 2016. The Renault listings are for the team that ran from 1977 to 1985, the stats for Red Bull Racing include those of the Stewart Grand Prix and Jaguar Racing teams from which it evolved, and those for Mercedes GP for the team that started as BAR in 1999, ran as Honda GP from 2006 and then as Brawn GP in 2009. Aston Martin II's stats include those of Jordan, Midland, Spyker, Force India and Racing Point, while Scuderia AlphaTauri's include those of its forerunner Minardi and Scuderia Toro Rosso. Alfa Romeo II's figures are for the team created in 2019 from Sauber, with no connection to the two iterations of the works team that ran from 1950-1951 and 1979-1985.

DRIVER	TEAM	Round 1 – March 5 BAHRAIN GP	Round 2 – March 19 SAUDI ARABIAN GP	Round 3 – April 2 AUSTRALIAN GP	Round 4 – April 30 AZERBAIJAN GP	Round 5 – May 7 MIAMI GP	Round 6 – May 21 EMILIA ROMAGNA GP	Round 7 – May 28 MONACO GP	Round 8 – June 4 SPANISH GP	Round 9 – June 18 CANADIAN GP	Round 10 – July 2 AUSTRIAN GP
MAX VERSTAPPEN	Red Bull										
SERGIO PEREZ	Red Bull										
CHARLES LECLERC	Ferrari										
CARLOS SAINZ JR	Ferrari										
GEORGE RUSSELL	Mercedes										
LEWIS HAMILTON	Mercedes										
ESTEBAN OCON	Alpine										
PIERRE GASLY	Alpine										
LANDO NORRIS	McLaren										
OSCAR PIASTRI	McLaren										
VALTTERI BOTTAS	Alfa Romeo										
GUANYU ZHOU	Alfa Romeo										
FERNANDO ALONSO	Aston Martin										
LANCE STROLL	Aston Martin										
KEVIN MAGNUSSEN	Haas F1										
NICO HULKENBERG	Haas F1										
YUKI TSUNODA	AlphaTauri										
NYCK DE VRIES	AlphaTauri										
ALEX ALBON	Williams										
LOGAN SARGEANT	Williams										

SCORING SYSTEM: 25, 18, 15, 12, 10, 8, 6, 4, 2, 1 POINTS FOR THE FIRST 10 FINISHERS IN EACH GRAND PRIX & 1 POINT FOR FASTEST LAP SET BY A DRIVER FINISHING IN TOP 10

Round 11 – July 9 BRITISH GP	Round 12 – July 23 HUNGARIAN GP	Round 13 – July 30 BELGIAN GP	Round 14 – August 27 DUTCH GP	Round 15 – September 3 ITALIAN GP	Round 16 – September 17 SINGAPORE GP	Round 17 – September 24 JAPANESE GP	Round 18 – October 8 QATAR GP	Round 19 – October 22 UNITED STATES GP	Round 20 – October 29 MEXICAN GP	Round 21 – November 5 SAO PAOLO GP	Round 22 – November 18 LAS VEGAS GP	Round 23 – November 26 ABU DHABI GP	POINTS TOTAL

128

The publishers would like to thank the following sources for their kind permission to reproduce the photographs and artwork in this book.

GETTY IMAGES: Peter J Fox 47L, 52L, 116; Bryn Lennon 93; Joe Portlock / Formula 1 63R

GRAPHIC NEWS: 11T, 12R, 13R, 15T, 16R, 17R, 21T, 22R, 23R, 25T, 26R, 27R, 31T, 32R, 33R, 35T, 36R, 37R, 41T, 42R, 43R, 45T, 46R, 47R, 51T, 52R, 53R, 55T, 56R, 57R, 68, 69, 70, 71, 72, 73, 74, 75, 78, 79, 80, 81, 82, 83, 84, 85, 86, 87, 88, 89, 90, 91, 92

MOTORSPORT IMAGES: 61TL, 63L, 98, 109, 123, 124; Lorenzo Bellanca 121; Carl Bingham 32L, 33L, 36L, 37L, 38-39, 42L, 44, 50, 54, 56L, 96, 107; Sam Bloxham 12L, 17L, 18-19, 48-49, 53L, 61C, 76-77, 115; Charles Coates 23L, 65TL; Emily Davenport 65TR; Glenn Dunbar 10, 14, 16L, 24, 34, 58-59; Steve Etherington 22L, 25B, 66-67, 103, 112, 128; Jake Galstad 63B; Andy Hone 5, 6-7, 13L, 30, 45B, 99, 102, 106, 111, 117; JEP 105; Zak Mauger 2, 20, 27L, 43L, 65B; James Moy 31B, 122; David Phipps 63T; Rainer Schlegelmilch 15B, 35B, 41B, 61TR; Alastair Staley 110; Sutton Images 11B, 21B, 55B; Mark Sutton 26L, 40, 46L, 51B, 57L, 61B, 97, 100, 101, 104, 108; Steven Tee: 8-9, 28-29, 65C, 94-95, 113, 114

Every effort has been made to acknowledge correctly and contact the source and/or copyright holder of each picture. Any unintentional errors or omissions will be corrected in future editions of this book.

George Russell took until the penultimate round to take his first win for previously dominant Mercedes, but before then took pole in Hungary.